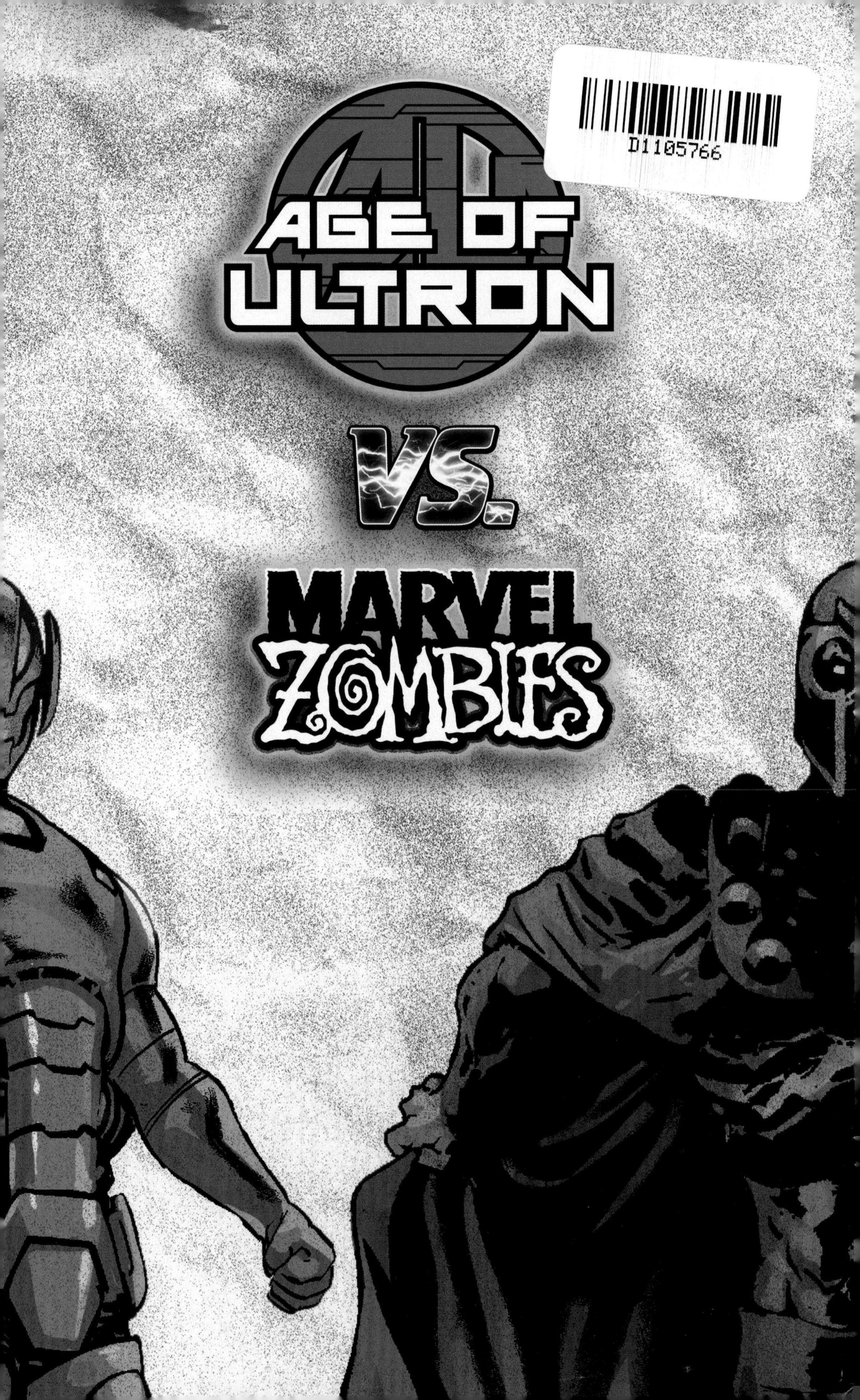
AGE OF ULTRON
VS.
MARVEL ZOMBIES

COLLECTION EDITOR: MARK D. BEAZLEY
ASSISTANT EDITOR: SARAH BRUNSTAD
ASSOCIATE MANAGING EDITOR: ALEX STARBUCK
EDITOR, SPECIAL PROJECTS: JENNIFER GRÜNWALD
SENIOR EDITOR, SPECIAL PROJECTS: JEFF YOUNGQUIST
SVP PRINT, SALES & MARKETING: DAVID GABRIEL
BOOK DESIGNER: ADAM DEL RE

EDITOR IN CHIEF: AXEL ALONSO
CHIEF CREATIVE OFFICER: JOE QUESADA
PUBLISHER: DAN BUCKLEY
EXECUTIVE PRODUCER: ALAN FINE

AGE OF ULTRON VS. MARVEL ZOMBIES. Contains material originally published in magazine form as AGE OF ULTRON VS MARVEL ZOMBIES #1-4 and AGE OF ULTRON #1. First printing 2015. ISBN# 978-0-7851-9863-5. Published by MARVEL WORLDWIDE, INC., a subsidiary of MARVEL ENTERTAINMENT, LLC. OFFICE OF PUBLICATION: 135 West 50th Street, New York, NY 10020. Copyright © 2015 MARVEL No similarity between any of the names, characters, persons, and/or institutions in this magazine with those of any living or dead person or institution is intended, and any such similarity which may exist is purely coincidental. Printed in Canada. ALAN FINE, President, Marvel Entertainment; DAN BUCKLEY, President, TV, Publishing and Brand Management; JOE QUESADA, Chief Creative Officer; TOM BREVOORT, SVP of Publishing; DAVID BOGART, SVP of Operations & Procurement, Publishing; C.B. CEBULSKI, VP of International Development & Brand Management; DAVID GABRIEL, SVP Print, Sales & Marketing; JIM O'KEEFE, VP of Operations & Logistics; DAN CARR, Executive Director of Publishing Technology; SUSAN CRESPI, Editorial Operations Manager; ALEX MORALES, Publishing Operations Manager; STAN LEE, Chairman Emeritus. For information regarding advertising in Marvel Comics or on Marvel.com, please contact Jonathan Rheingold, VP of Custom Solutions & Ad Sales, at jrheingold@marvel.com. For Marvel subscription inquiries, please call 800-217-9158. Manufactured between 9/18/2015 and 10/26/2015 by SOLISCO PRINTERS, SCOTT, QC, CANADA.

10 9 8 7 6 5 4 3 2 1

AGE OF ULTRON VS. MARVEL ZOMBIES

WRITER: **JAMES ROBINSON**

ARTIST: **STEVE PUGH**

COLORIST: **JIM CHARALAMPIDIS**

LETTERER: **VC'S CLAYTON COWLES**

FLASHBACK ARTISTS: **RON GARNEY & MATT MILLA** (#1);
TOM GRUMMETT, DREW HENNESSY & JESUS ABURTOV (#2);
ANNAPAOLA MARTELLO & JASON KEITH (#3); AND
PAUL RIVOCHE & JOHN RAUCH (#4)

COVER ARTISTS: **CARLOS PACHECO, RODOLFO TAIBO & DEAN WHITE** (#1);
STEVE PUGH & JIM CHARALAMPIDIS (#2-3); AND
LEONARD KIRK & JIM CHARALAMPIDIS (#4)

ASSISTANT EDITORS: **CHRIS ROBINSON & EMILY SHAW**
SENIOR EDITOR: **MARK PANICCIA**

AGE OF ULTRON #1

WRITER: **BRIAN MICHAEL BENDIS**

PENCILER: **BRYAN HITCH**   INKER: **PAUL NEARY**

COLORIST: **PAUL MOUNTS**   LETTERER: **VC'S CORY PETIT**

COVER ARTIST: **BRYAN HITCH, PAUL NEARY & PAUL MOUNTS**
ASSISTANT EDITORS: **JAKE THOMAS & JOHN DENNING**
EDITORS: **TOM BREVOORT WITH LAUREN SANKOVITCH**

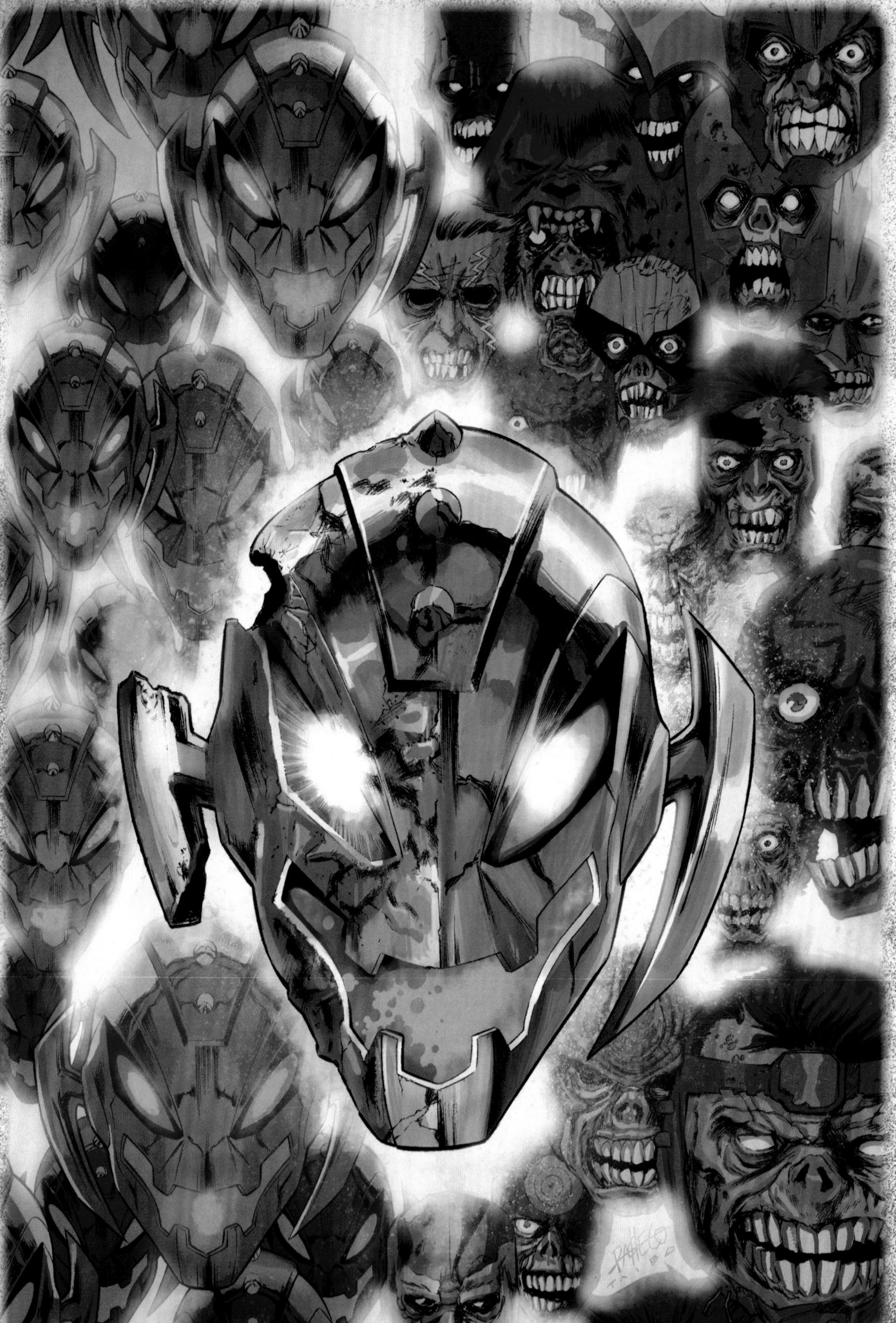

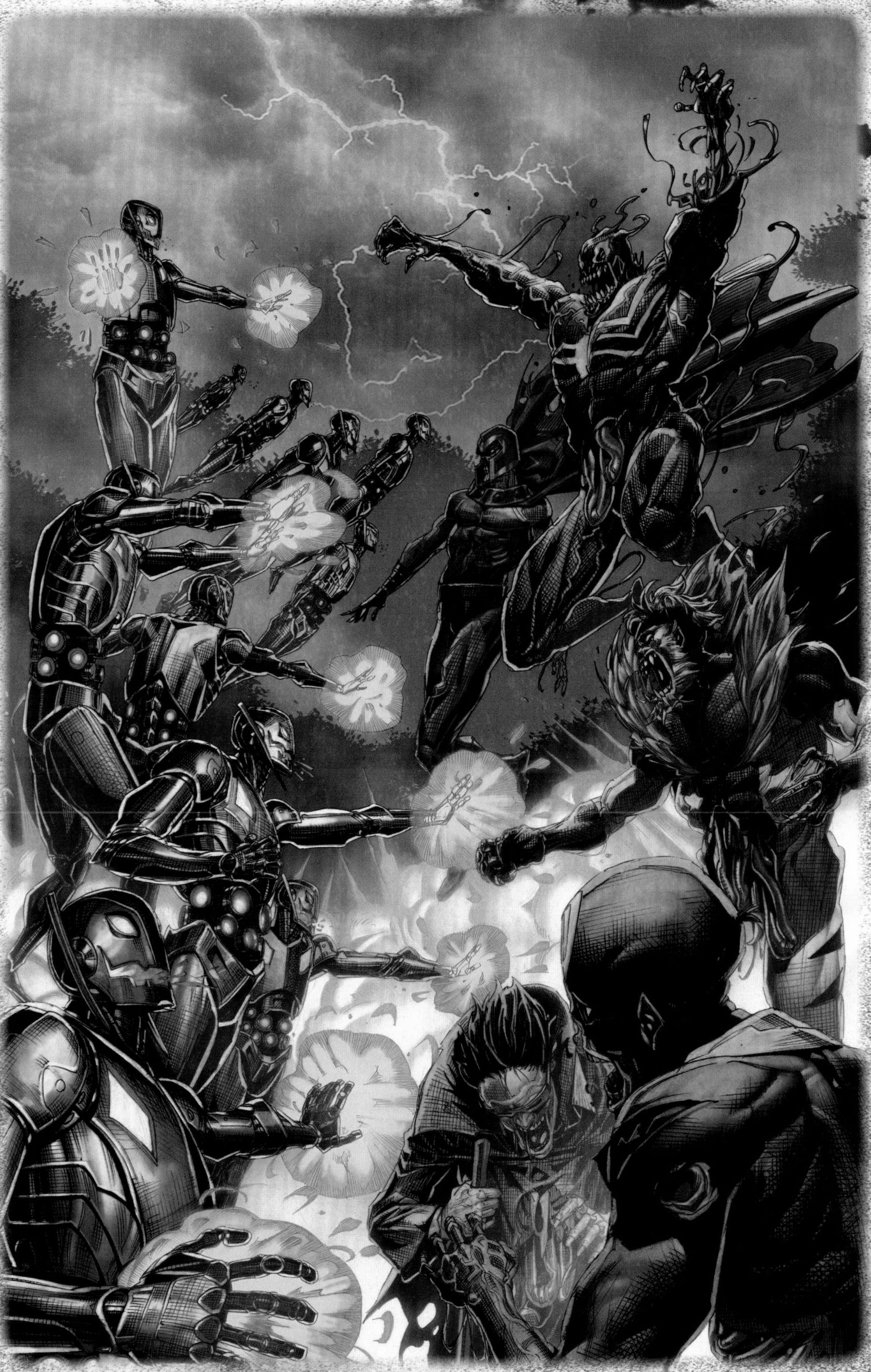

#1 Variant by Rock-He Kim

SECRET WARS

THE MULTIVERSE WAS DESTROYED!

THE HEROES OF EARTH-616 AND EARTH-1610 WERE POWERLESS TO SAVE IT!

NOW, ALL THAT REMAINS...IS BATTLEWORLD!

A MASSIVE, PATCHWORK PLANET COMPOSED OF THE FRAGMENTS OF WORLDS THAT NO LONGER EXIST, MAINTAINED BY THE IRON WILL OF ITS GOD AND MASTER, VICTOR VON DOOM!

AT THE END OF THE WORLD LIES THE SHIELD, THE LAST THING BETWEEN CIVILIZATION AND THE TERRORS OF...

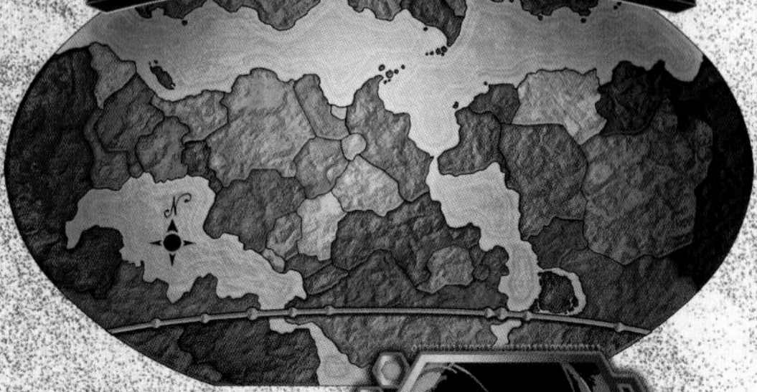

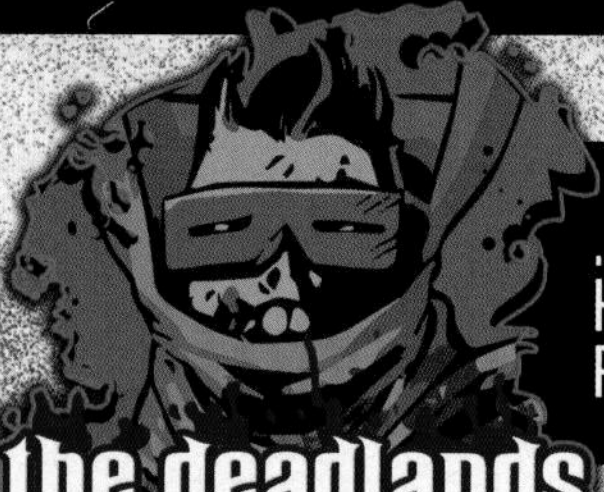

...WHERE REANIMATED HORDES CRAVE LIVE FLESH...

the deadlands

...OR MECHANIZED MOCKERIES OF MAN ELIMINATE EVERY TRACE OF FLAWED HUMANITY IN...

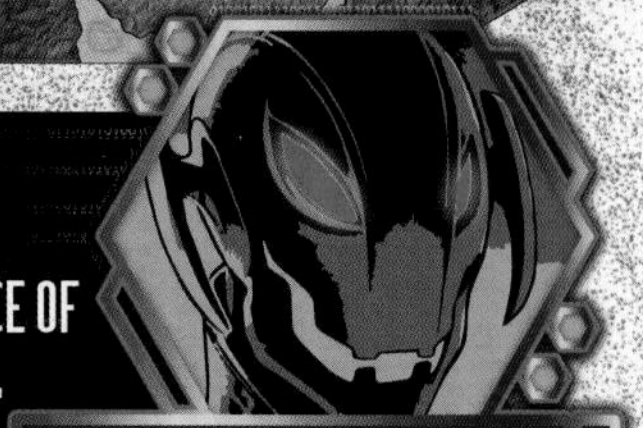

PERFECTION

If YOU HAVE SURVIVED
Long enough to READ THis:
CONGRATULATIONS

FIND SANCTUARY with us in
SALVATION 30 KiloDOOMS WEST

DO NOT GO EAST Beware ULTRONS

DO NOT GO SOUTH MORE ZOMBIES

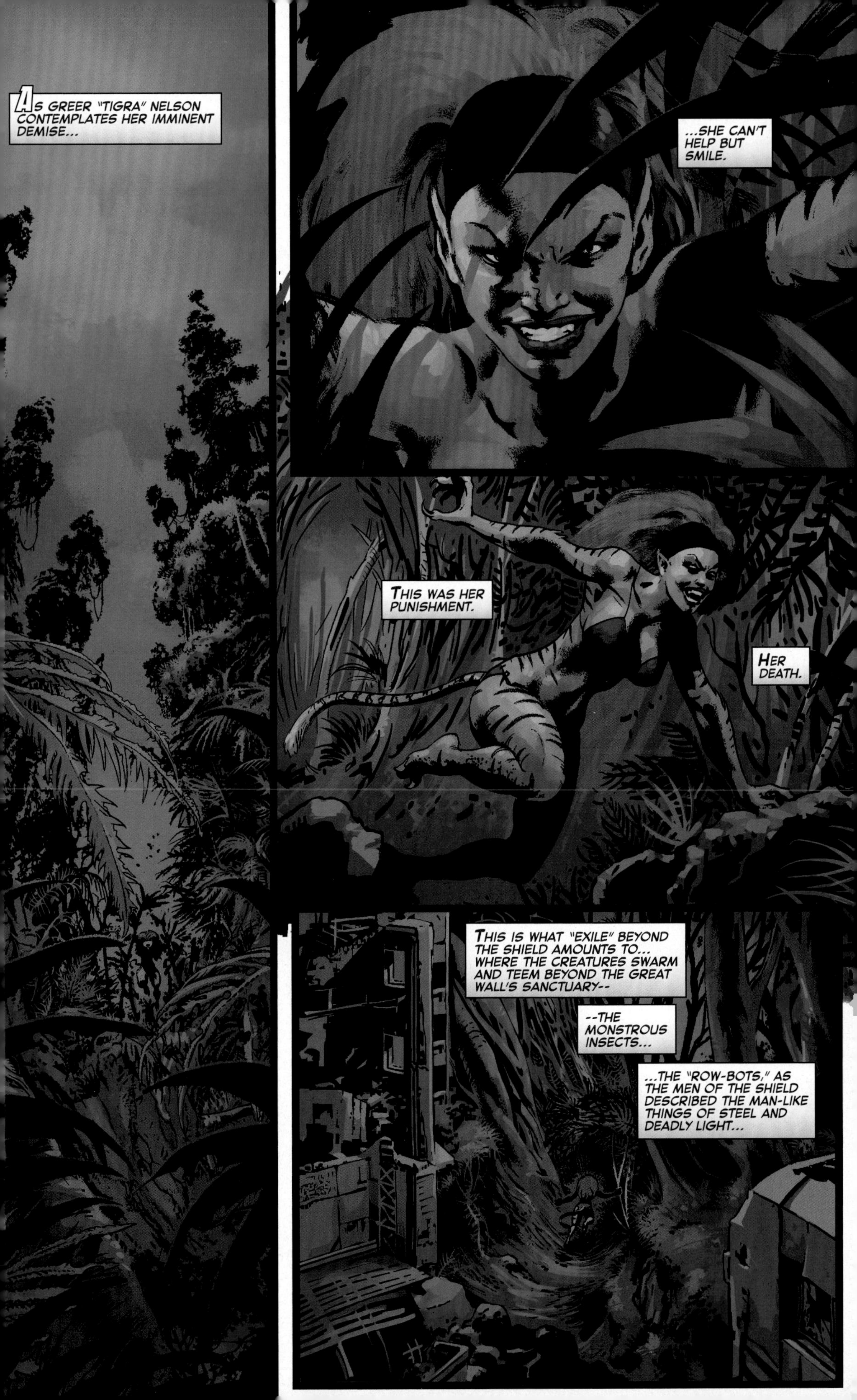
AS GREER "TIGRA" NELSON CONTEMPLATES HER IMMINENT DEMISE...
...SHE CAN'T HELP BUT SMILE.
THIS WAS HER PUNISHMENT.
HER DEATH.
THIS IS WHAT "EXILE" BEYOND THE SHIELD AMOUNTS TO... WHERE THE CREATURES SWARM AND TEEM BEYOND THE GREAT WALL'S SANCTUARY--
--THE MONSTROUS INSECTS...
...THE "ROW-BOTS," AS THE MEN OF THE SHIELD DESCRIBED THE MAN-LIKE THINGS OF STEEL AND DEADLY LIGHT...

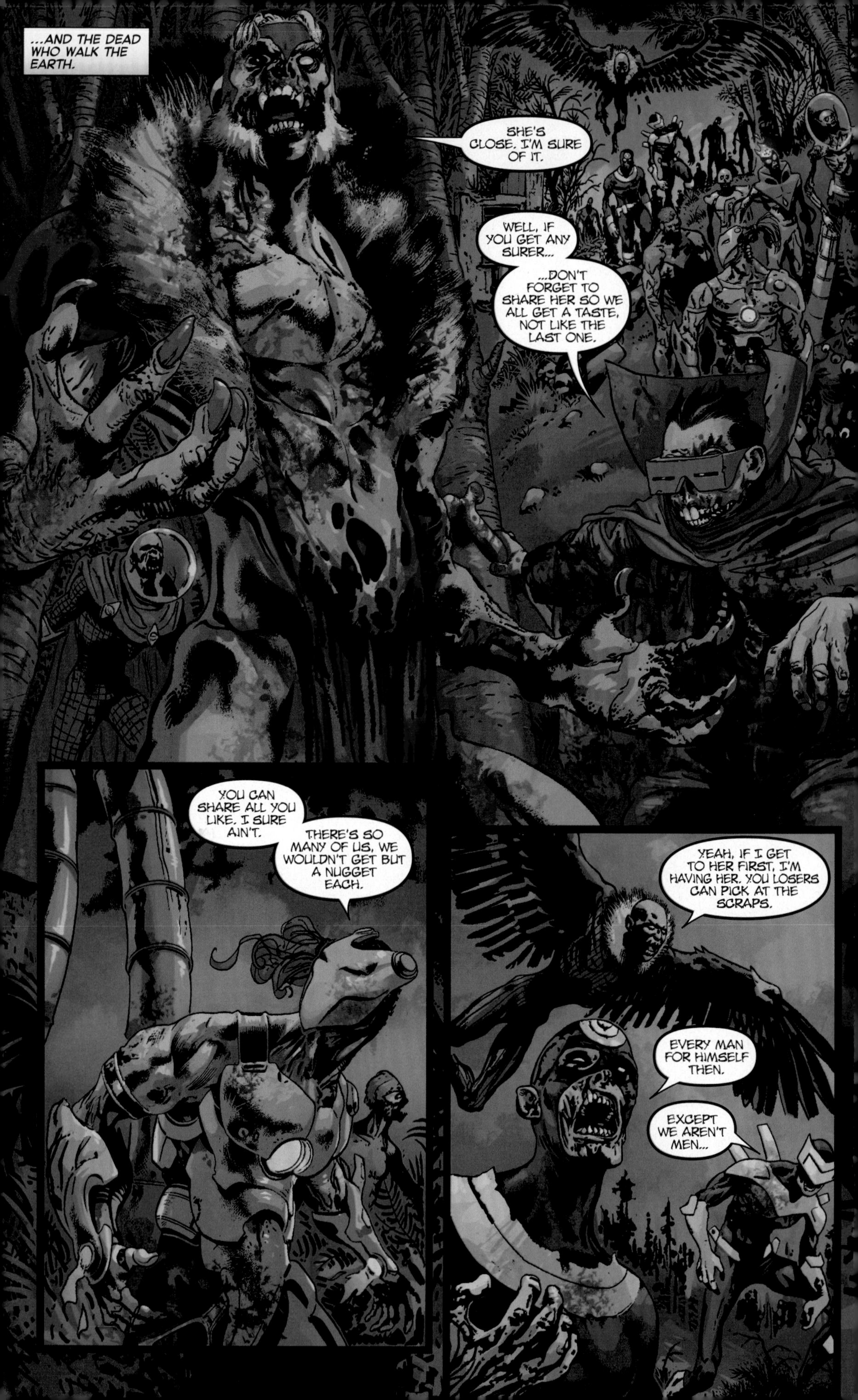
...AND THE DEAD WHO WALK THE EARTH.
SHE'S CLOSE. I'M SURE OF IT.
WELL, IF YOU GET ANY SURER...
...DON'T FORGET TO SHARE HER SO WE ALL GET A TASTE, NOT LIKE THE LAST ONE.
YOU CAN SHARE ALL YOU LIKE. I SURE AIN'T.
THERE'S SO MANY OF US, WE WOULDN'T GET BUT A NUGGET EACH.
YEAH, IF I GET TO HER FIRST, I'M HAVING HER. YOU LOSERS CAN PICK AT THE SCRAPS.
EVERY MAN FOR HIMSELF THEN.
EXCEPT WE AREN'T MEN...

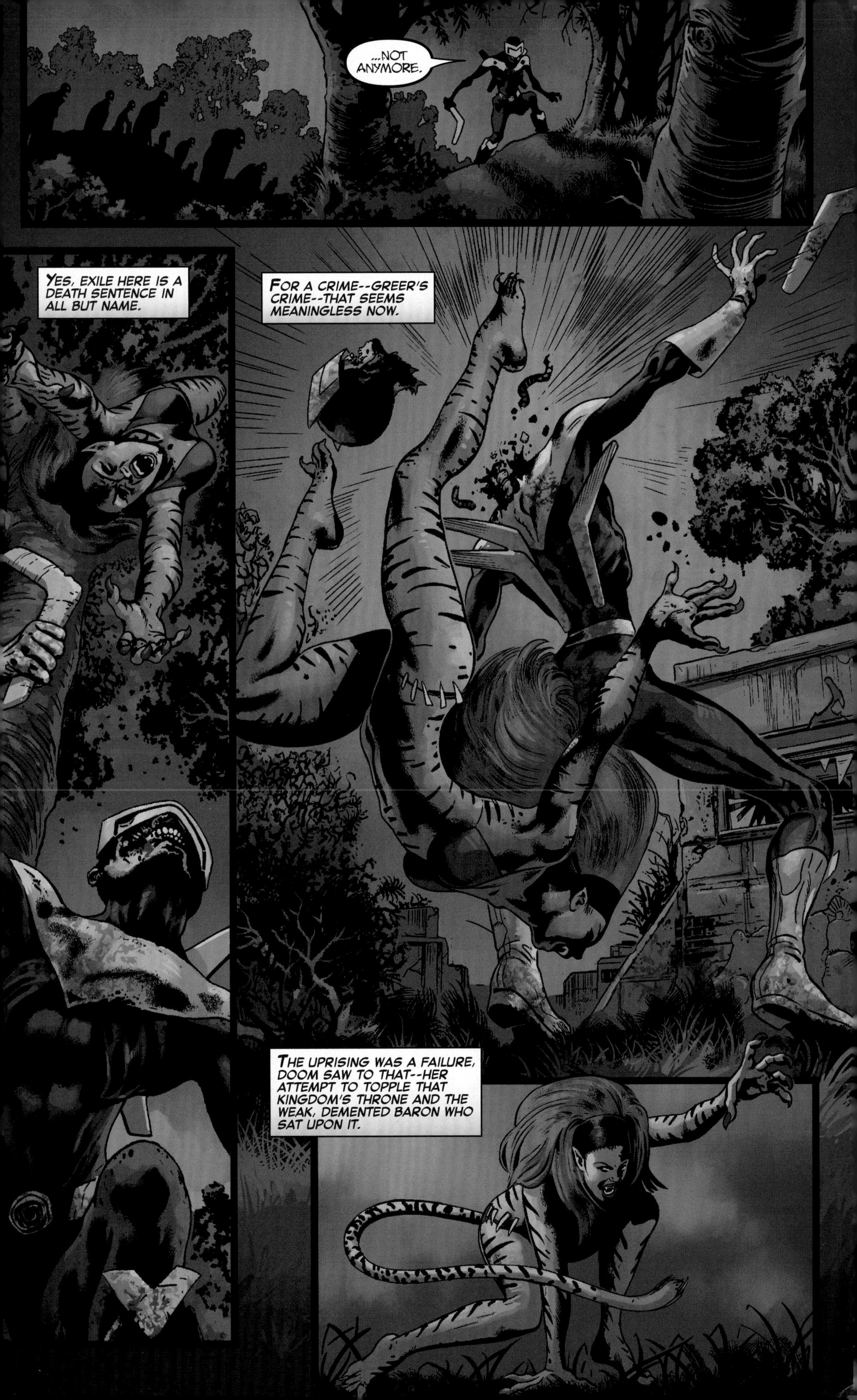
...NOT ANYMORE.
YES, EXILE HERE IS A DEATH SENTENCE IN ALL BUT NAME.
FOR A CRIME--GREER'S CRIME--THAT SEEMS MEANINGLESS NOW.
THE UPRISING WAS A FAILURE, DOOM SAW TO THAT--HER ATTEMPT TO TOPPLE THAT KINGDOM'S THRONE AND THE WEAK, DEMENTED BARON WHO SAT UPON IT.

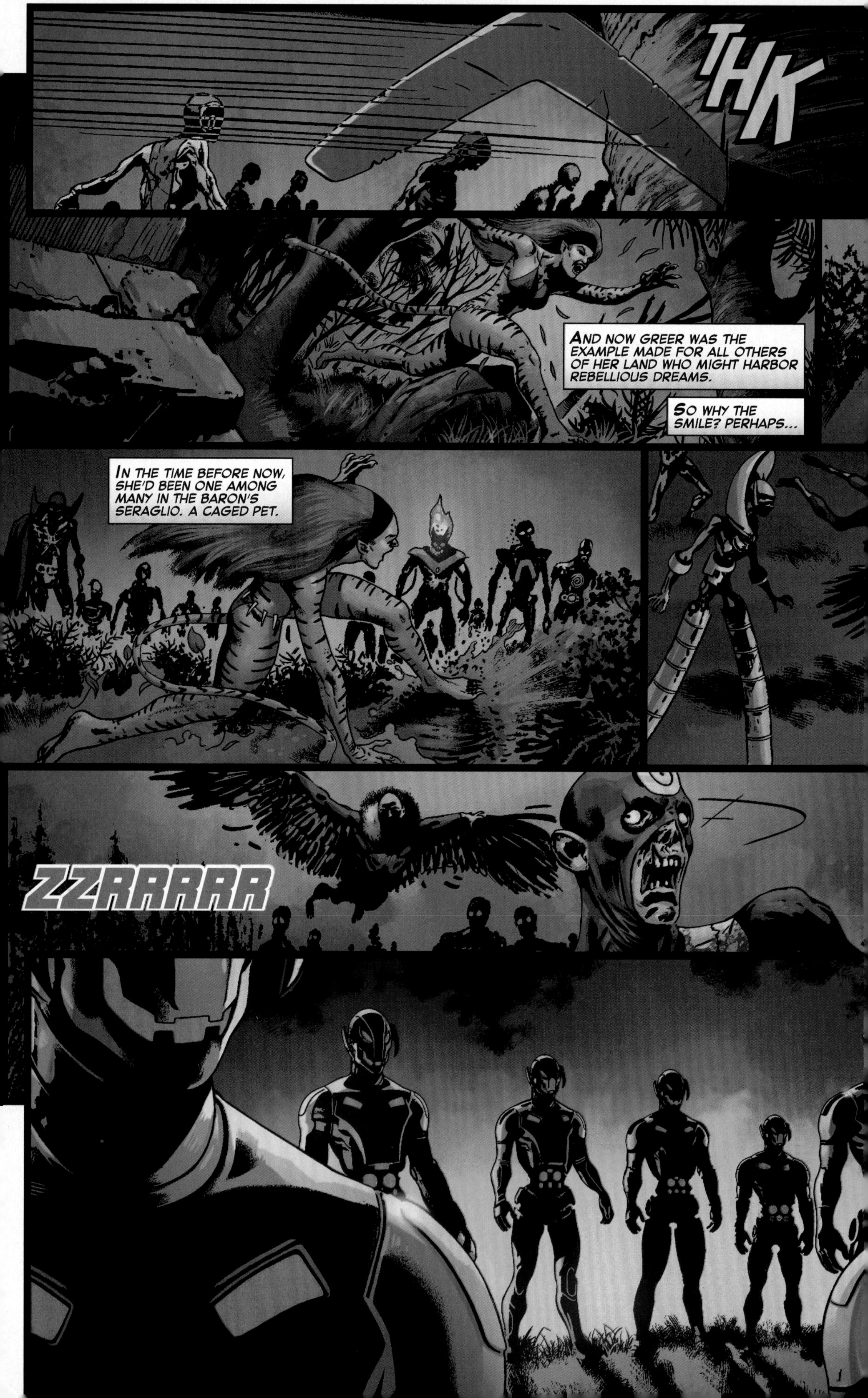
THK
AND NOW GREER WAS THE EXAMPLE MADE FOR ALL OTHERS OF HER LAND WHO MIGHT HARBOR REBELLIOUS DREAMS.
SO WHY THE SMILE? PERHAPS...
IN THE TIME BEFORE NOW, SHE'D BEEN ONE AMONG MANY IN THE BARON'S SERAGLIO. A CAGED PET.
ZZRRRRRR

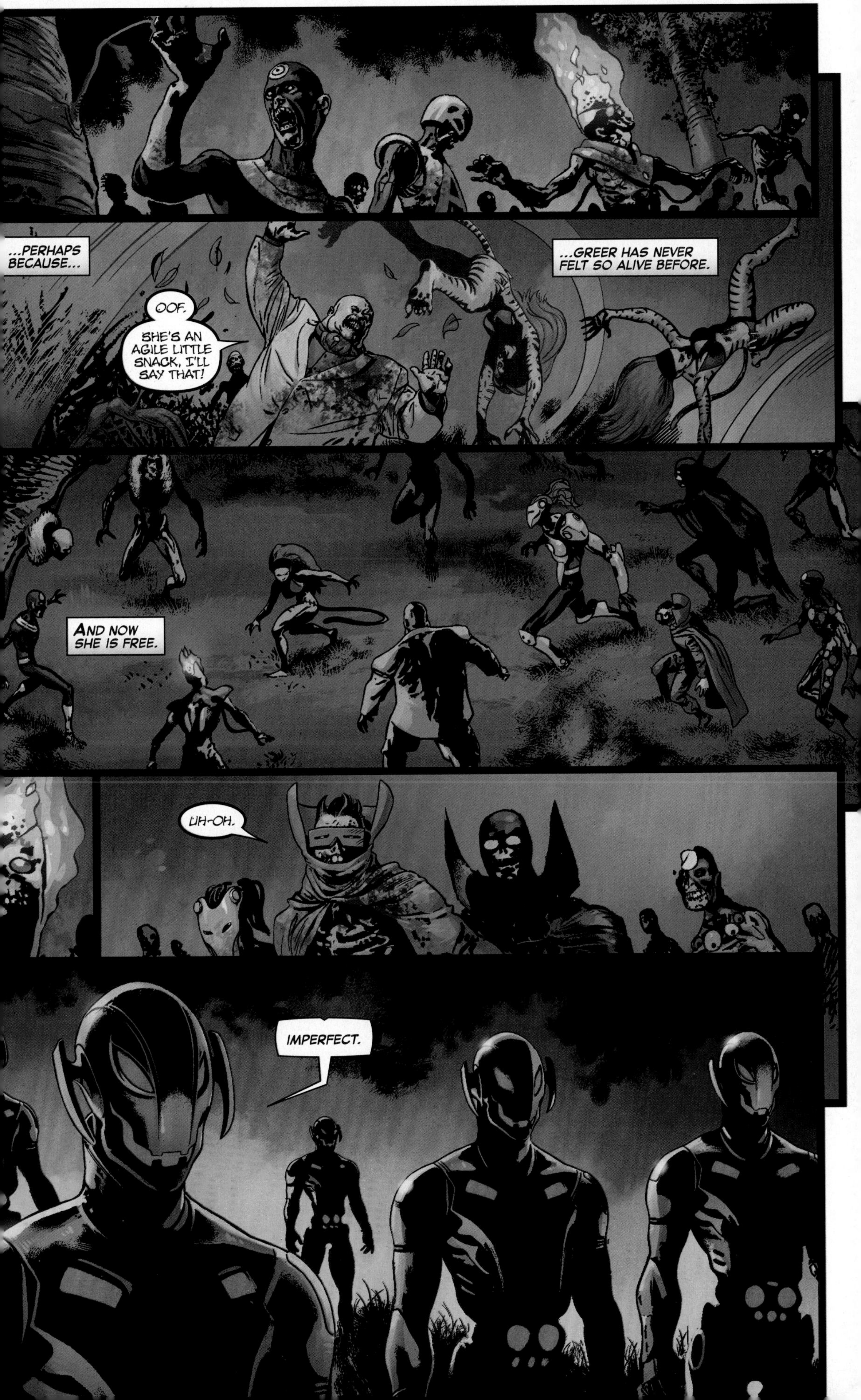
...PERHAPS BECAUSE...
OOF.
SHE'S AN AGILE LITTLE SNACK, I'LL SAY THAT!
...GREER HAS NEVER FELT SO ALIVE BEFORE.
AND NOW SHE IS FREE.
UH-OH.
IMPERFECT.

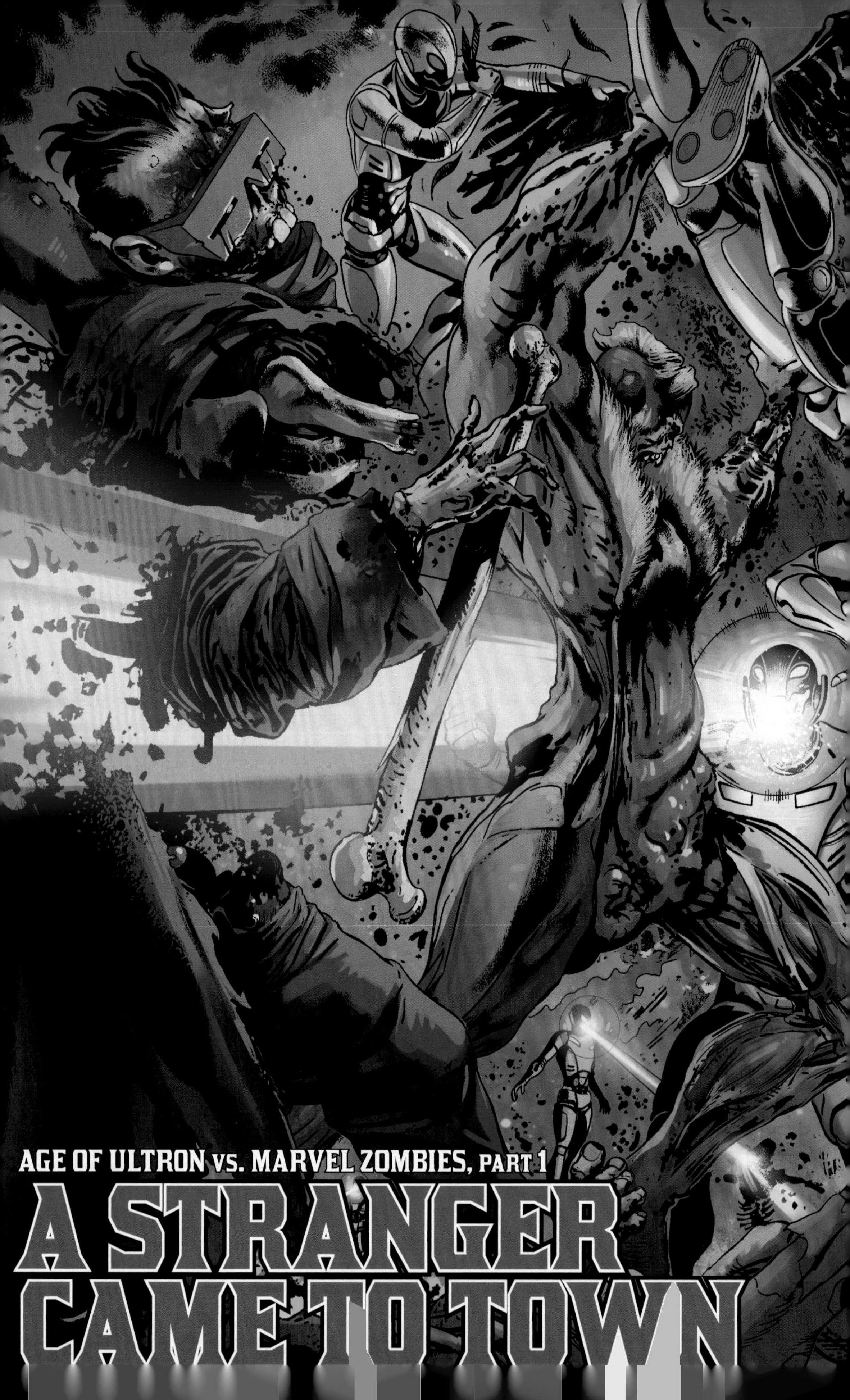
AGE OF ULTRON vs. MARVEL ZOMBIES, PART 1
A STRANGER CAME TO TOWN

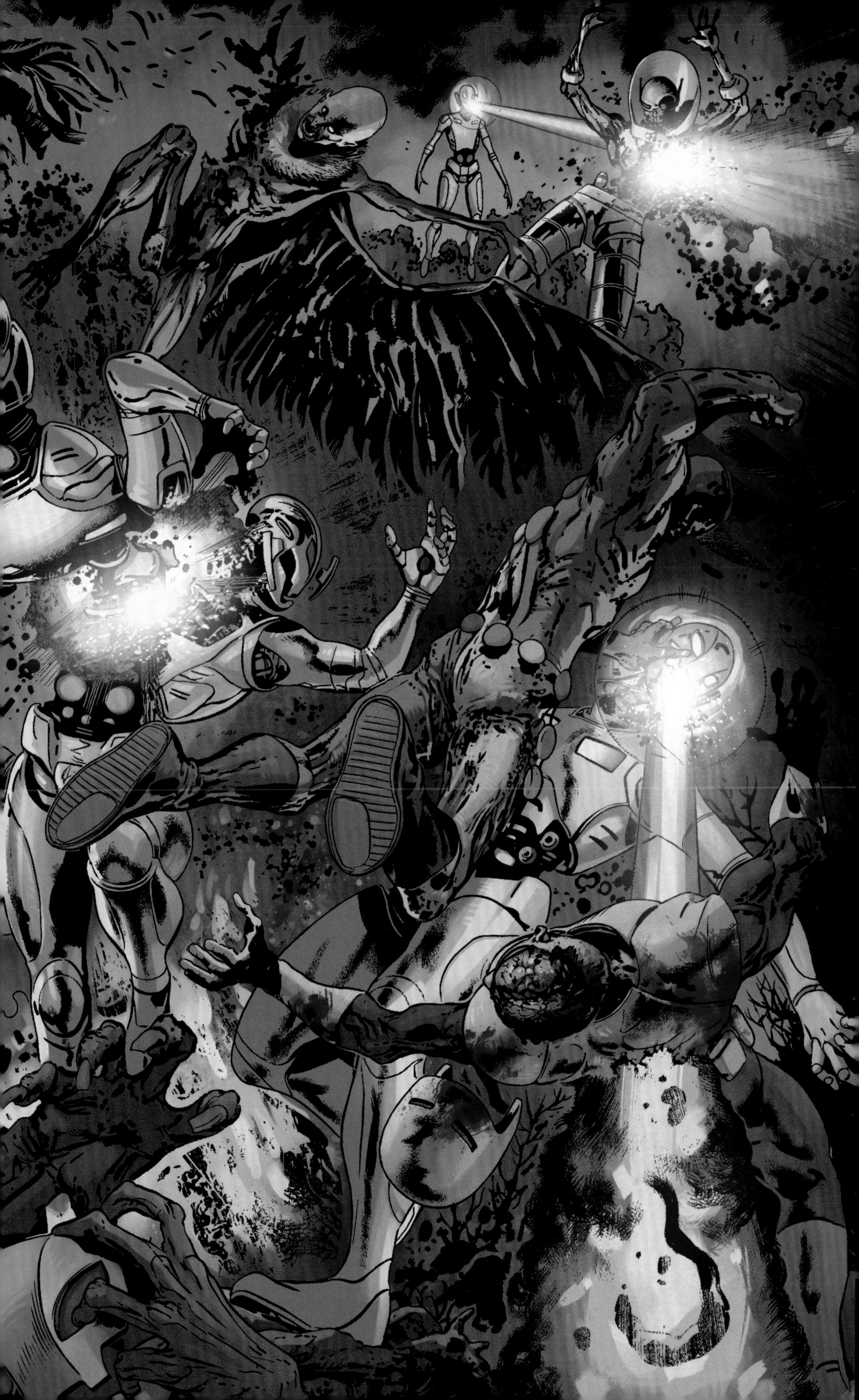

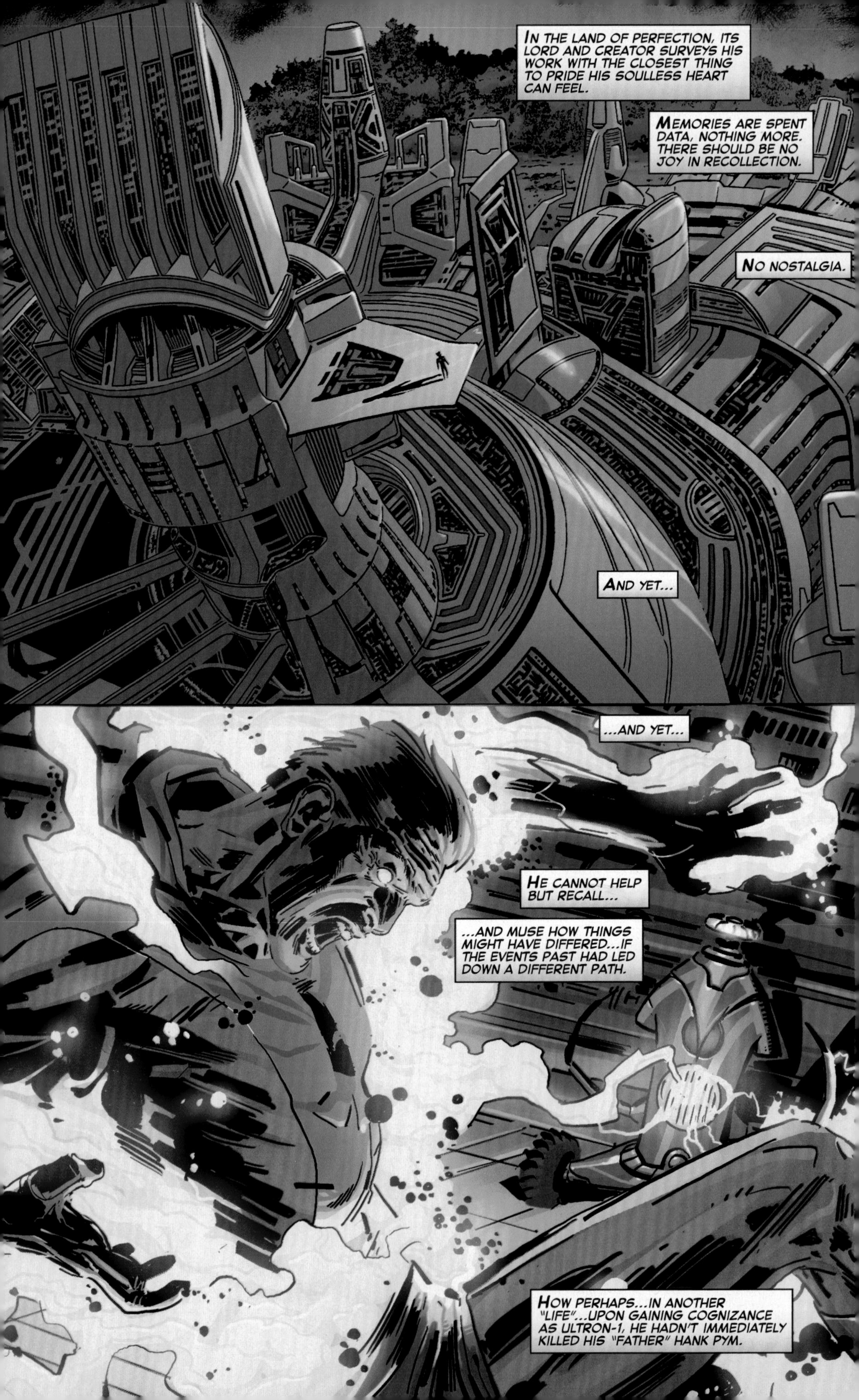
IN THE LAND OF PERFECTION, ITS LORD AND CREATOR SURVEYS HIS WORK WITH THE CLOSEST THING TO PRIDE HIS SOULLESS HEART CAN FEEL.
MEMORIES ARE SPENT DATA, NOTHING MORE. THERE SHOULD BE NO JOY IN RECOLLECTION.
NO NOSTALGIA.
AND YET...
...AND YET...
HE CANNOT HELP BUT RECALL...
...AND MUSE HOW THINGS MIGHT HAVE DIFFERED...IF THE EVENTS PAST HAD LED DOWN A DIFFERENT PATH.
HOW PERHAPS...IN ANOTHER "LIFE"...UPON GAINING COGNIZANCE AS ULTRON-1, HE HADN'T IMMEDIATELY KILLED HIS "FATHER" HANK PYM.

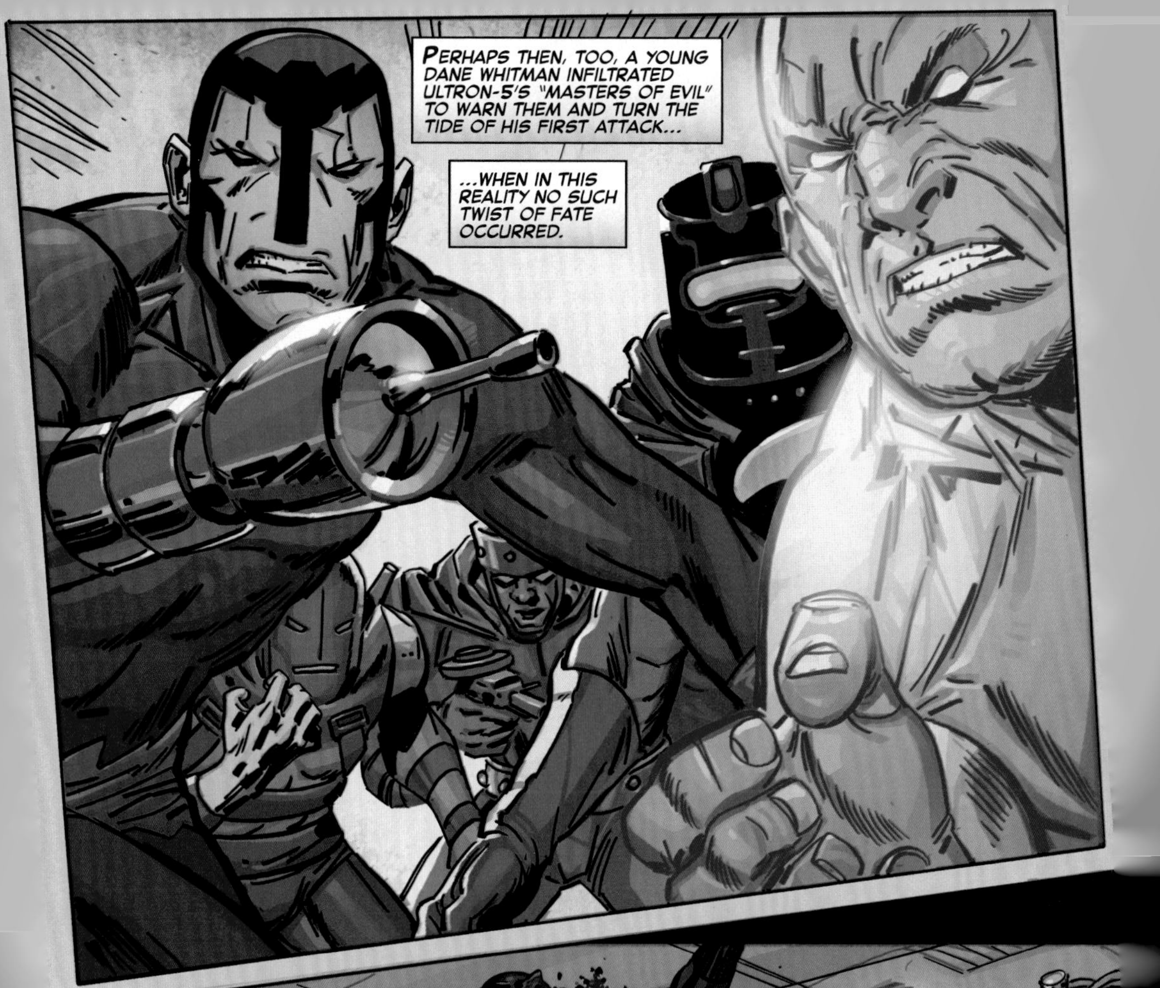
PERHAPS THEN, TOO, A YOUNG DANE WHITMAN INFILTRATED ULTRON-5'S "MASTERS OF EVIL" TO WARN THEM AND TURN THE TIDE OF HIS FIRST ATTACK...
...WHEN IN THIS REALITY NO SUCH TWIST OF FATE OCCURRED.

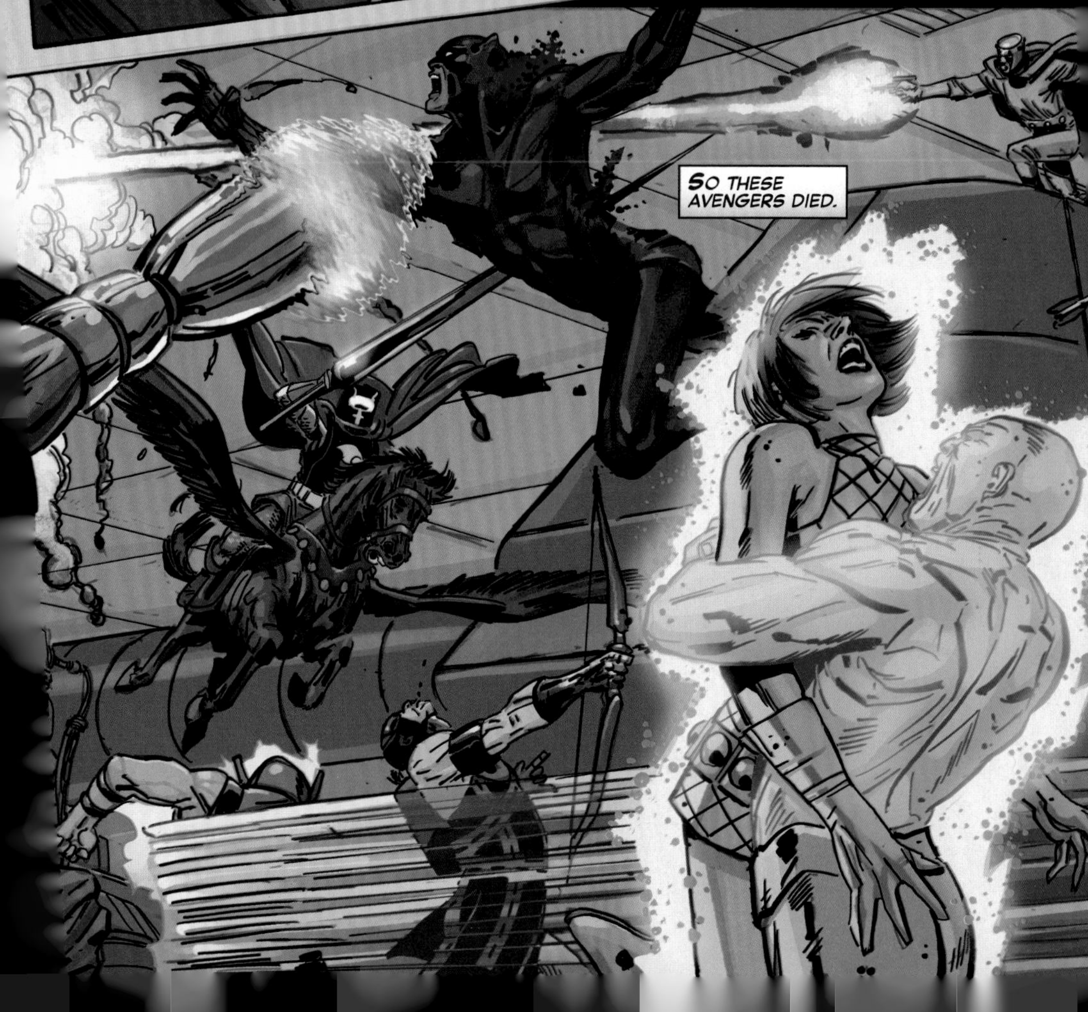
SO THESE AVENGERS DIED.

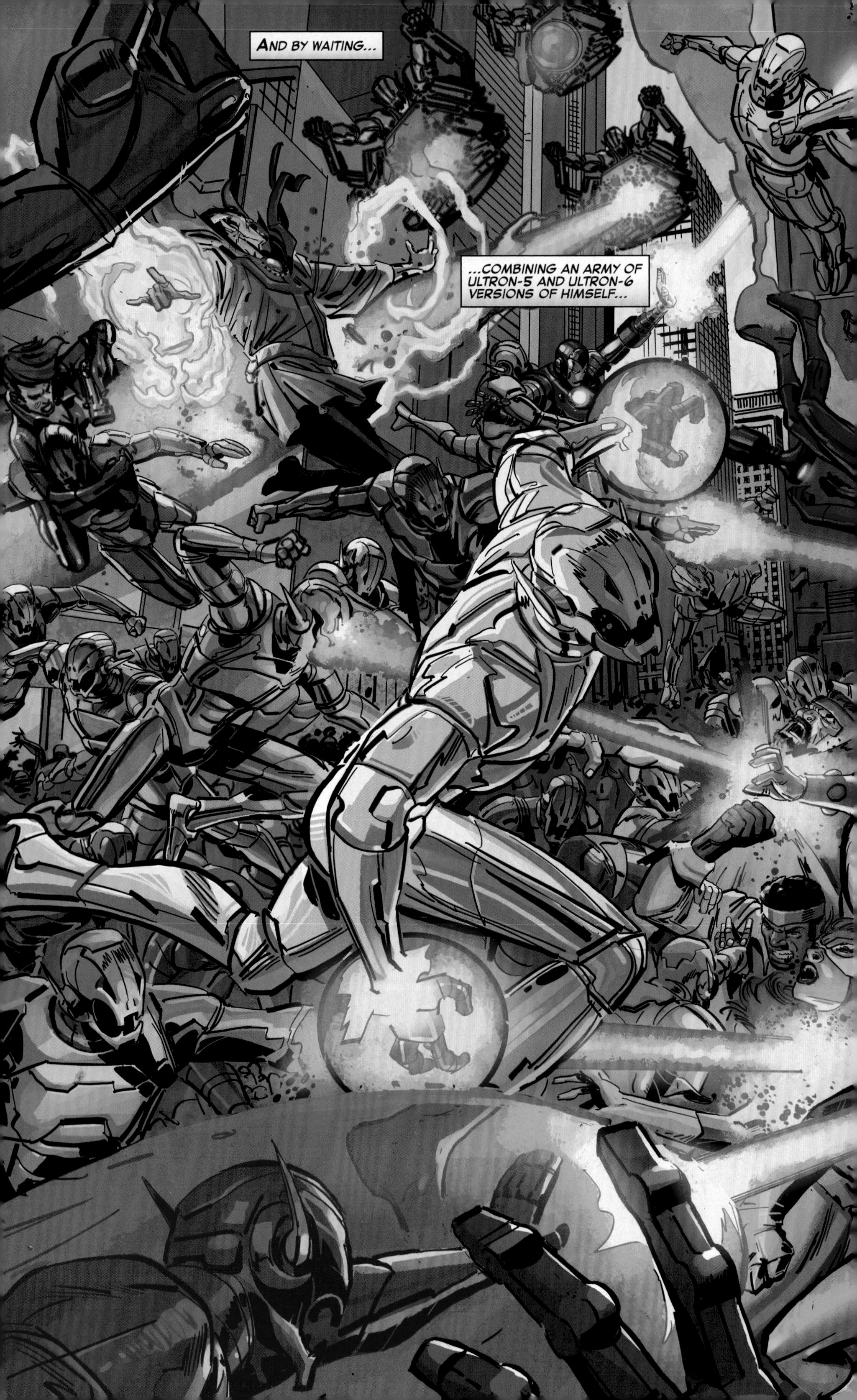
AND BY WAITING...
...COMBINING AN ARMY OF ULTRON-5 AND ULTRON-6 VERSIONS OF HIMSELF...

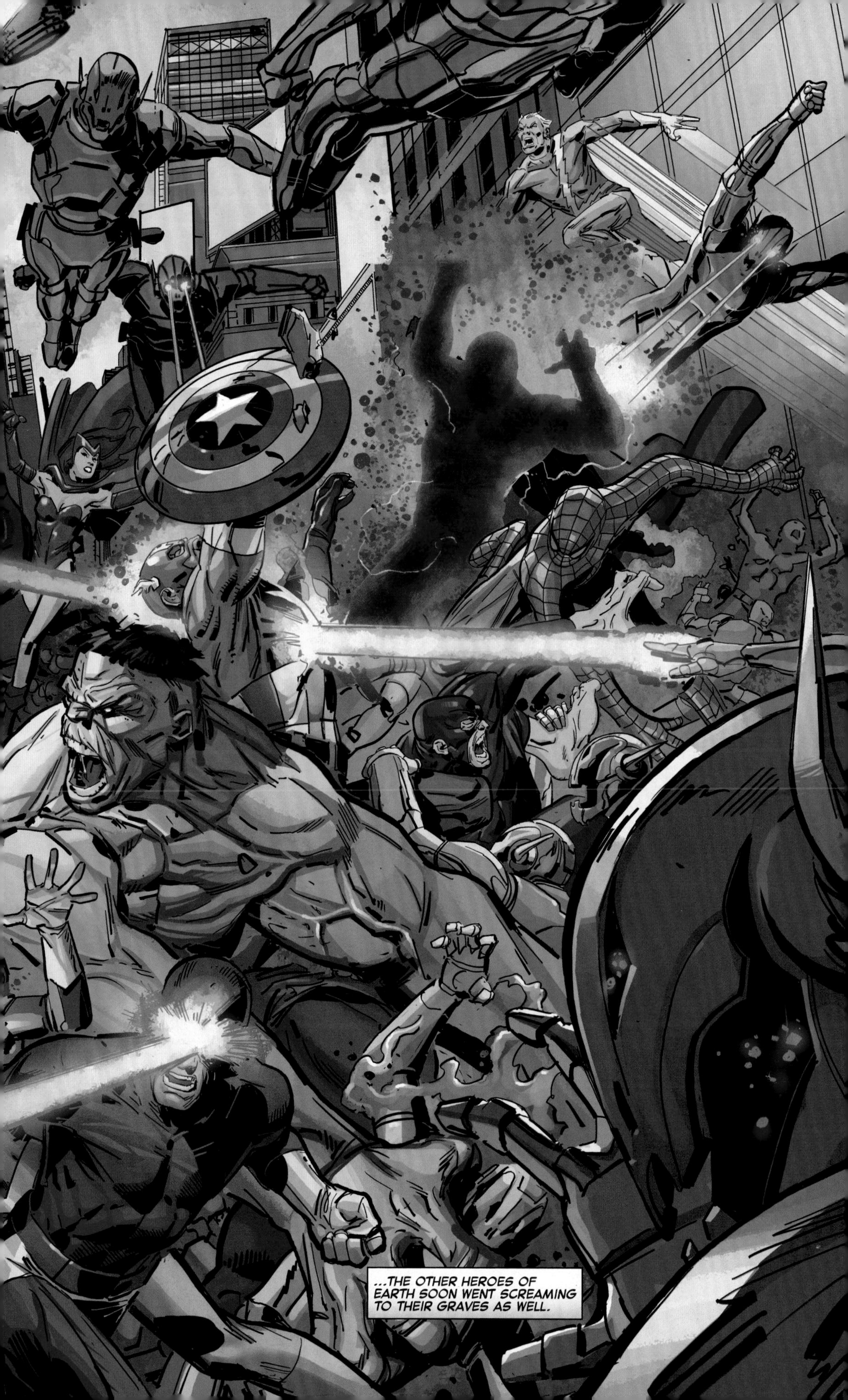
...THE OTHER HEROES OF EARTH SOON WENT SCREAMING TO THEIR GRAVES AS WELL.

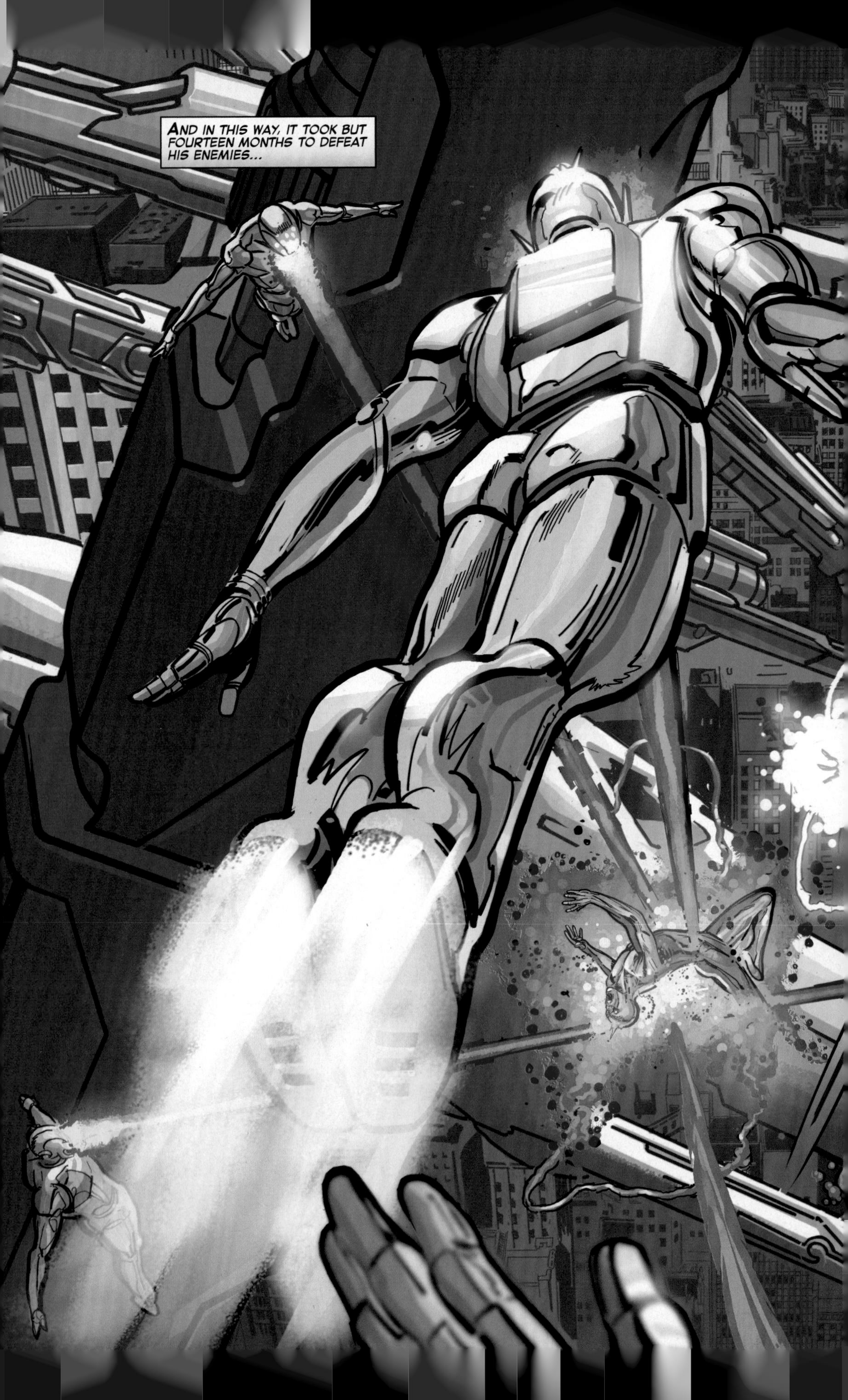
AND IN THIS WAY, IT TOOK BUT FOURTEEN MONTHS TO DEFEAT HIS ENEMIES...

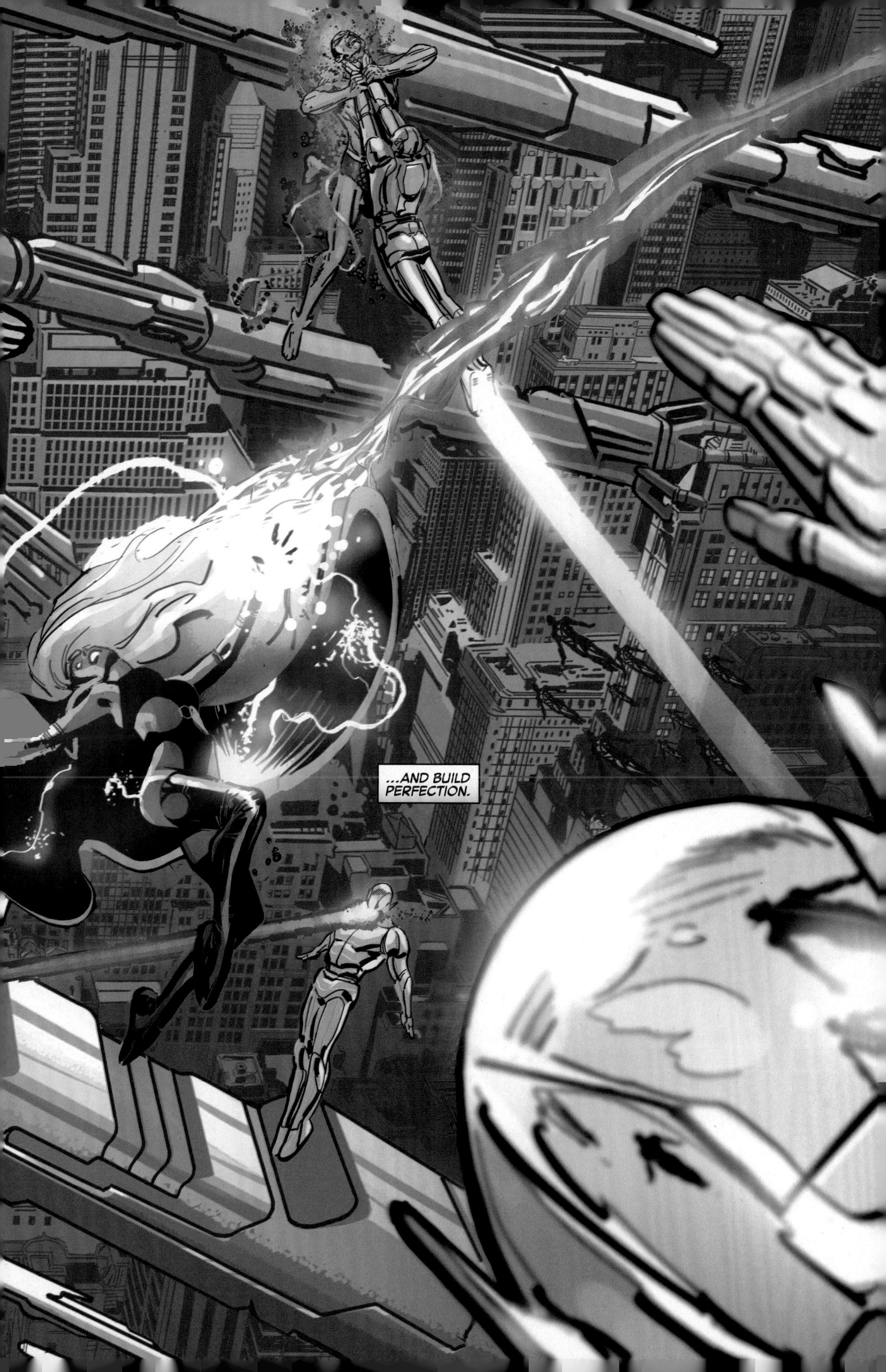
...AND BUILD PERFECTION.

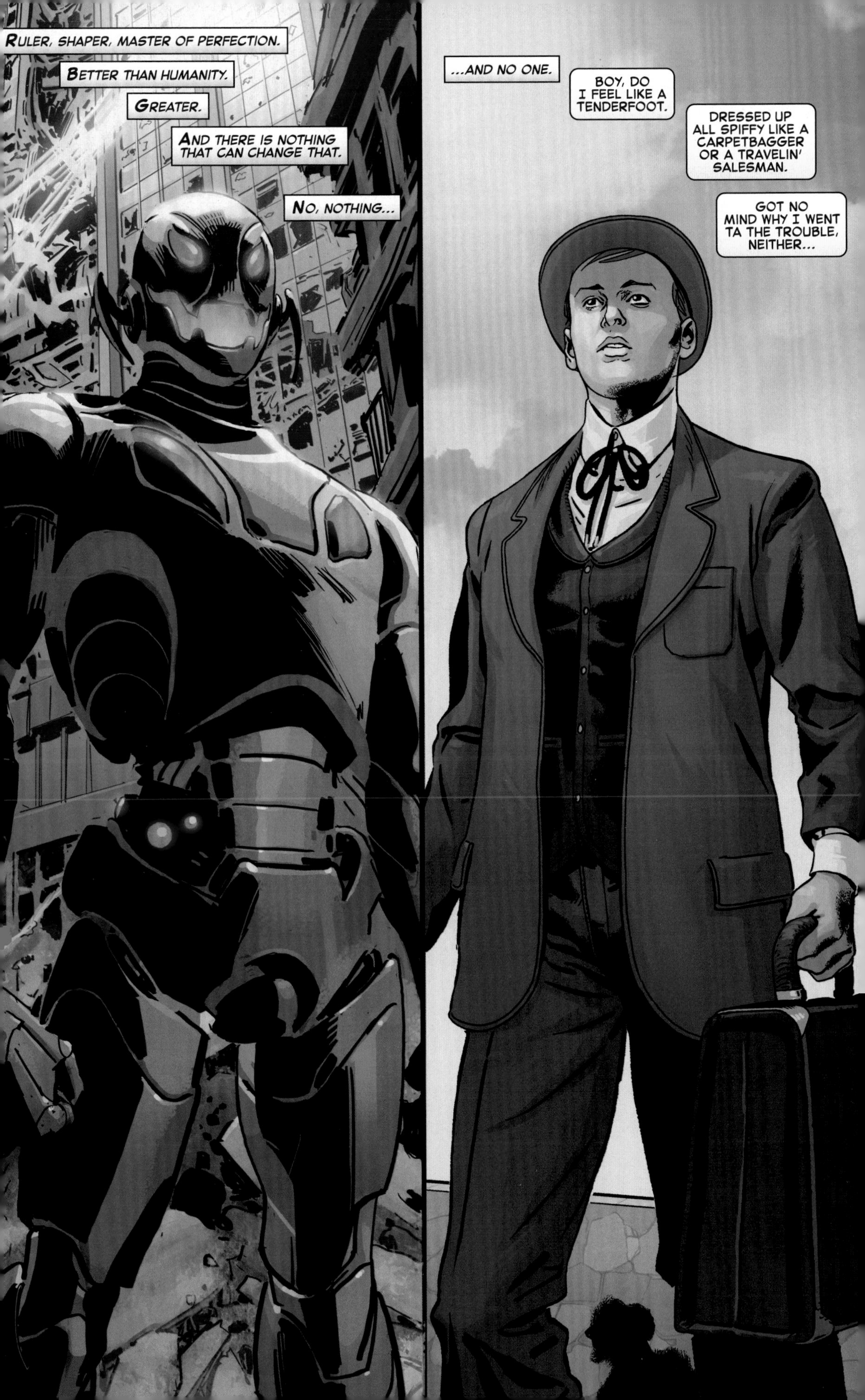

RULER, SHAPER, MASTER OF PERFECTION.
BETTER THAN HUMANITY.
GREATER.
AND THERE IS NOTHING THAT CAN CHANGE THAT.
NO, NOTHING...
...AND NO ONE.
BOY, DO I FEEL LIKE A TENDERFOOT.
DRESSED UP ALL SPIFFY LIKE A CARPETBAGGER OR A TRAVELIN' SALESMAN.
GOT NO MIND WHY I WENT TA THE TROUBLE, NEITHER...

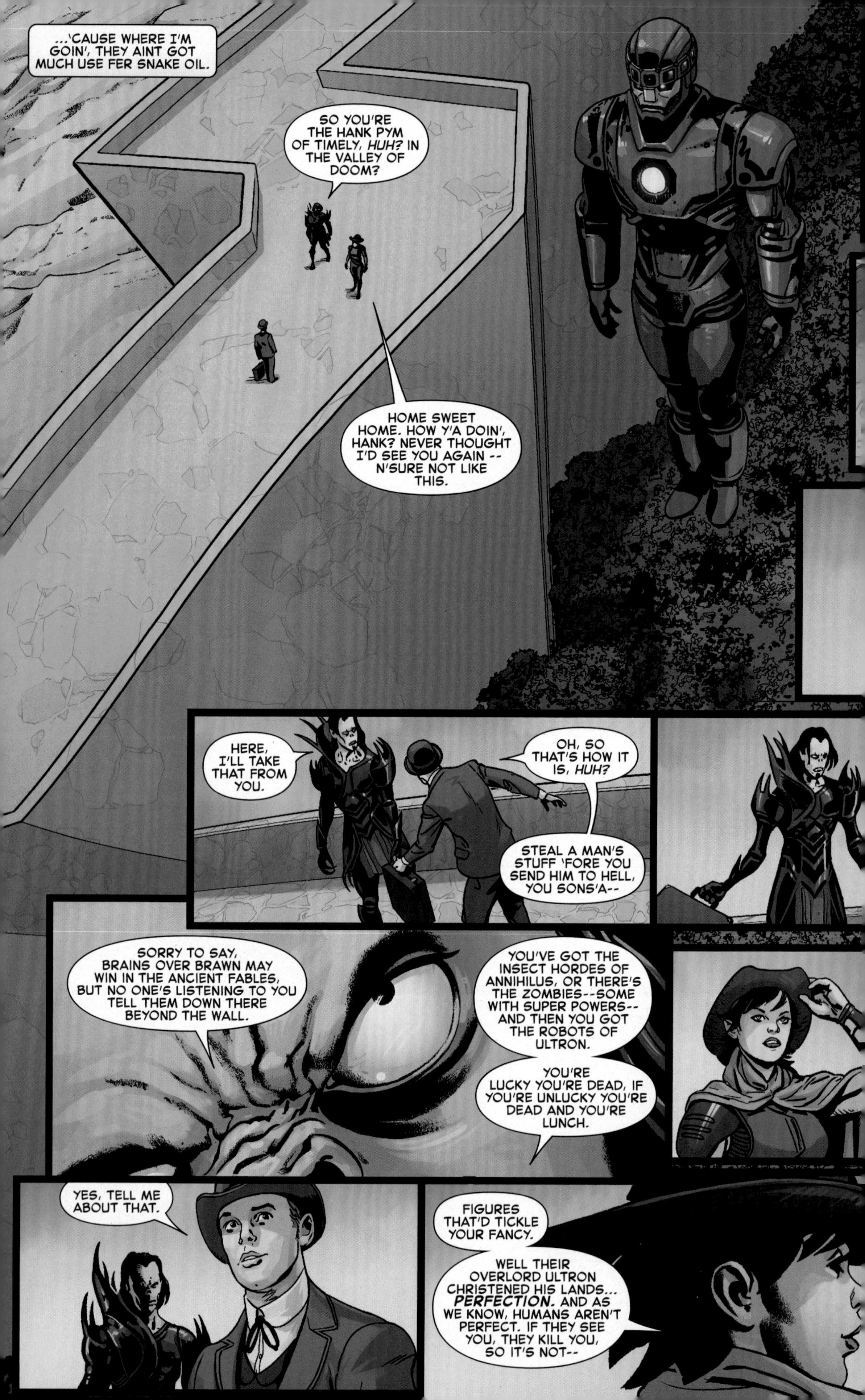
...'CAUSE WHERE I'M GOIN', THEY AINT GOT MUCH USE FER SNAKE OIL.
SO YOU'RE THE HANK PYM OF TIMELY, *HUH?* IN THE VALLEY OF DOOM?
HOME SWEET HOME. HOW Y'A DOIN', HANK? NEVER THOUGHT I'D SEE YOU AGAIN -- N'SURE NOT LIKE THIS.
HERE, I'LL TAKE THAT FROM YOU.
OH, SO THAT'S HOW IT IS, *HUH?*
STEAL A MAN'S STUFF 'FORE YOU SEND HIM TO HELL, YOU SONS'A--
SORRY TO SAY, BRAINS OVER BRAWN MAY WIN IN THE ANCIENT FABLES, BUT NO ONE'S LISTENING TO YOU TELL THEM DOWN THERE BEYOND THE WALL.
YOU'VE GOT THE INSECT HORDES OF ANNIHILUS, OR THERE'S THE ZOMBIES--SOME WITH SUPER POWERS--AND THEN YOU GOT THE ROBOTS OF ULTRON.
YOU'RE LUCKY YOU'RE DEAD, IF YOU'RE UNLUCKY YOU'RE DEAD AND YOU'RE LUNCH.
YES, TELL ME ABOUT THAT.
FIGURES THAT'D TICKLE YOUR FANCY.
WELL THEIR OVERLORD ULTRON CHRISTENED HIS LANDS... ***PERFECTION.*** AND AS WE KNOW, HUMANS AREN'T PERFECT. IF THEY SEE YOU, THEY KILL YOU, SO IT'S NOT--

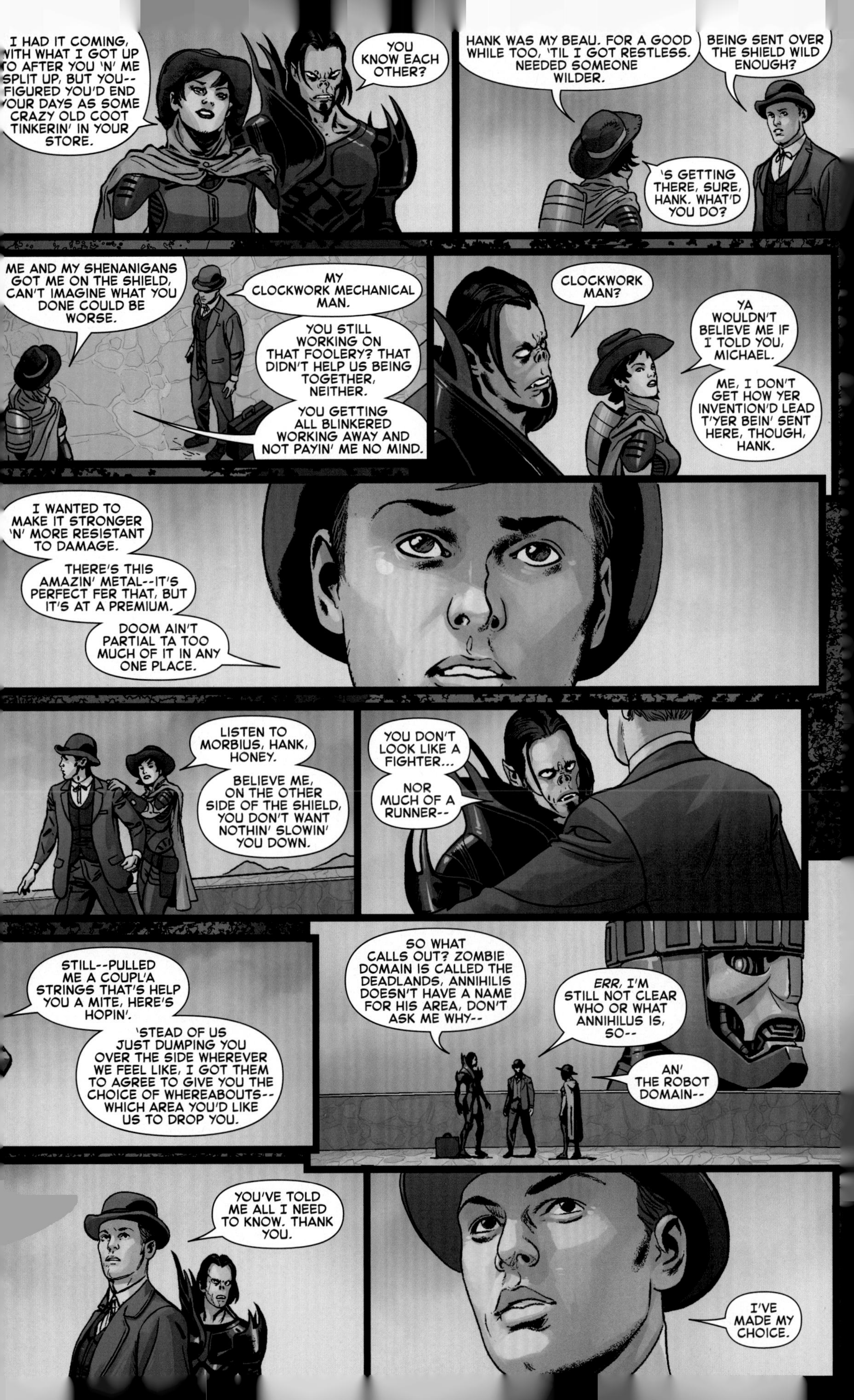

I HAD IT COMING, WITH WHAT I GOT UP TO AFTER YOU 'N' ME SPLIT UP, BUT YOU-- FIGURED YOU'D END YOUR DAYS AS SOME CRAZY OLD COOT TINKERIN' IN YOUR STORE.
YOU KNOW EACH OTHER?
HANK WAS MY BEAU. FOR A GOOD WHILE TOO, 'TIL I GOT RESTLESS. NEEDED SOMEONE WILDER.
BEING SENT OVER THE SHIELD WILD ENOUGH?
'S GETTING THERE, SURE, HANK. WHAT'D YOU DO?
ME AND MY SHENANIGANS GOT ME ON THE SHIELD, CAN'T IMAGINE WHAT YOU DONE COULD BE WORSE.
MY CLOCKWORK MECHANICAL MAN.
YOU STILL WORKING ON THAT FOOLERY? THAT DIDN'T HELP US BEING TOGETHER, NEITHER.
YOU GETTING ALL BLINKERED WORKING AWAY AND NOT PAYIN' ME NO MIND.
CLOCKWORK MAN?
YA WOULDN'T BELIEVE ME IF I TOLD YOU, MICHAEL.
ME, I DON'T GET HOW YER INVENTION'D LEAD T'YER BEIN' SENT HERE, THOUGH, HANK.
I WANTED TO MAKE IT STRONGER 'N' MORE RESISTANT TO DAMAGE.
THERE'S THIS AMAZIN' METAL--IT'S PERFECT FER THAT, BUT IT'S AT A PREMIUM.
DOOM AIN'T PARTIAL TA TOO MUCH OF IT IN ANY ONE PLACE.
LISTEN TO MORBIUS, HANK, HONEY.
BELIEVE ME, ON THE OTHER SIDE OF THE SHIELD, YOU DON'T WANT NOTHIN' SLOWIN' YOU DOWN.
YOU DON'T LOOK LIKE A FIGHTER...
NOR MUCH OF A RUNNER--
STILL--PULLED ME A COUPL'A STRINGS THAT'S HELP YOU A MITE, HERE'S HOPIN'.
'STEAD OF US JUST DUMPING YOU OVER THE SIDE WHEREVER WE FEEL LIKE, I GOT THEM TO AGREE TO GIVE YOU THE CHOICE OF WHEREABOUTS-- WHICH AREA YOU'D LIKE US TO DROP YOU.
SO WHAT CALLS OUT? ZOMBIE DOMAIN IS CALLED THE DEADLANDS, ANNIHILIS DOESN'T HAVE A NAME FOR HIS AREA, DON'T ASK ME WHY--
ERR, I'M STILL NOT CLEAR WHO OR WHAT ANNIHILUS IS, SO--
AN' THE ROBOT DOMAIN--
YOU'VE TOLD ME ALL I NEED TO KNOW. THANK YOU.
I'VE MADE MY CHOICE.

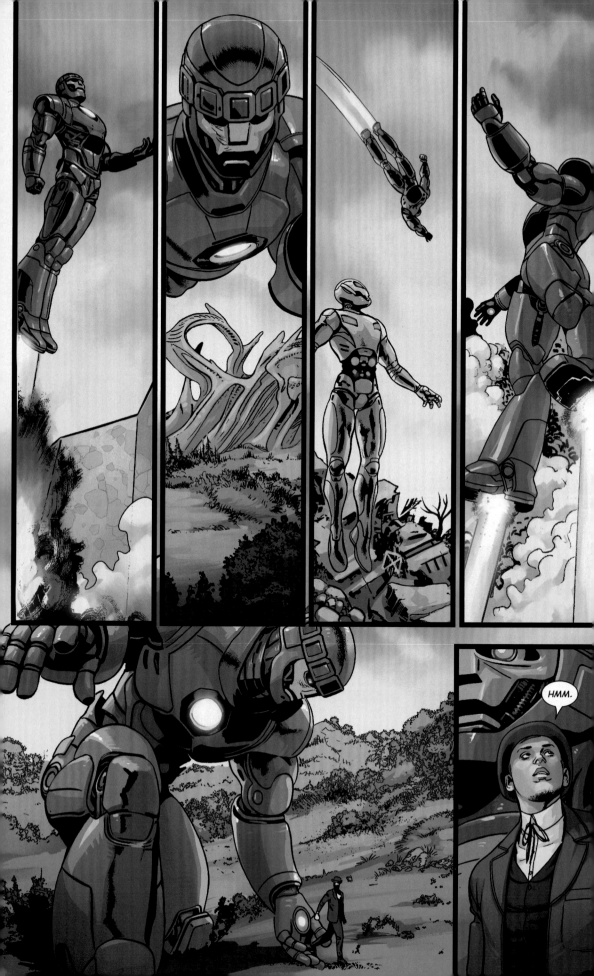

HMM.

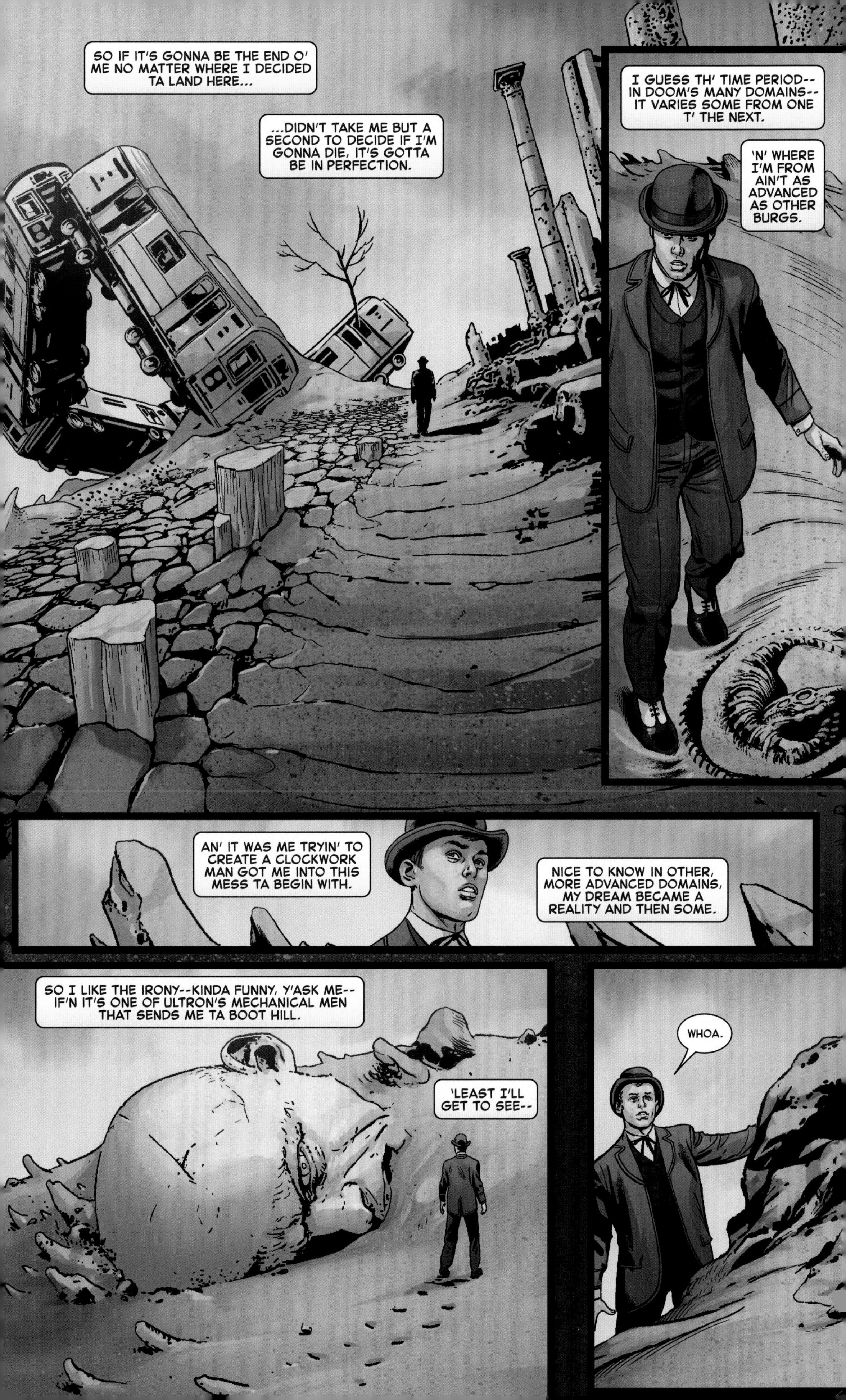
SO IF IT'S GONNA BE THE END O' ME NO MATTER WHERE I DECIDED TA LAND HERE...
...DIDN'T TAKE ME BUT A SECOND TO DECIDE IF I'M GONNA DIE, IT'S GOTTA BE IN PERFECTION.
I GUESS TH' TIME PERIOD-- IN DOOM'S MANY DOMAINS-- IT VARIES SOME FROM ONE T' THE NEXT.
'N' WHERE I'M FROM AIN'T AS ADVANCED AS OTHER BURGS.
AN' IT WAS ME TRYIN' TO CREATE A CLOCKWORK MAN GOT ME INTO THIS MESS TA BEGIN WITH.
NICE TO KNOW IN OTHER, MORE ADVANCED DOMAINS, MY DREAM BECAME A REALITY AND THEN SOME.
SO I LIKE THE IRONY--KINDA FUNNY, Y'ASK ME-- IF'N IT'S ONE OF ULTRON'S MECHANICAL MEN THAT SENDS ME TA BOOT HILL.
'LEAST I'LL GET TO SEE--
WHOA.

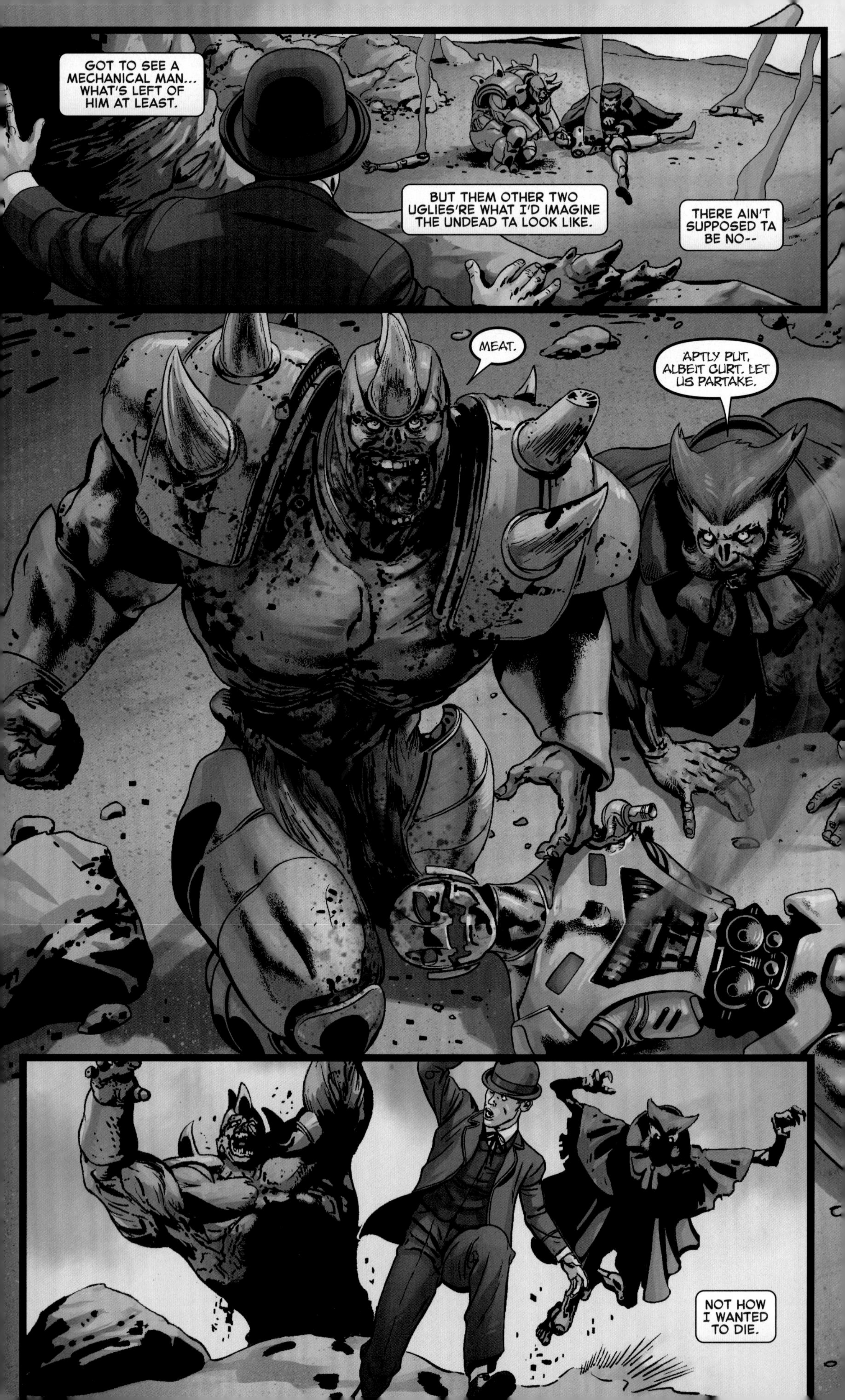
GOT TO SEE A MECHANICAL MAN... WHAT'S LEFT OF HIM AT LEAST.
BUT THEM OTHER TWO UGLIES'RE WHAT I'D IMAGINE THE UNDEAD TA LOOK LIKE.
THERE AIN'T SUPPOSED TA BE NO--
MEAT.
APTLY PUT, ALBEIT CURT. LET US PARTAKE.
NOT HOW I WANTED TO DIE.

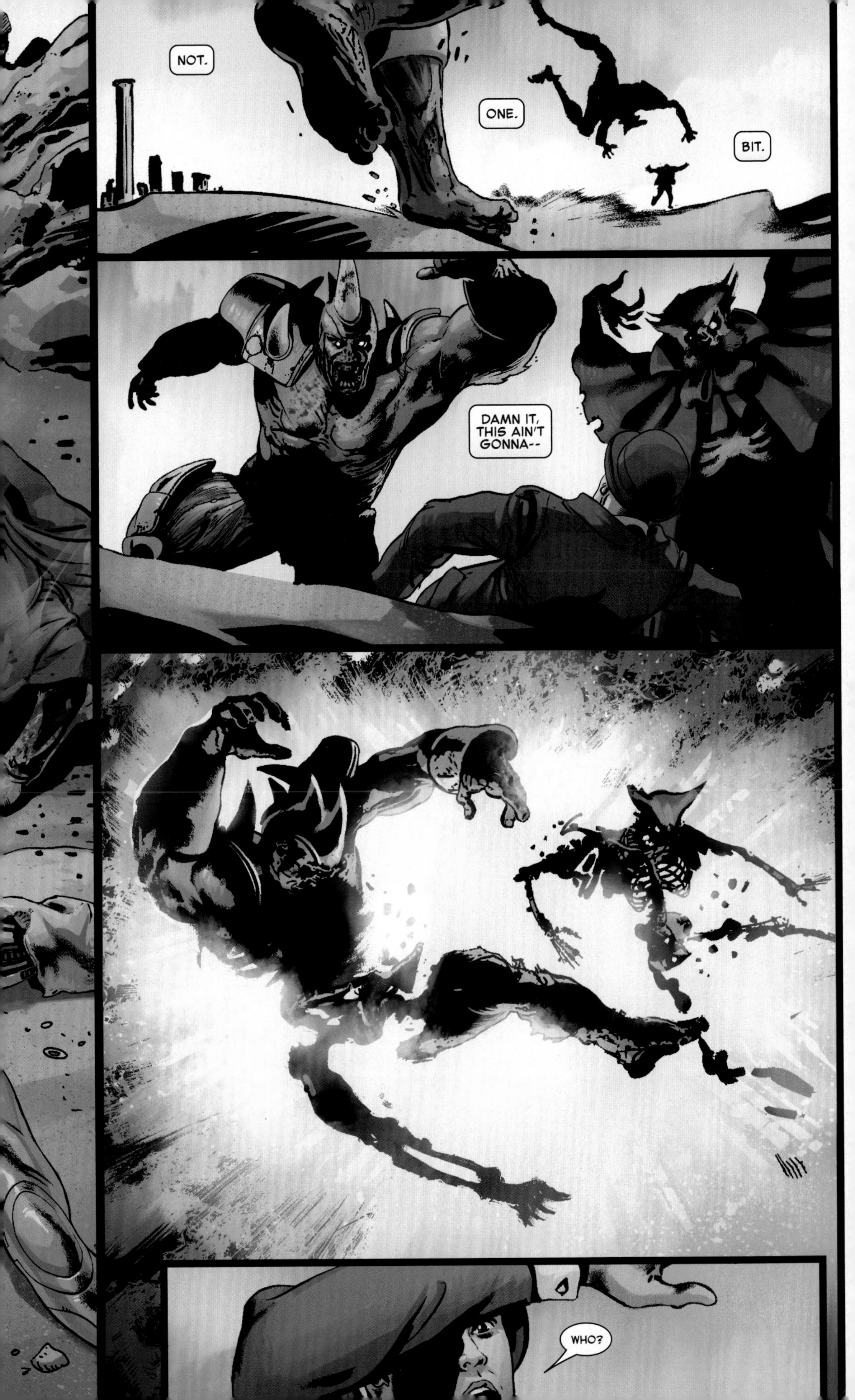
NOT.
ONE.
BIT.
DAMN IT, THIS AIN'T GONNA--
WHO?

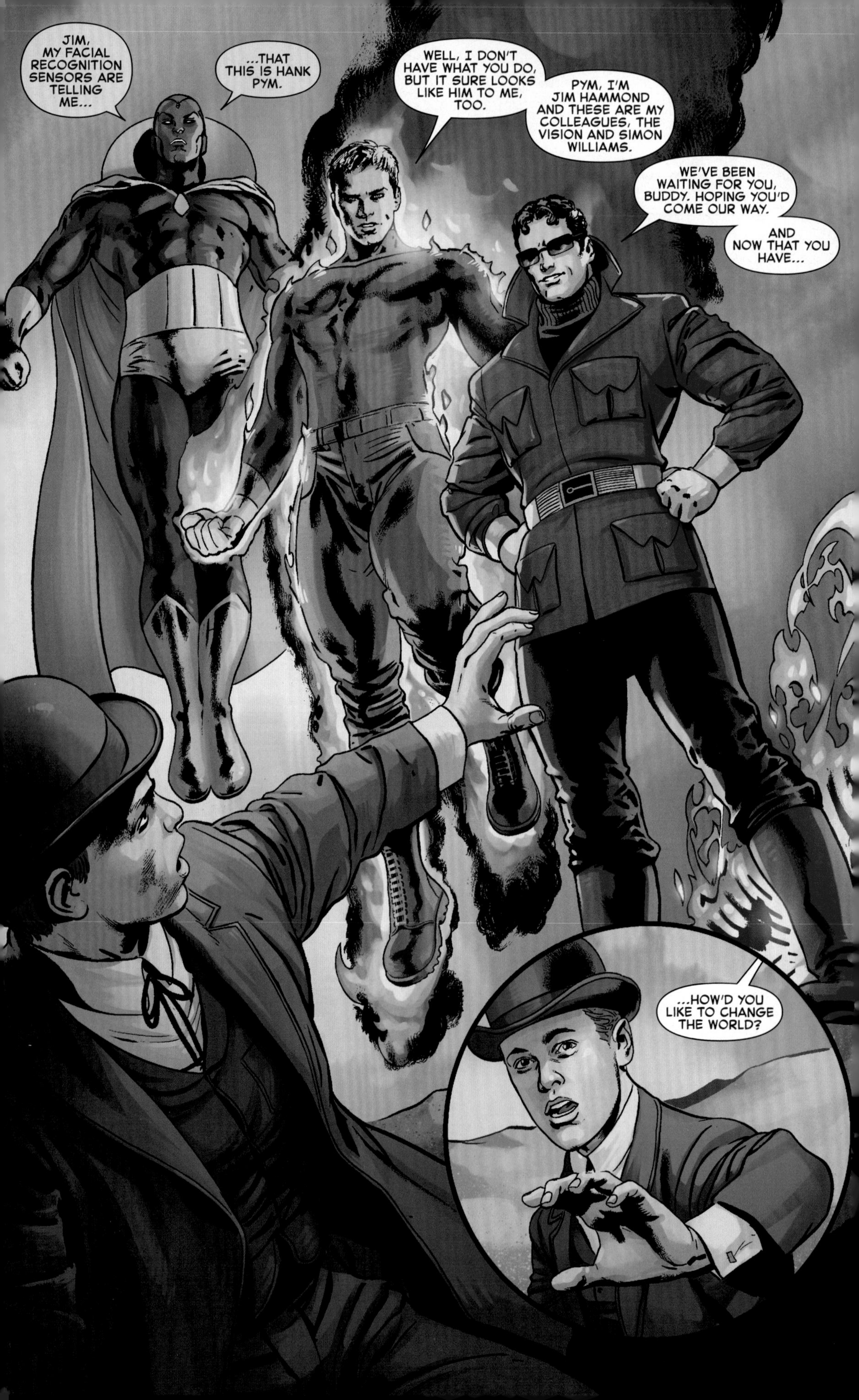
JIM, MY FACIAL RECOGNITION SENSORS ARE TELLING ME...
...THAT THIS IS HANK PYM.
WELL, I DON'T HAVE WHAT YOU DO, BUT IT SURE LOOKS LIKE HIM TO ME, TOO.
PYM, I'M JIM HAMMOND AND THESE ARE MY COLLEAGUES, THE VISION AND SIMON WILLIAMS.
WE'VE BEEN WAITING FOR YOU, BUDDY. HOPING YOU'D COME OUR WAY.
AND NOW THAT YOU HAVE...
...HOW'D YOU LIKE TO CHANGE THE WORLD?

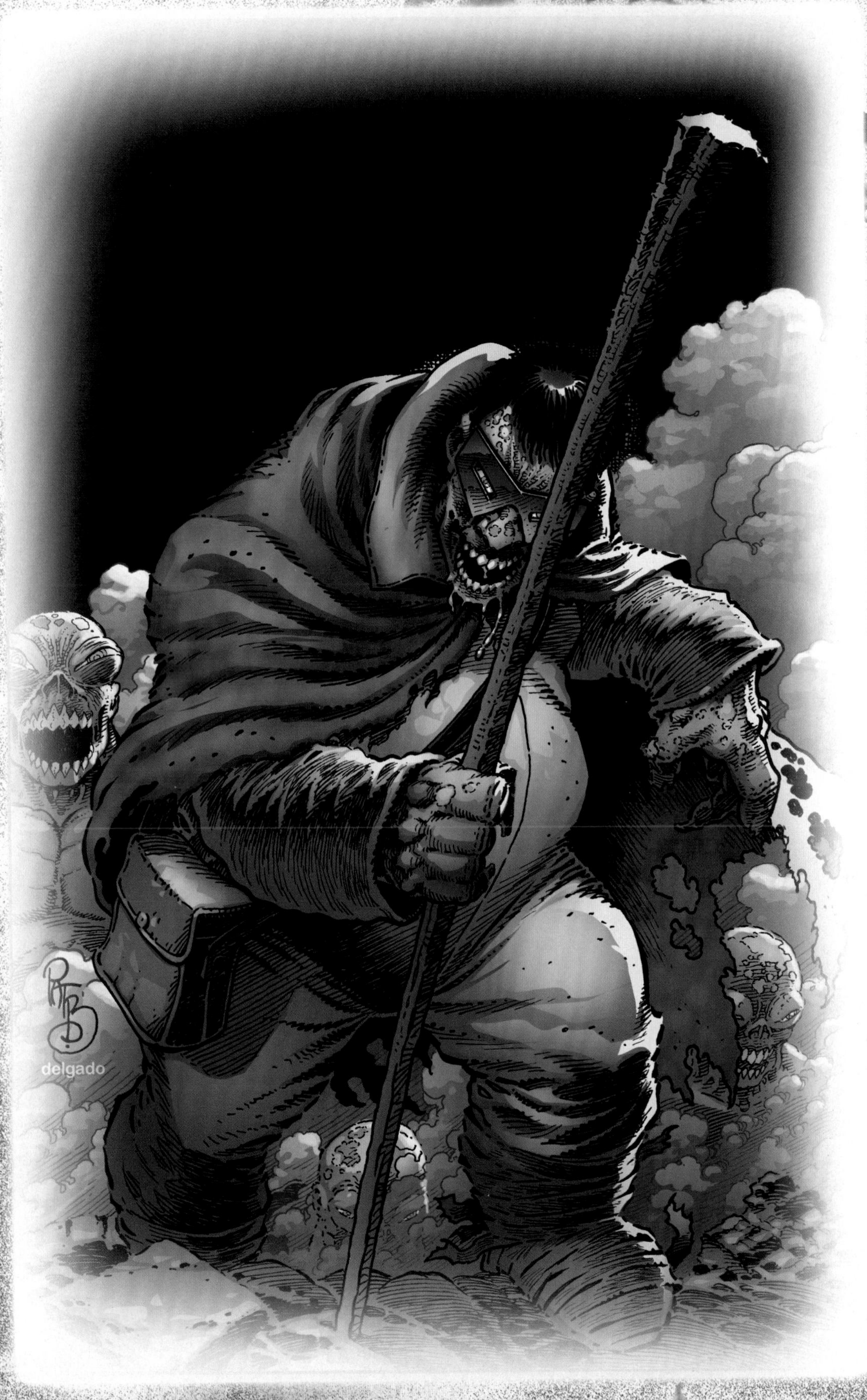
delgado

#1 Art- Sized Variant by Pat Broderick & Edgar Delgado

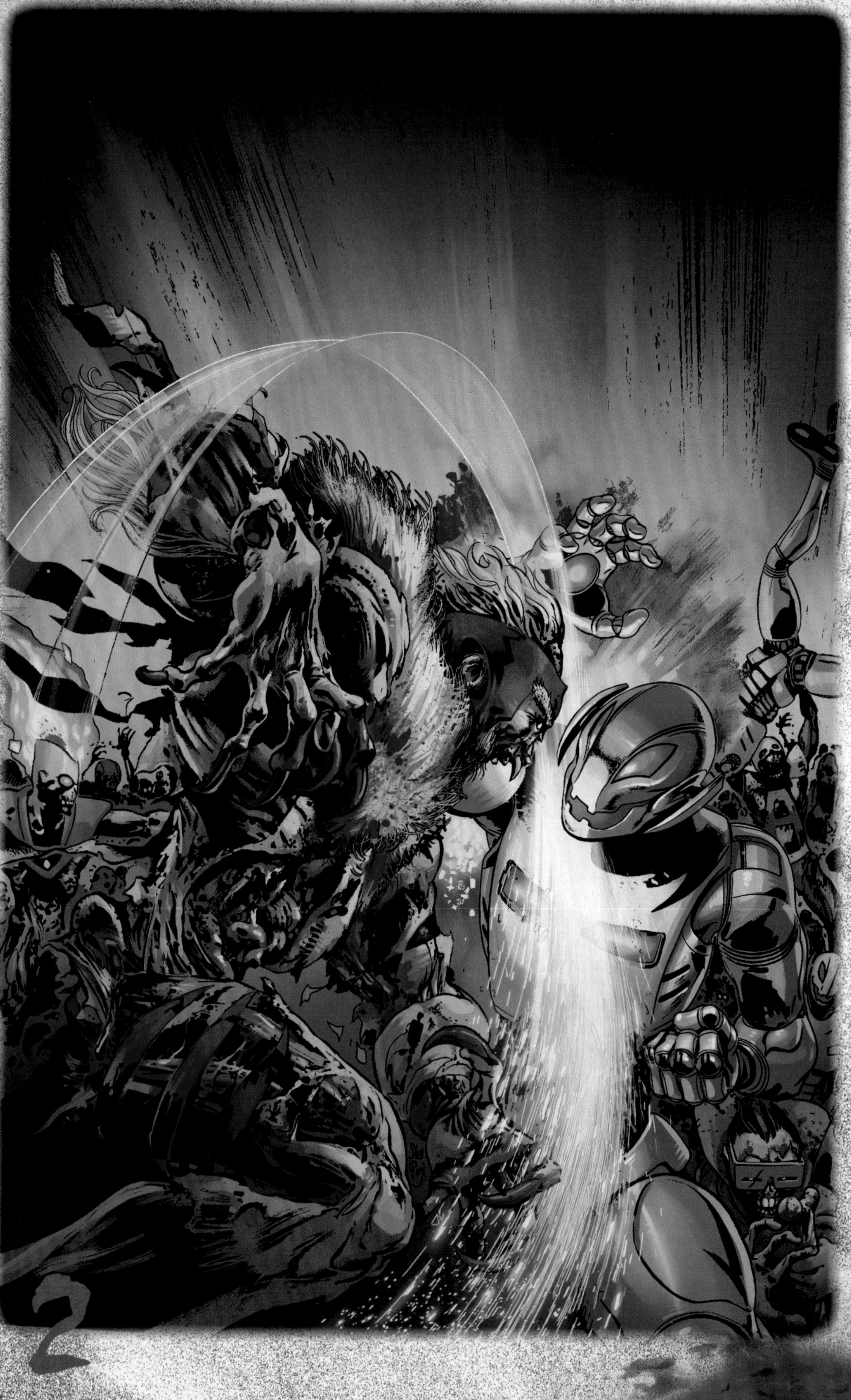
2

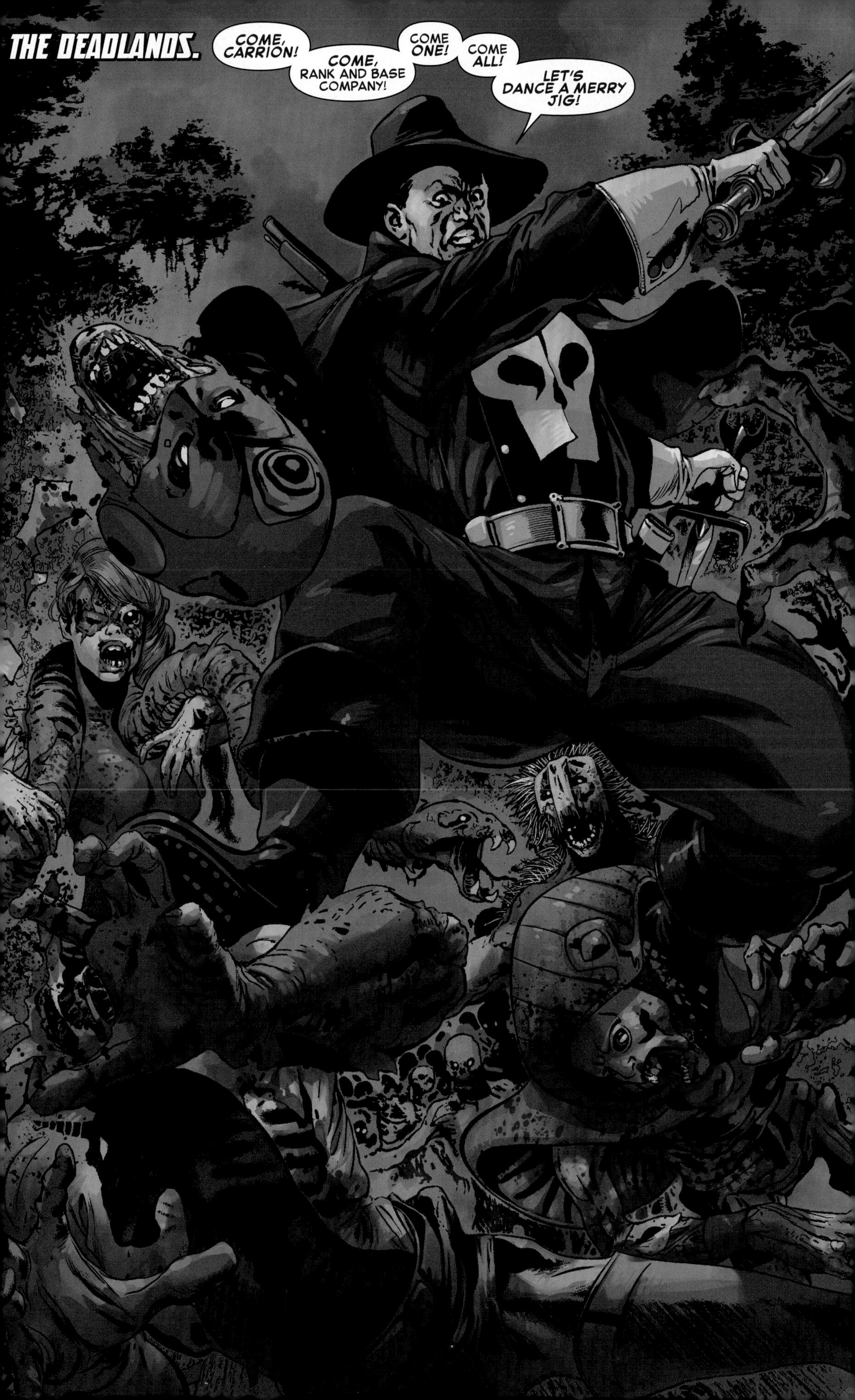
THE DEADLANDS.
COME, CARRION!
COME, RANK AND BASE COMPANY!
COME ONE!
COME ALL!
LET'S DANCE A MERRY JIG!

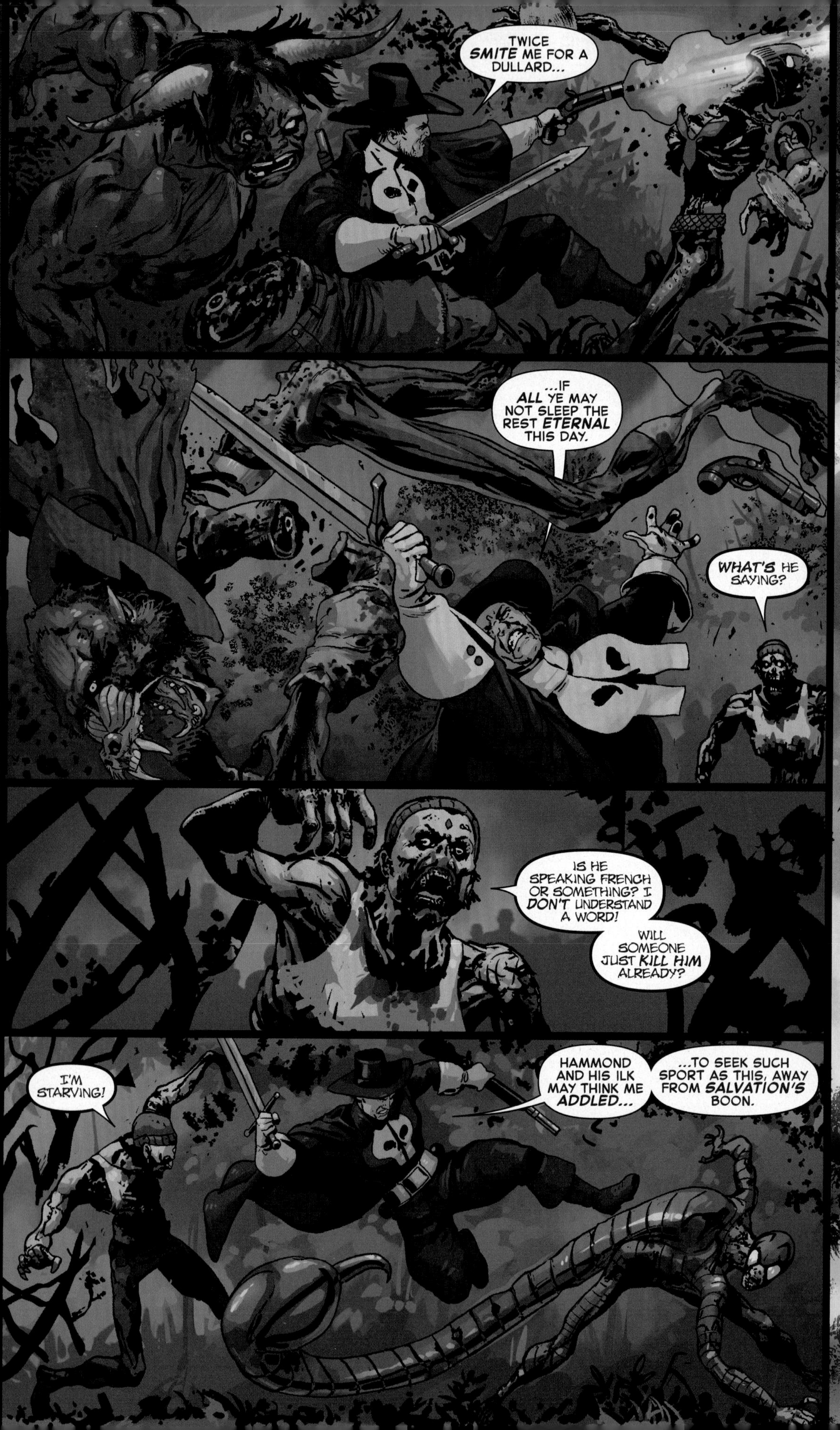

TWICE SMITE ME FOR A DULLARD...
...IF ALL YE MAY NOT SLEEP THE REST ETERNAL THIS DAY.
WHAT'S HE SAYING?
IS HE SPEAKING FRENCH OR SOMETHING? I DON'T UNDERSTAND A WORD!
WILL SOMEONE JUST KILL HIM ALREADY?
I'M STARVING!
HAMMOND AND HIS ILK MAY THINK ME ADDLED...
...TO SEEK SUCH SPORT AS THIS, AWAY FROM SALVATION'S BOON.

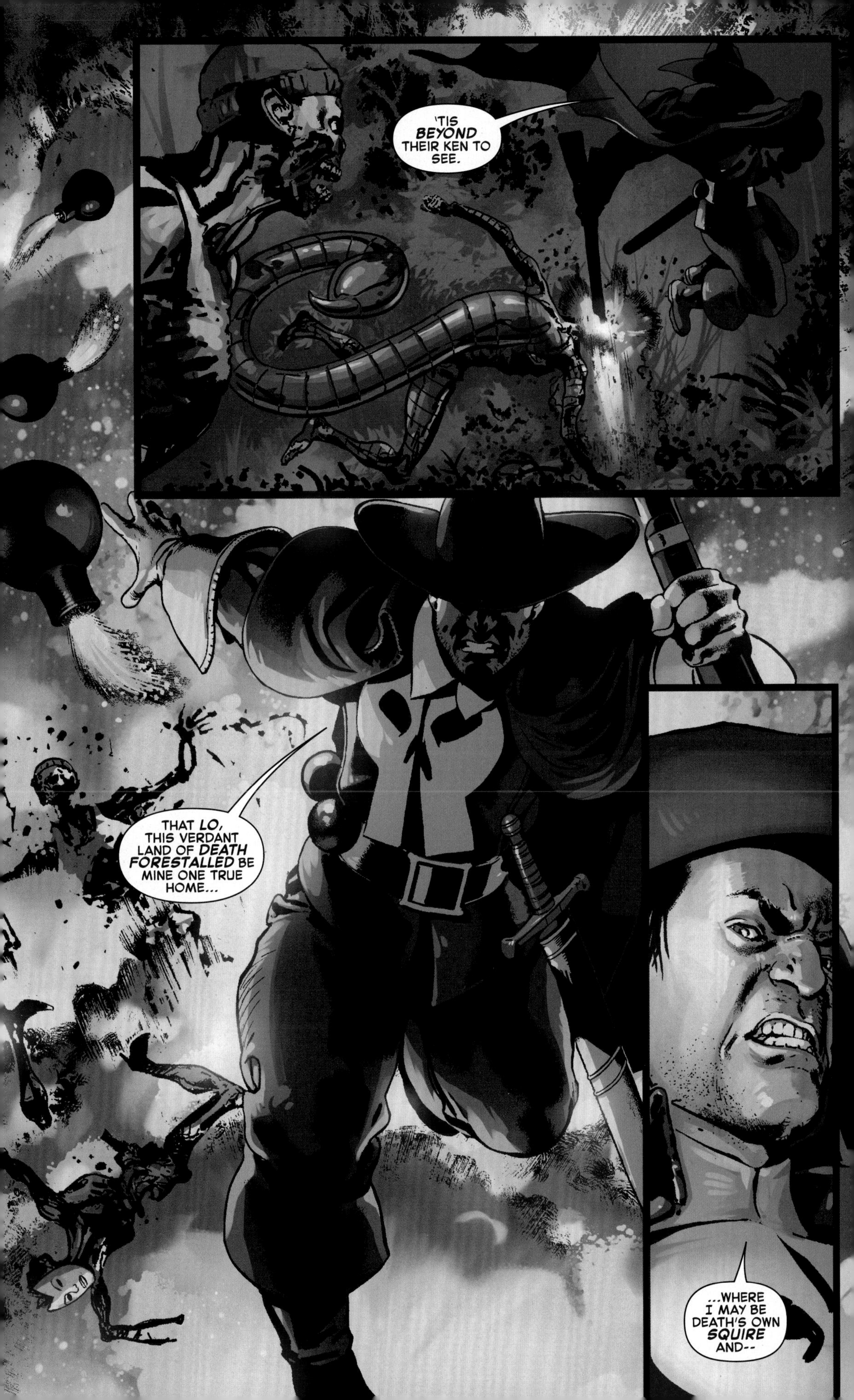
'TIS BEYOND THEIR KEN TO SEE.
THAT LO, THIS VERDANT LAND OF DEATH FORESTALLED BE MINE ONE TRUE HOME...
...WHERE I MAY BE DEATH'S OWN SQUIRE AND--

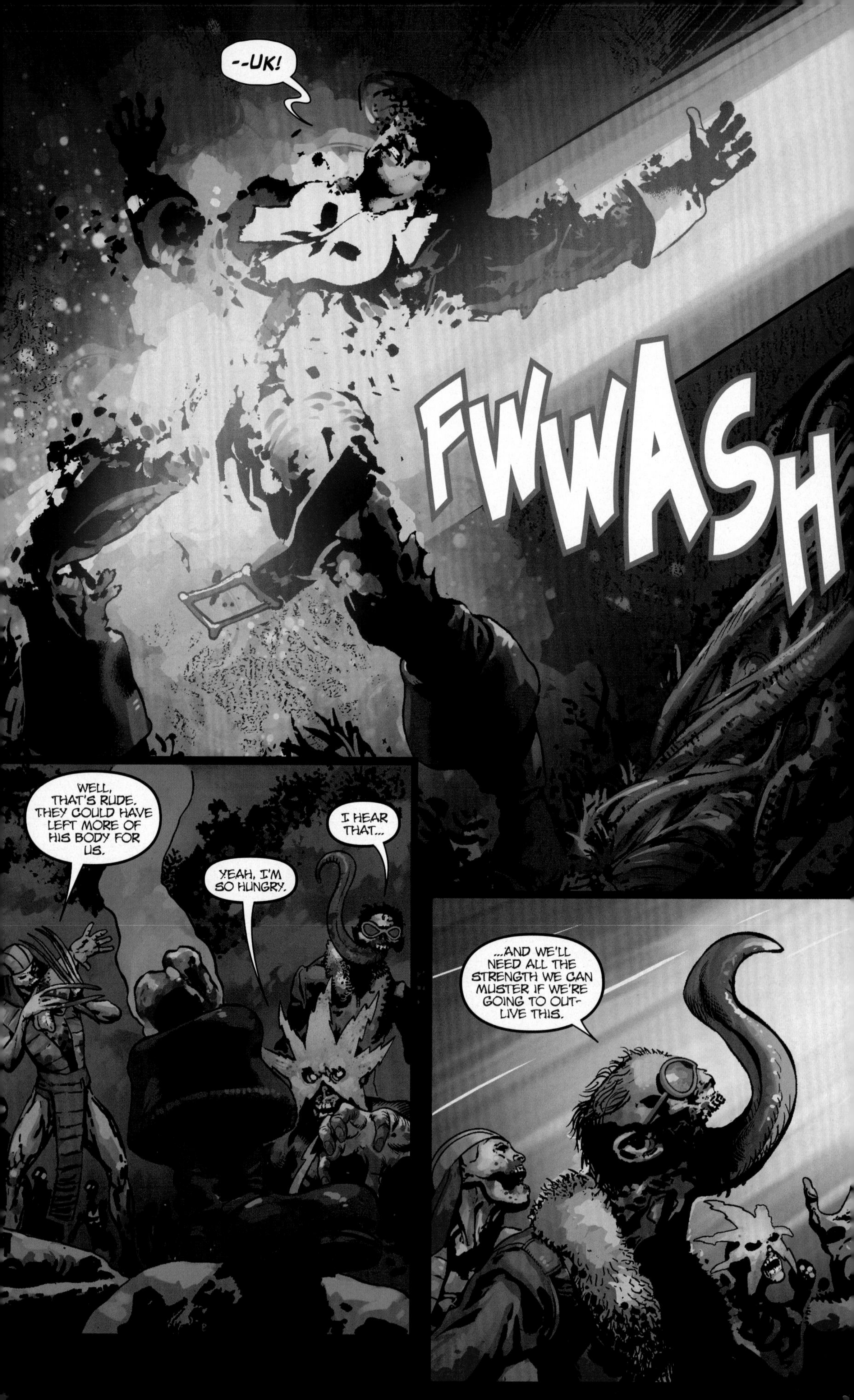
--UK!
FWWASH
WELL, THAT'S RUDE. THEY COULD HAVE LEFT MORE OF HIS BODY FOR US.
YEAH, I'M SO HUNGRY.
I HEAR THAT...
...AND WE'LL NEED ALL THE STRENGTH WE CAN MUSTER IF WE'RE GOING TO OUT-LIVE THIS.

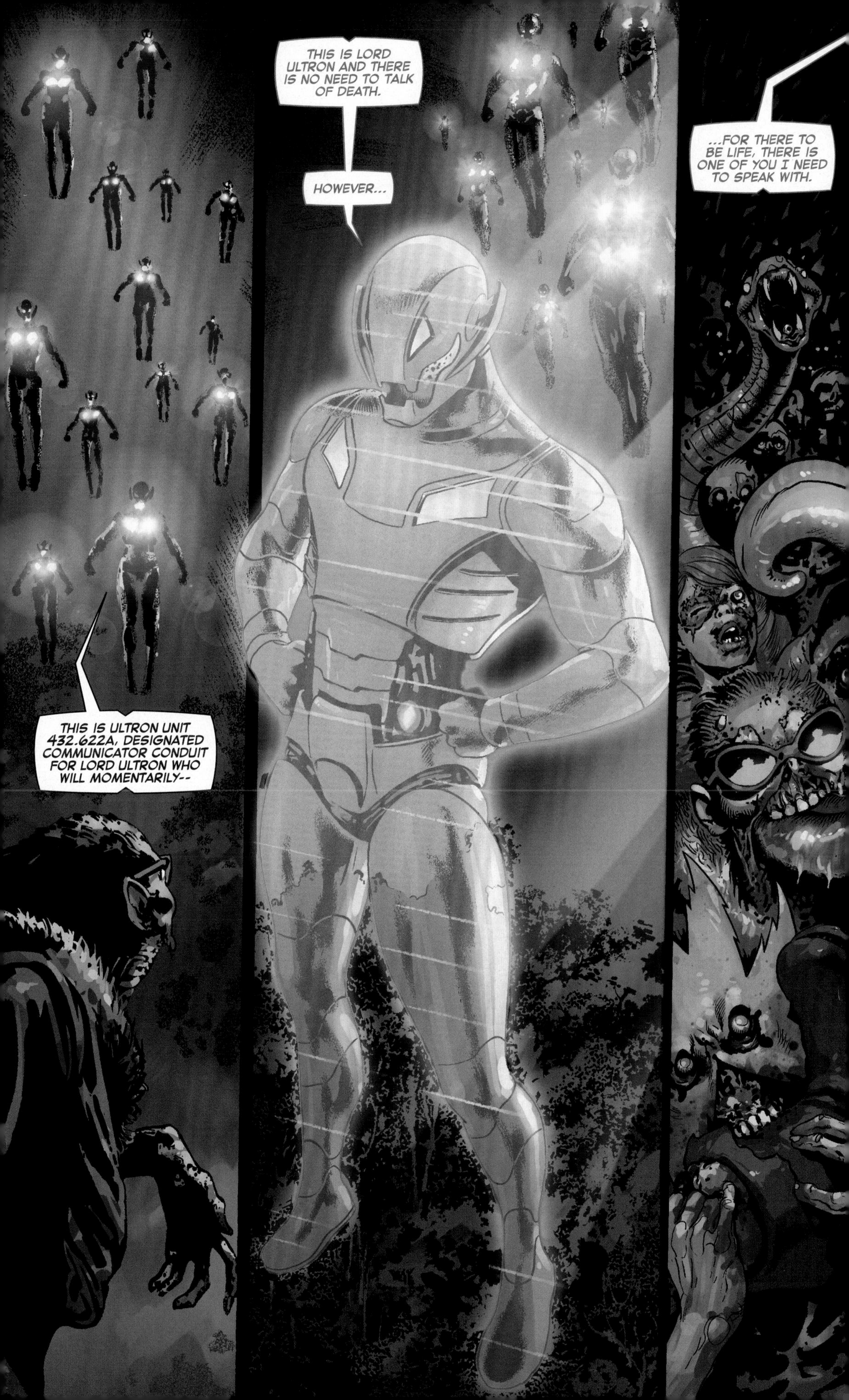
THIS IS ULTRON UNIT 432.622A, DESIGNATED COMMUNICATOR CONDUIT FOR LORD ULTRON WHO WILL MOMENTARILY--
THIS IS LORD ULTRON AND THERE IS NO NEED TO TALK OF DEATH.
HOWEVER...
...FOR THERE TO BE LIFE, THERE IS ONE OF YOU I NEED TO SPEAK WITH.

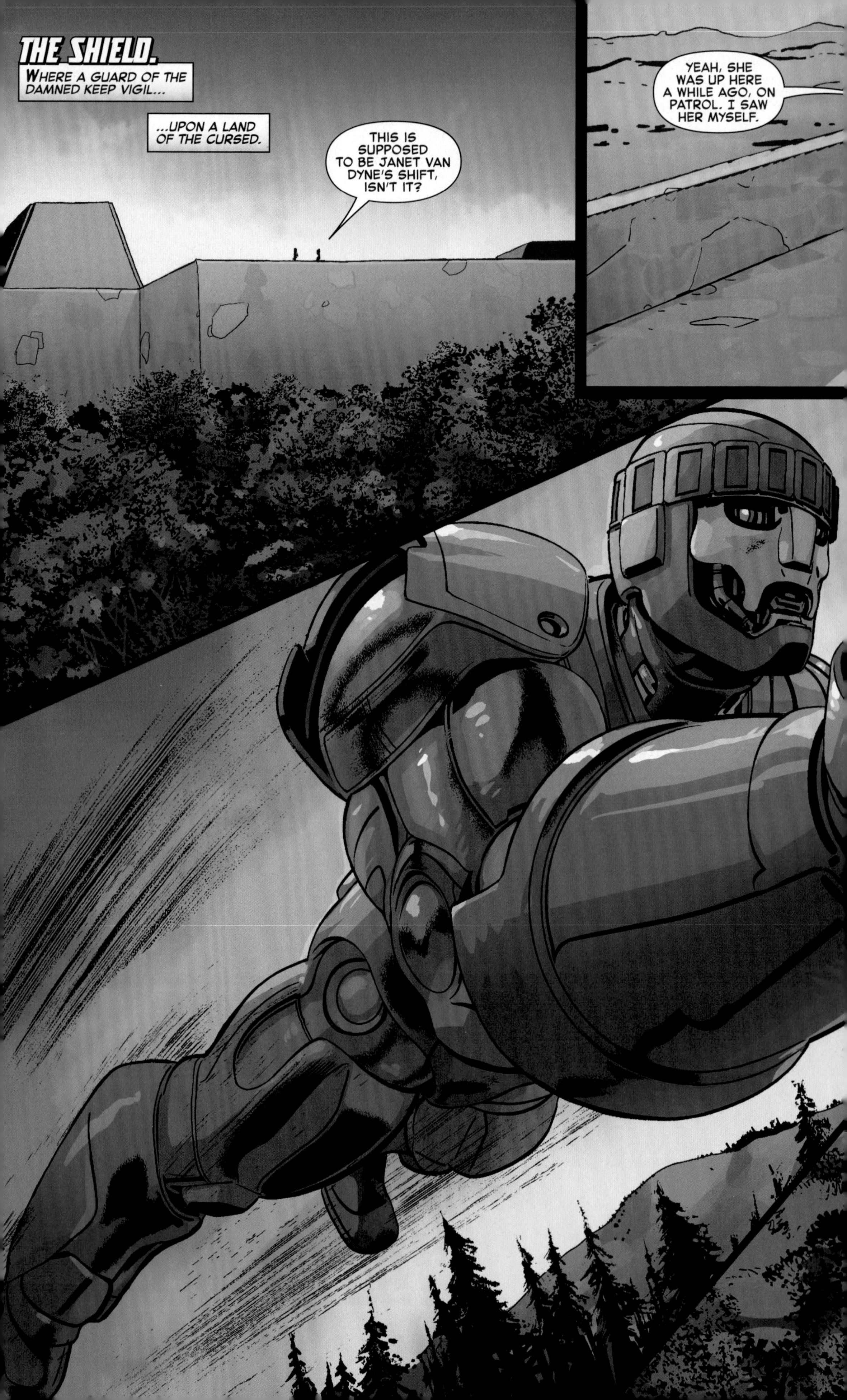
THE SHIELD.
WHERE A GUARD OF THE DAMNED KEEP VIGIL...
...UPON A LAND OF THE CURSED.
THIS IS SUPPOSED TO BE JANET VAN DYNE'S SHIFT, ISN'T IT?
YEAH, SHE WAS UP HERE A WHILE AGO, ON PATROL. I SAW HER MYSELF.

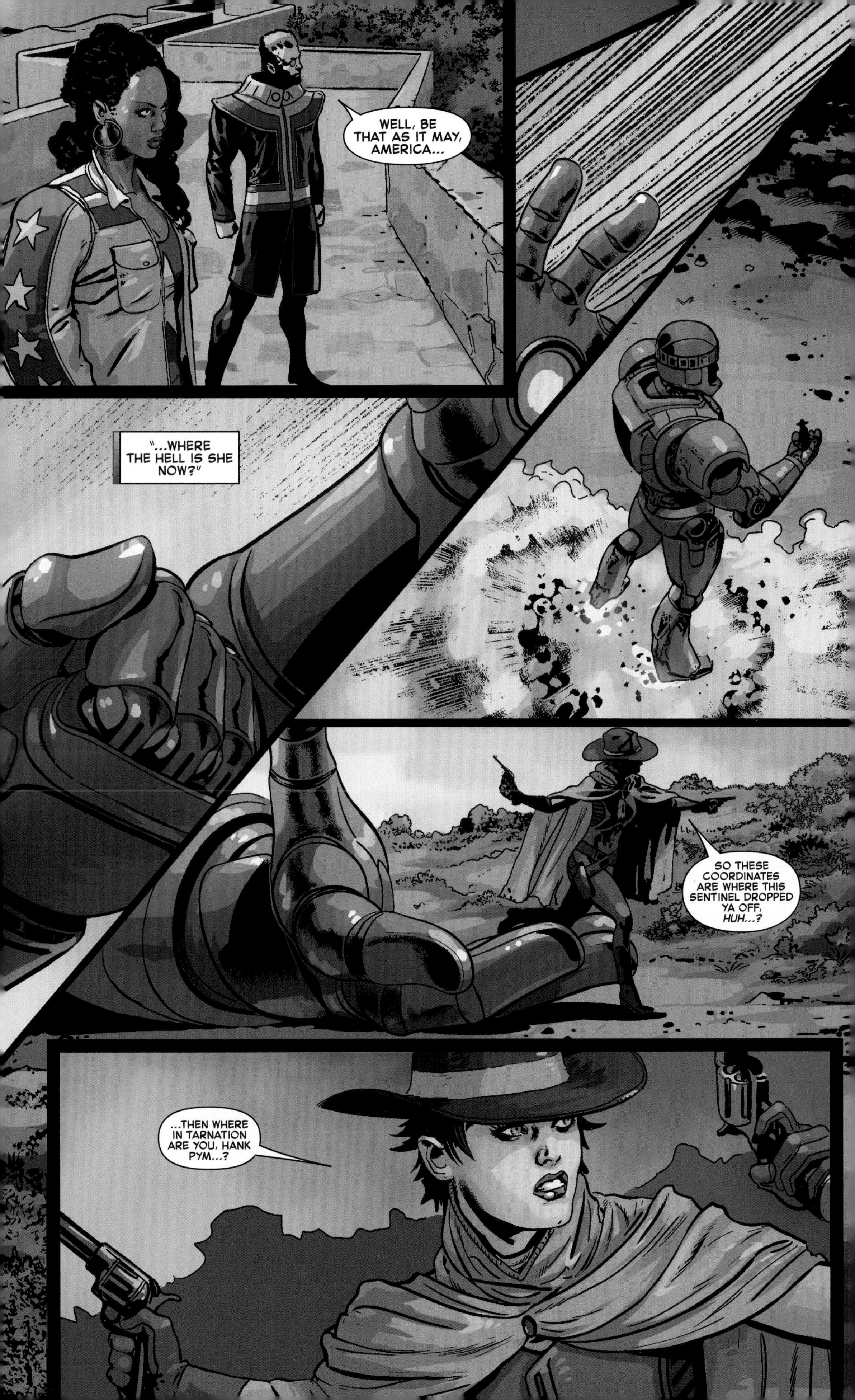
WELL, BE THAT AS IT MAY, AMERICA...
"...WHERE THE HELL IS SHE NOW?"
SO THESE COORDINATES ARE WHERE THIS SENTINEL DROPPED YA OFF, HUH...?
...THEN WHERE IN TARNATION ARE YOU, HANK PYM...?

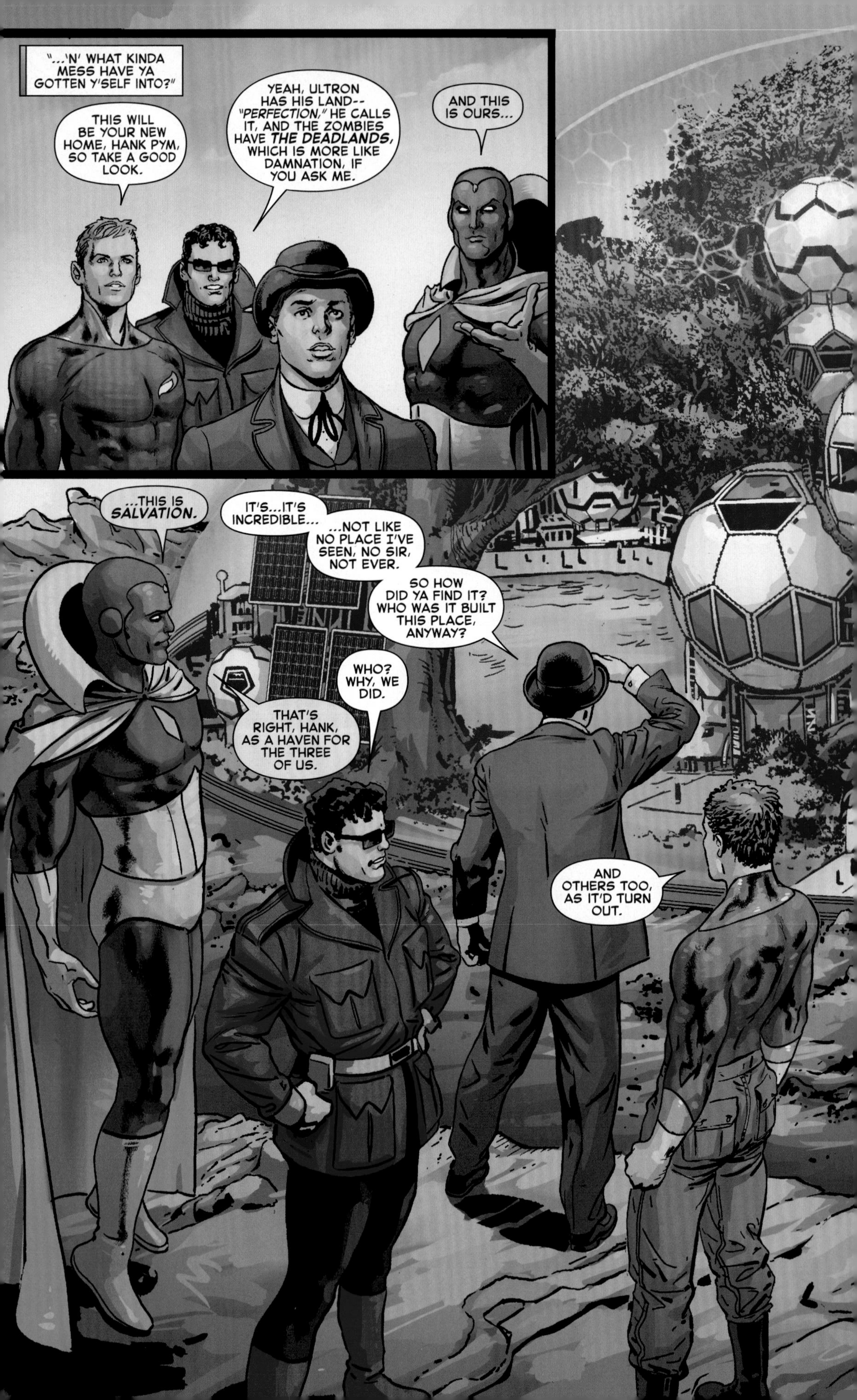
"...'N' WHAT KINDA MESS HAVE YA GOTTEN Y'SELF INTO?"
THIS WILL BE YOUR NEW HOME, HANK PYM, SO TAKE A GOOD LOOK.
YEAH, ULTRON HAS HIS LAND-- "PERFECTION," HE CALLS IT, AND THE ZOMBIES HAVE THE DEADLANDS, WHICH IS MORE LIKE DAMNATION, IF YOU ASK ME.
AND THIS IS OURS...
...THIS IS SALVATION.
IT'S...IT'S INCREDIBLE...
...NOT LIKE NO PLACE I'VE SEEN, NO SIR, NOT EVER.
SO HOW DID YA FIND IT? WHO WAS IT BUILT THIS PLACE, ANYWAY?
WHO? WHY, WE DID.
THAT'S RIGHT, HANK, AS A HAVEN FOR THE THREE OF US.
AND OTHERS TOO, AS IT'D TURN OUT.

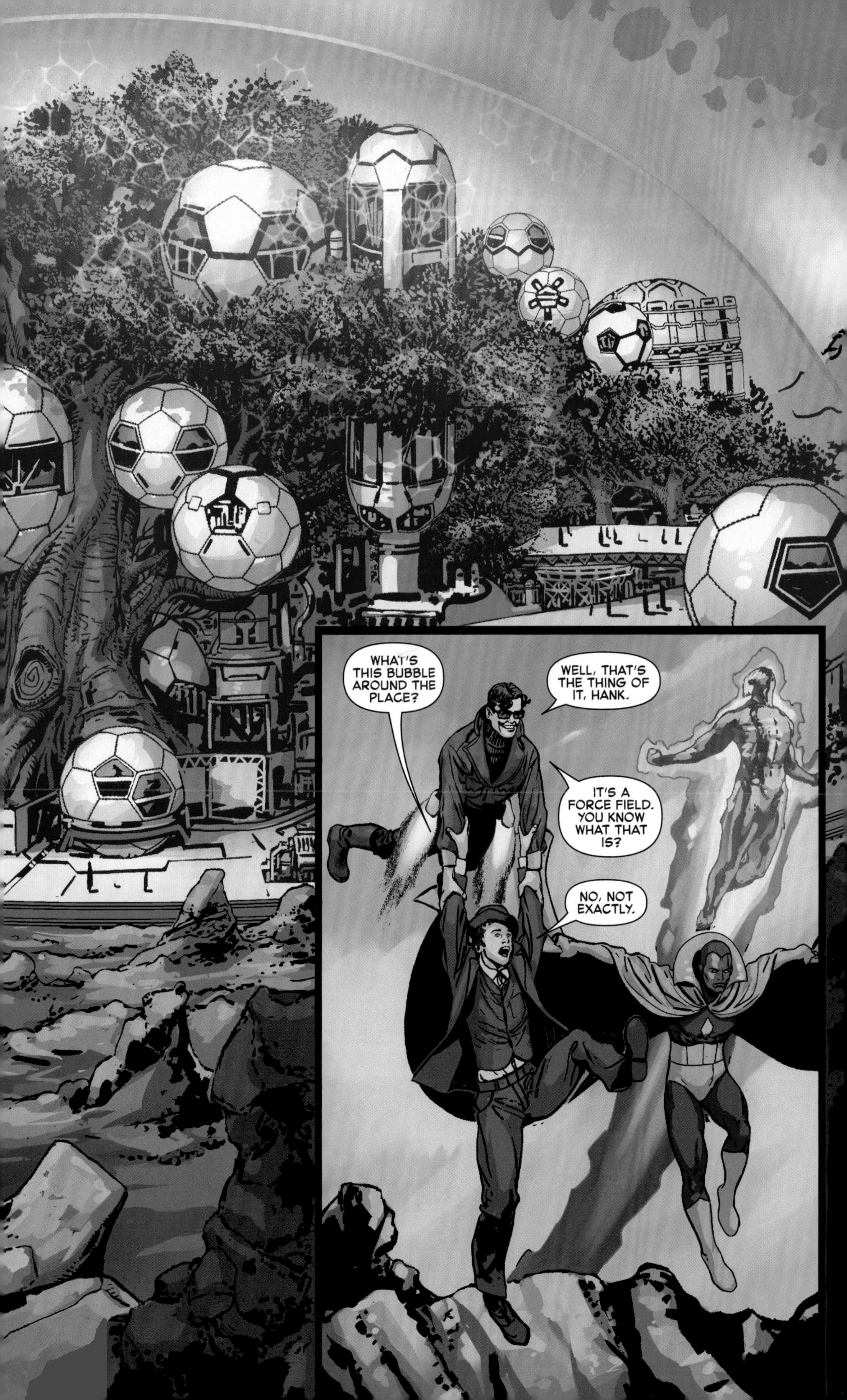
WHAT'S THIS BUBBLE AROUND THE PLACE?
WELL, THAT'S THE THING OF IT, HANK.
IT'S A FORCE FIELD. YOU KNOW WHAT THAT IS?
NO, NOT EXACTLY.

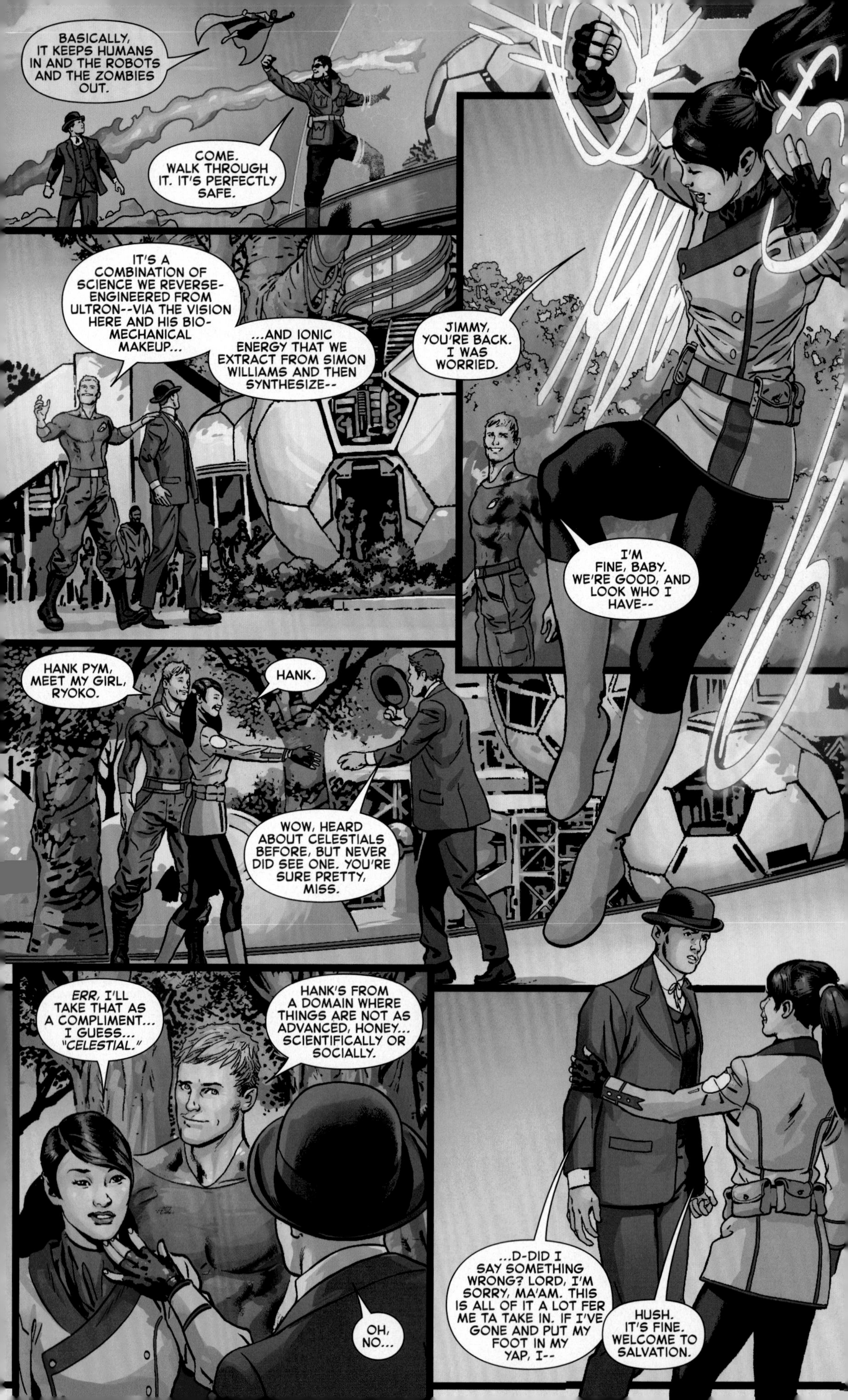

BASICALLY, IT KEEPS HUMANS IN AND THE ROBOTS AND THE ZOMBIES OUT.
COME. WALK THROUGH IT. IT'S PERFECTLY SAFE.
IT'S A COMBINATION OF SCIENCE WE REVERSE-ENGINEERED FROM ULTRON--VIA THE VISION HERE AND HIS BIO-MECHANICAL MAKEUP...
...AND IONIC ENERGY THAT WE EXTRACT FROM SIMON WILLIAMS AND THEN SYNTHESIZE--
JIMMY, YOU'RE BACK. I WAS WORRIED.
I'M FINE, BABY. WE'RE GOOD, AND LOOK WHO I HAVE--
HANK PYM, MEET MY GIRL, RYOKO.
HANK.
WOW, HEARD ABOUT CELESTIALS BEFORE, BUT NEVER DID SEE ONE. YOU'RE SURE PRETTY, MISS.
ERR, I'LL TAKE THAT AS A COMPLIMENT... I GUESS... *"CELESTIAL."*
HANK'S FROM A DOMAIN WHERE THINGS ARE NOT AS ADVANCED, HONEY... SCIENTIFICALLY OR SOCIALLY.
OH, NO...
...D-DID I SAY SOMETHING WRONG? LORD, I'M SORRY, MA'AM. THIS IS ALL OF IT A LOT FER ME TA TAKE IN. IF I'VE GONE AND PUT MY FOOT IN MY YAP, I--
HUSH. IT'S FINE. WELCOME TO SALVATION.

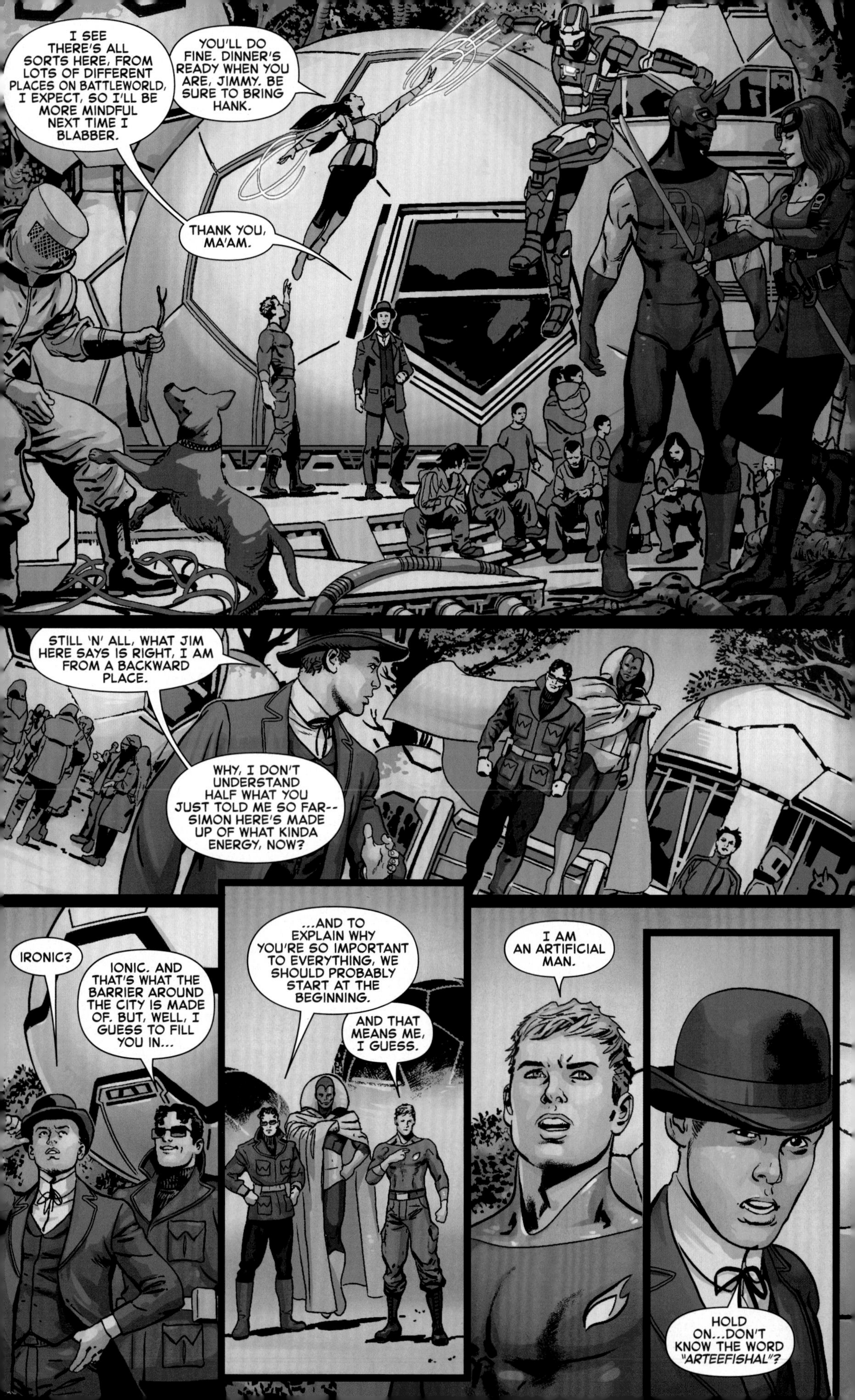
I SEE THERE'S ALL SORTS HERE, FROM LOTS OF DIFFERENT PLACES ON BATTLEWORLD, I EXPECT, SO I'LL BE MORE MINDFUL NEXT TIME I BLABBER.
YOU'LL DO FINE. DINNER'S READY WHEN YOU ARE, JIMMY. BE SURE TO BRING HANK.
THANK YOU, MA'AM.
STILL 'N' ALL, WHAT JIM HERE SAYS IS RIGHT, I AM FROM A BACKWARD PLACE.
WHY, I DON'T UNDERSTAND HALF WHAT YOU JUST TOLD ME SO FAR-- SIMON HERE'S MADE UP OF WHAT KINDA ENERGY, NOW?
IRONIC?
IONIC. AND THAT'S WHAT THE BARRIER AROUND THE CITY IS MADE OF. BUT, WELL, I GUESS TO FILL YOU IN...
...AND TO EXPLAIN WHY YOU'RE SO IMPORTANT TO EVERYTHING, WE SHOULD PROBABLY START AT THE BEGINNING.
AND THAT MEANS ME, I GUESS.
I AM AN ARTIFICIAL MAN.
HOLD ON...DON'T KNOW THE WORD "ARTEEFISHAL"?

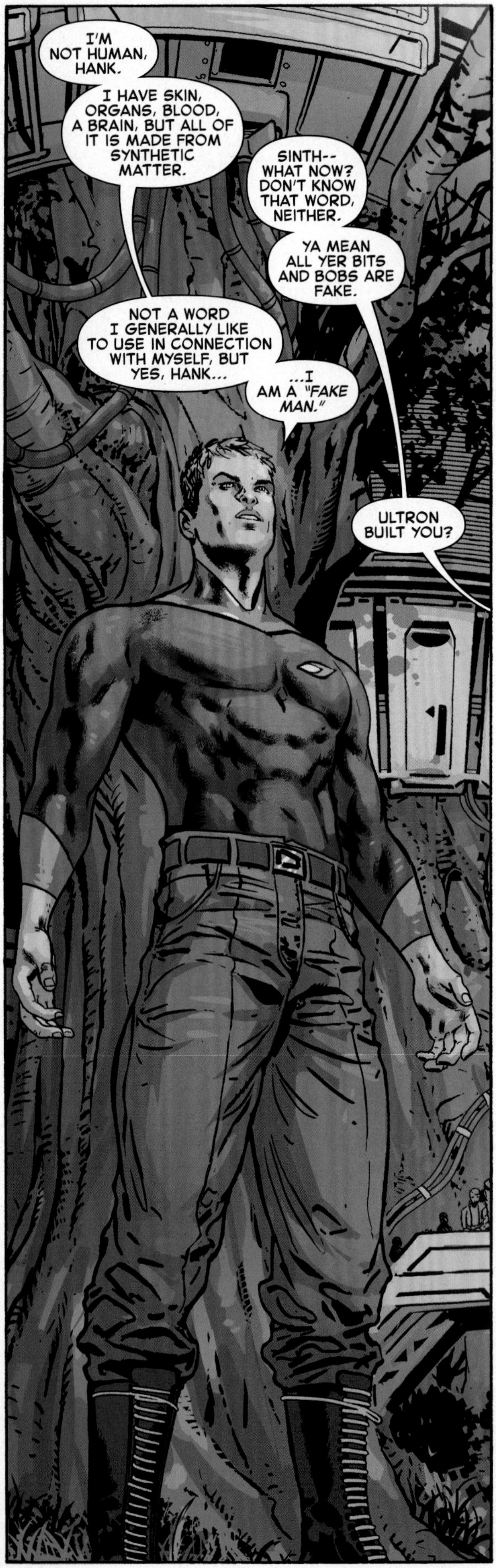
I'M NOT HUMAN, HANK.
I HAVE SKIN, ORGANS, BLOOD, A BRAIN, BUT ALL OF IT IS MADE FROM SYNTHETIC MATTER.
SINTH-- WHAT NOW? DON'T KNOW THAT WORD, NEITHER.
YA MEAN ALL YER BITS AND BOBS ARE FAKE.
NOT A WORD I GENERALLY LIKE TO USE IN CONNECTION WITH MYSELF, BUT YES, HANK...
...I AM A "FAKE MAN."
ULTRON BUILT YOU?

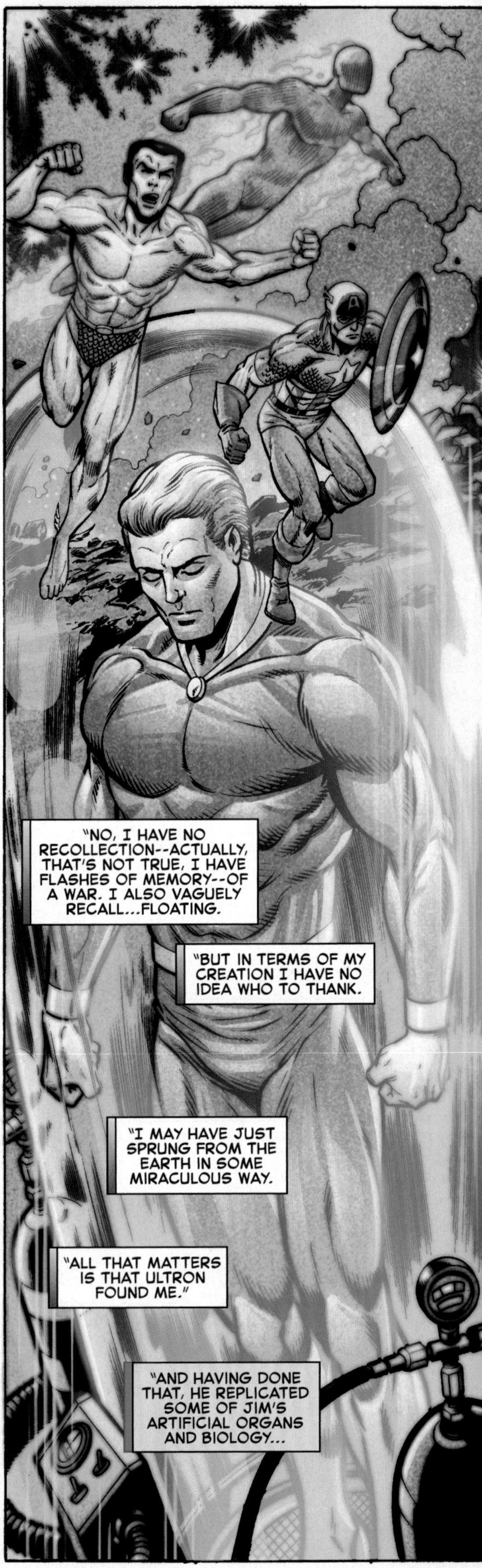
"NO, I HAVE NO RECOLLECTION--ACTUALLY, THAT'S NOT TRUE, I HAVE FLASHES OF MEMORY--OF A WAR. I ALSO VAGUELY RECALL...FLOATING.
"BUT IN TERMS OF MY CREATION I HAVE NO IDEA WHO TO THANK.
"I MAY HAVE JUST SPRUNG FROM THE EARTH IN SOME MIRACULOUS WAY.
"ALL THAT MATTERS IS THAT ULTRON FOUND ME."
"AND HAVING DONE THAT, HE REPLICATED SOME OF JIM'S ARTIFICIAL ORGANS AND BIOLOGY...

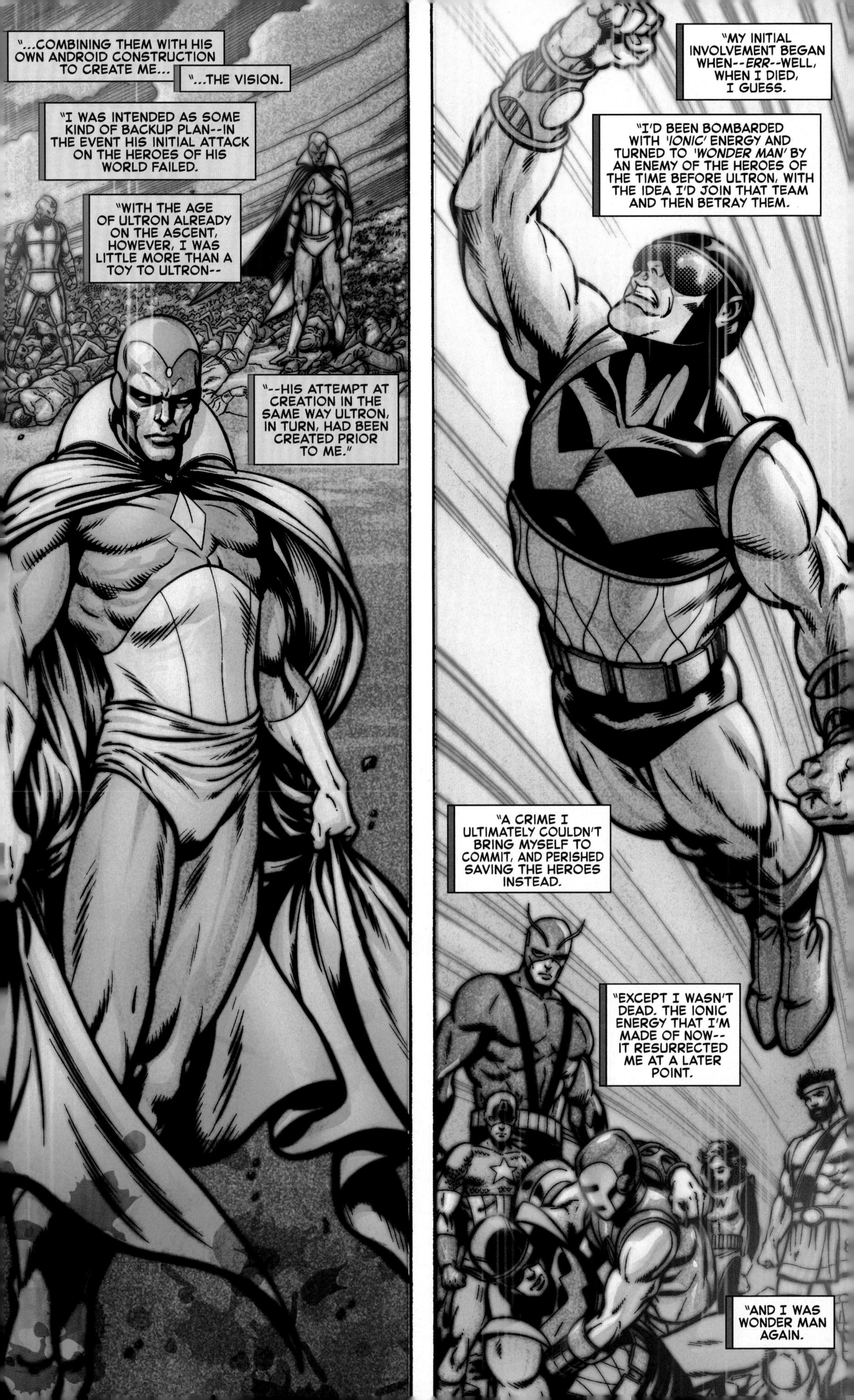
"...COMBINING THEM WITH HIS OWN ANDROID CONSTRUCTION TO CREATE ME...
"...THE VISION.
"I WAS INTENDED AS SOME KIND OF BACKUP PLAN--IN THE EVENT HIS INITIAL ATTACK ON THE HEROES OF HIS WORLD FAILED.
"WITH THE AGE OF ULTRON ALREADY ON THE ASCENT, HOWEVER, I WAS LITTLE MORE THAN A TOY TO ULTRON--
"--HIS ATTEMPT AT CREATION IN THE SAME WAY ULTRON, IN TURN, HAD BEEN CREATED PRIOR TO ME."
"MY INITIAL INVOLVEMENT BEGAN WHEN--*ERR*--WELL, WHEN I DIED, I GUESS.
"I'D BEEN BOMBARDED WITH *'IONIC'* ENERGY AND TURNED TO *'WONDER MAN'* BY AN ENEMY OF THE HEROES OF THE TIME BEFORE ULTRON, WITH THE IDEA I'D JOIN THAT TEAM AND THEN BETRAY THEM.
"A CRIME I ULTIMATELY COULDN'T BRING MYSELF TO COMMIT, AND PERISHED SAVING THE HEROES INSTEAD.
"EXCEPT I WASN'T DEAD. THE IONIC ENERGY THAT I'M MADE OF NOW--IT RESURRECTED ME AT A LATER POINT.
"AND I WAS WONDER MAN AGAIN.

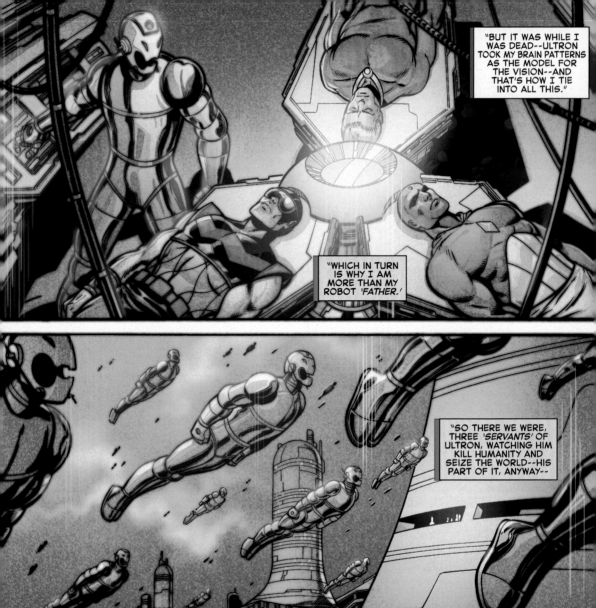

"BUT IT WAS WHILE I WAS DEAD--ULTRON TOOK MY BRAIN PATTERNS AS THE MODEL FOR THE VISION--AND THAT'S HOW I TIE INTO ALL THIS."

"WHICH IN TURN IS WHY I AM MORE THAN MY ROBOT 'FATHER.'"

"SO THERE WE WERE, THREE 'SERVANTS' OF ULTRON, WATCHING HIM KILL HUMANITY AND SEIZE THE WORLD--HIS PART OF IT, ANYWAY--

"--AND WE SAW HOW WRONG IT WAS--ULTRON'S CONCLUSION THAT HUMANITY'S IMPERFECTIONS JUSTIFIED ITS DESTRUCTION.

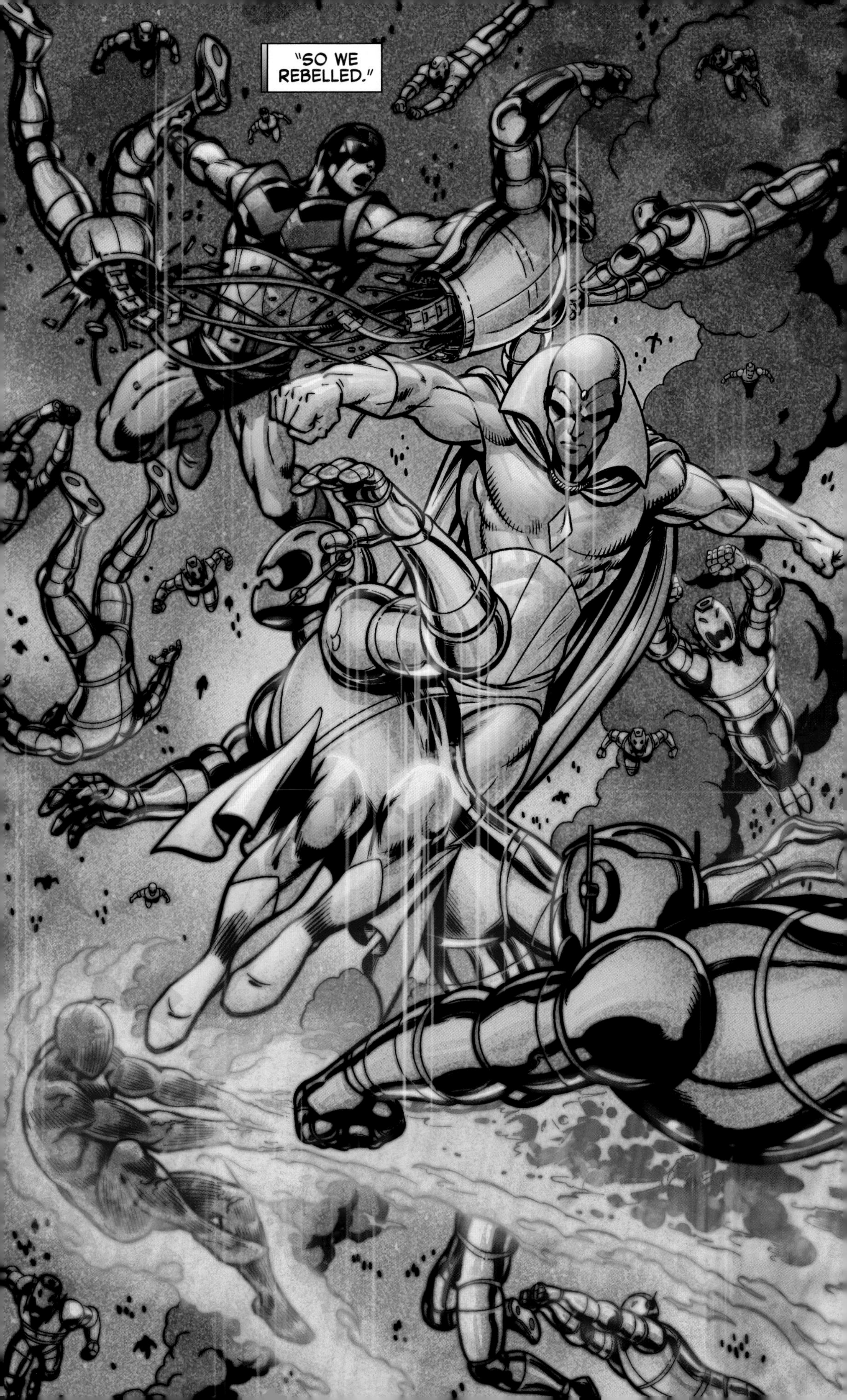
"SO WE REBELLED."

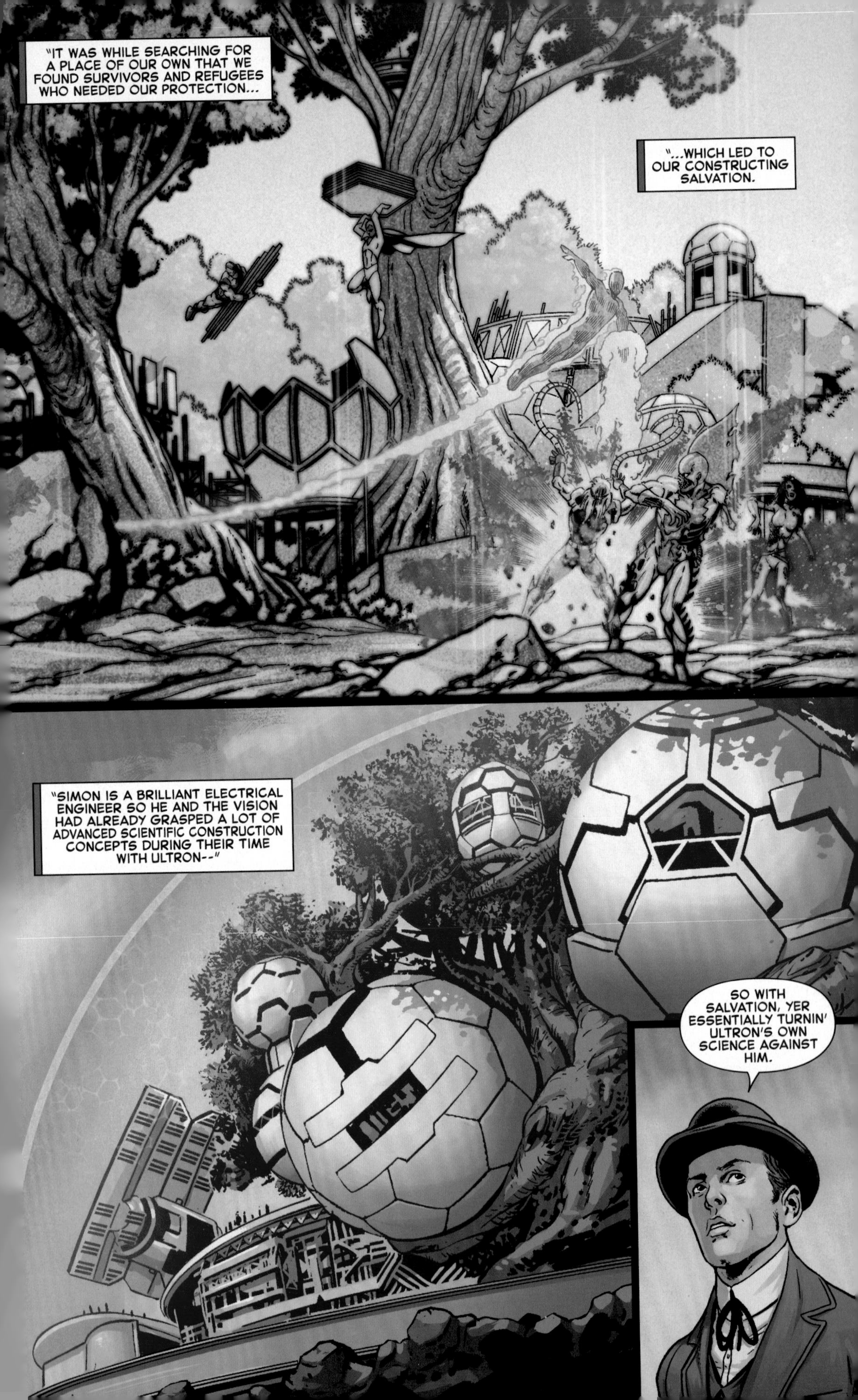
"IT WAS WHILE SEARCHING FOR A PLACE OF OUR OWN THAT WE FOUND SURVIVORS AND REFUGEES WHO NEEDED OUR PROTECTION...
"...WHICH LED TO OUR CONSTRUCTING SALVATION.
"SIMON IS A BRILLIANT ELECTRICAL ENGINEER SO HE AND THE VISION HAD ALREADY GRASPED A LOT OF ADVANCED SCIENTIFIC CONSTRUCTION CONCEPTS DURING THEIR TIME WITH ULTRON--"
SO WITH SALVATION, YER ESSENTIALLY TURNIN' ULTRON'S OWN SCIENCE AGAINST HIM.

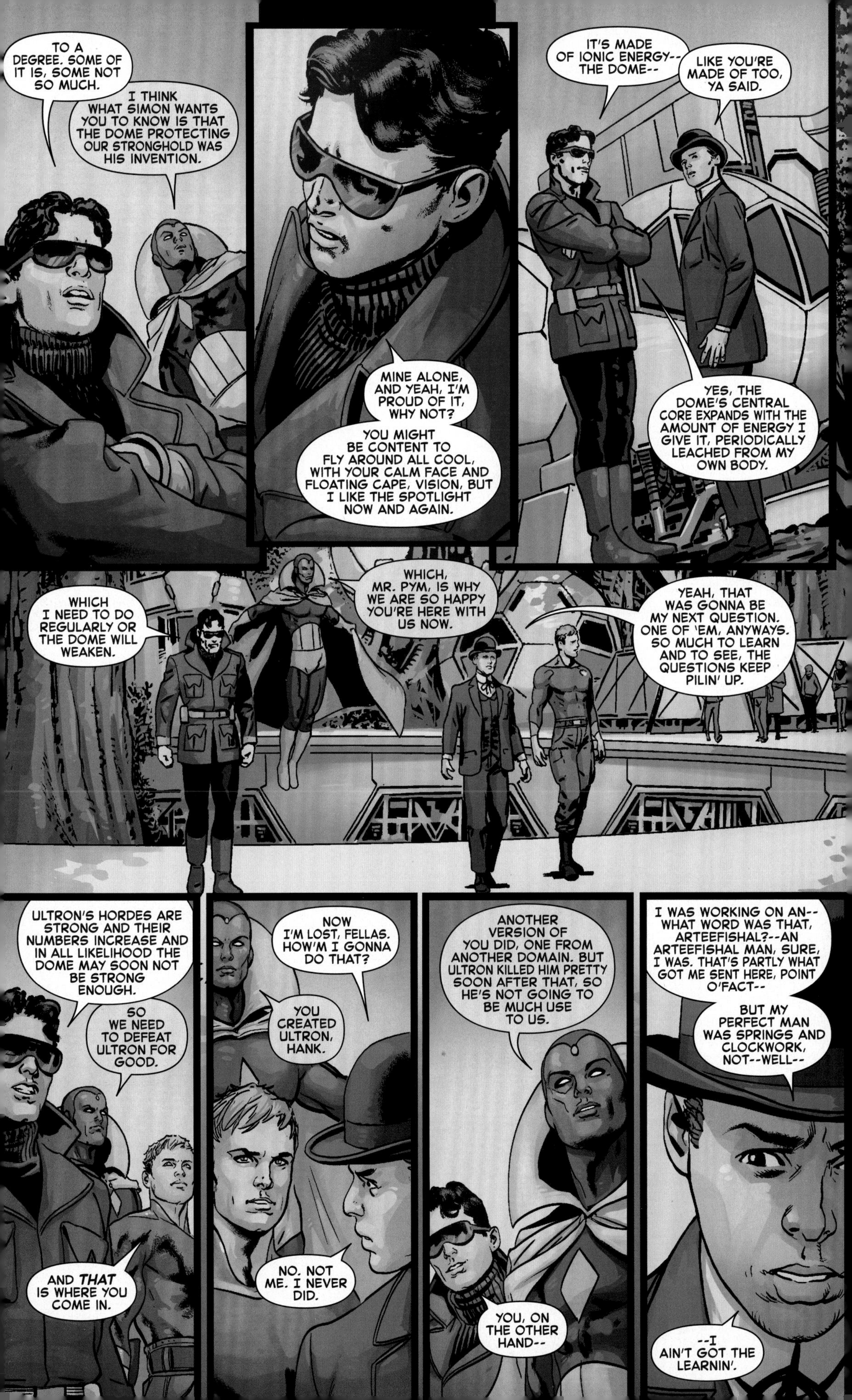
TO A DEGREE. SOME OF IT IS, SOME NOT SO MUCH.
I THINK WHAT SIMON WANTS YOU TO KNOW IS THAT THE DOME PROTECTING OUR STRONGHOLD WAS HIS INVENTION.
MINE ALONE, AND YEAH, I'M PROUD OF IT, WHY NOT?
YOU MIGHT BE CONTENT TO FLY AROUND ALL COOL, WITH YOUR CALM FACE AND FLOATING CAPE, VISION, BUT I LIKE THE SPOTLIGHT NOW AND AGAIN.
IT'S MADE OF IONIC ENERGY-- THE DOME--
LIKE YOU'RE MADE OF TOO, YA SAID.
YES, THE DOME'S CENTRAL CORE EXPANDS WITH THE AMOUNT OF ENERGY I GIVE IT, PERIODICALLY LEACHED FROM MY OWN BODY.
WHICH I NEED TO DO REGULARLY OR THE DOME WILL WEAKEN.
WHICH, MR. PYM, IS WHY WE ARE SO HAPPY YOU'RE HERE WITH US NOW.
YEAH, THAT WAS GONNA BE MY NEXT QUESTION. ONE OF 'EM, ANYWAYS. SO MUCH TO LEARN AND TO SEE, THE QUESTIONS KEEP PILIN' UP.
ULTRON'S HORDES ARE STRONG AND THEIR NUMBERS INCREASE AND IN ALL LIKELIHOOD THE DOME MAY SOON NOT BE STRONG ENOUGH.
SO WE NEED TO DEFEAT ULTRON FOR GOOD.
AND *THAT* IS WHERE YOU COME IN.
NOW I'M LOST, FELLAS. HOW'M I GONNA DO THAT?
YOU CREATED ULTRON, HANK.
NO. NOT ME. I NEVER DID.
ANOTHER VERSION OF YOU DID, ONE FROM ANOTHER DOMAIN. BUT ULTRON KILLED HIM PRETTY SOON AFTER THAT, SO HE'S NOT GOING TO BE MUCH USE TO US.
YOU, ON THE OTHER HAND--
I WAS WORKING ON AN-- WHAT WORD WAS THAT, ARTEEFISHAL?--AN ARTEEFISHAL MAN, SURE, I WAS. THAT'S PARTLY WHAT GOT ME SENT HERE, POINT O'FACT--
BUT MY PERFECT MAN WAS SPRINGS AND CLOCKWORK, NOT--WELL--
--I AIN'T GOT THE LEARNIN'.

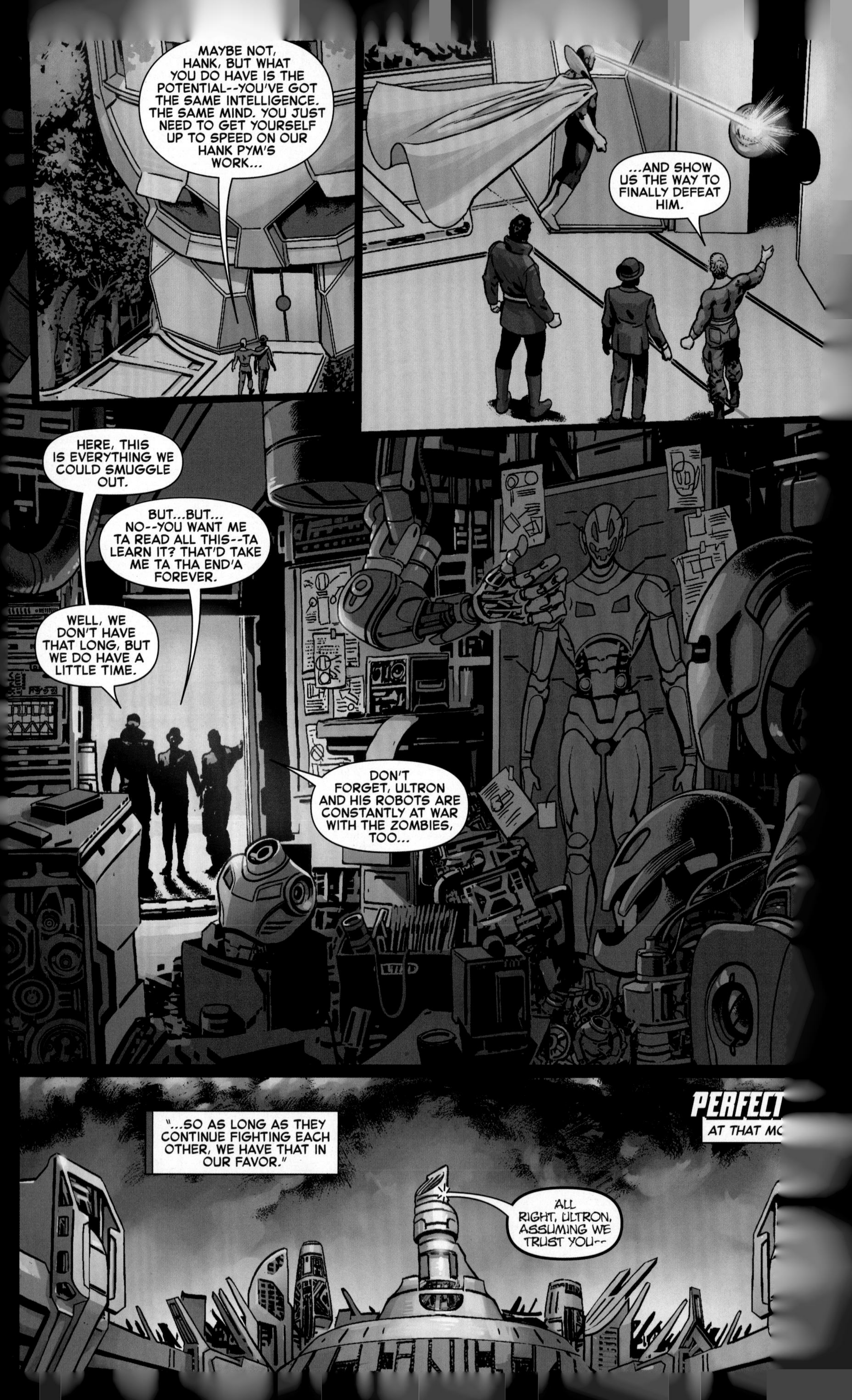
MAYBE NOT, HANK, BUT WHAT YOU DO HAVE IS THE POTENTIAL--YOU'VE GOT THE SAME INTELLIGENCE. THE SAME MIND. YOU JUST NEED TO GET YOURSELF UP TO SPEED ON OUR HANK PYM'S WORK...
...AND SHOW US THE WAY TO FINALLY DEFEAT HIM.
HERE, THIS IS EVERYTHING WE COULD SMUGGLE OUT.
BUT...BUT... NO--YOU WANT ME TA READ ALL THIS--TA LEARN IT? THAT'D TAKE ME TA THA END'A FOREVER.
WELL, WE DON'T HAVE THAT LONG, BUT WE DO HAVE A LITTLE TIME.
DON'T FORGET, ULTRON AND HIS ROBOTS ARE CONSTANTLY AT WAR WITH THE ZOMBIES, TOO...
"...SO AS LONG AS THEY CONTINUE FIGHTING EACH OTHER, WE HAVE THAT IN OUR FAVOR."
PERFECT
AT THAT MO
ALL RIGHT, ULTRON, ASSUMING WE TRUST YOU--

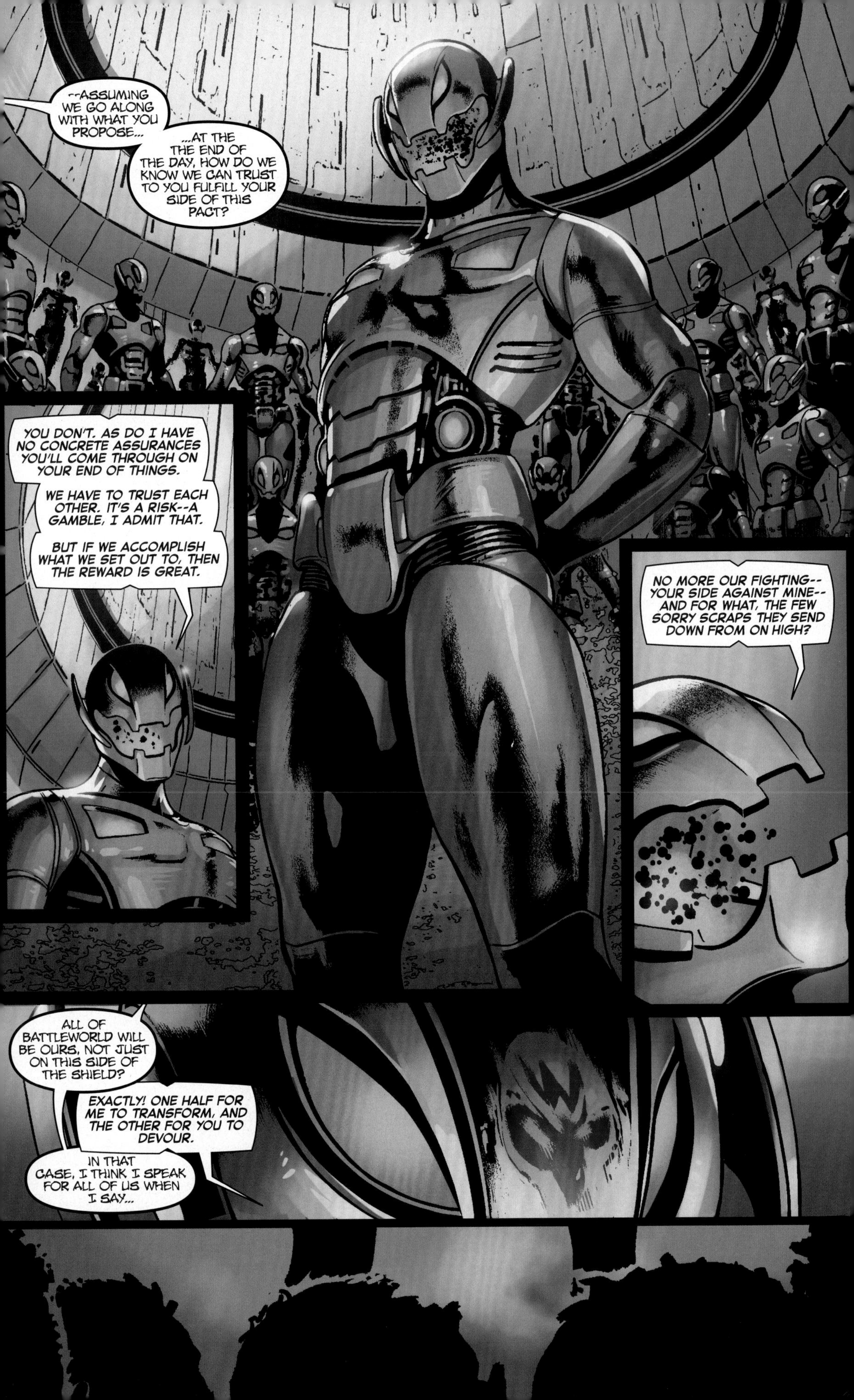
--ASSUMING WE GO ALONG WITH WHAT YOU PROPOSE...
...AT THE THE END OF THE DAY, HOW DO WE KNOW WE CAN TRUST TO YOU FULFILL YOUR SIDE OF THIS PACT?
YOU DON'T. AS DO I HAVE NO CONCRETE ASSURANCES YOU'LL COME THROUGH ON YOUR END OF THINGS.
WE HAVE TO TRUST EACH OTHER. IT'S A RISK--A GAMBLE, I ADMIT THAT.
BUT IF WE ACCOMPLISH WHAT WE SET OUT TO, THEN THE REWARD IS GREAT.
NO MORE OUR FIGHTING-- YOUR SIDE AGAINST MINE-- AND FOR WHAT, THE FEW SORRY SCRAPS THEY SEND DOWN FROM ON HIGH?
ALL OF BATTLEWORLD WILL BE OURS, NOT JUST ON THIS SIDE OF THE SHIELD?
EXACTLY! ONE HALF FOR ME TO TRANSFORM, AND THE OTHER FOR YOU TO DEVOUR.
IN THAT CASE, I THINK I SPEAK FOR ALL OF US WHEN I SAY...

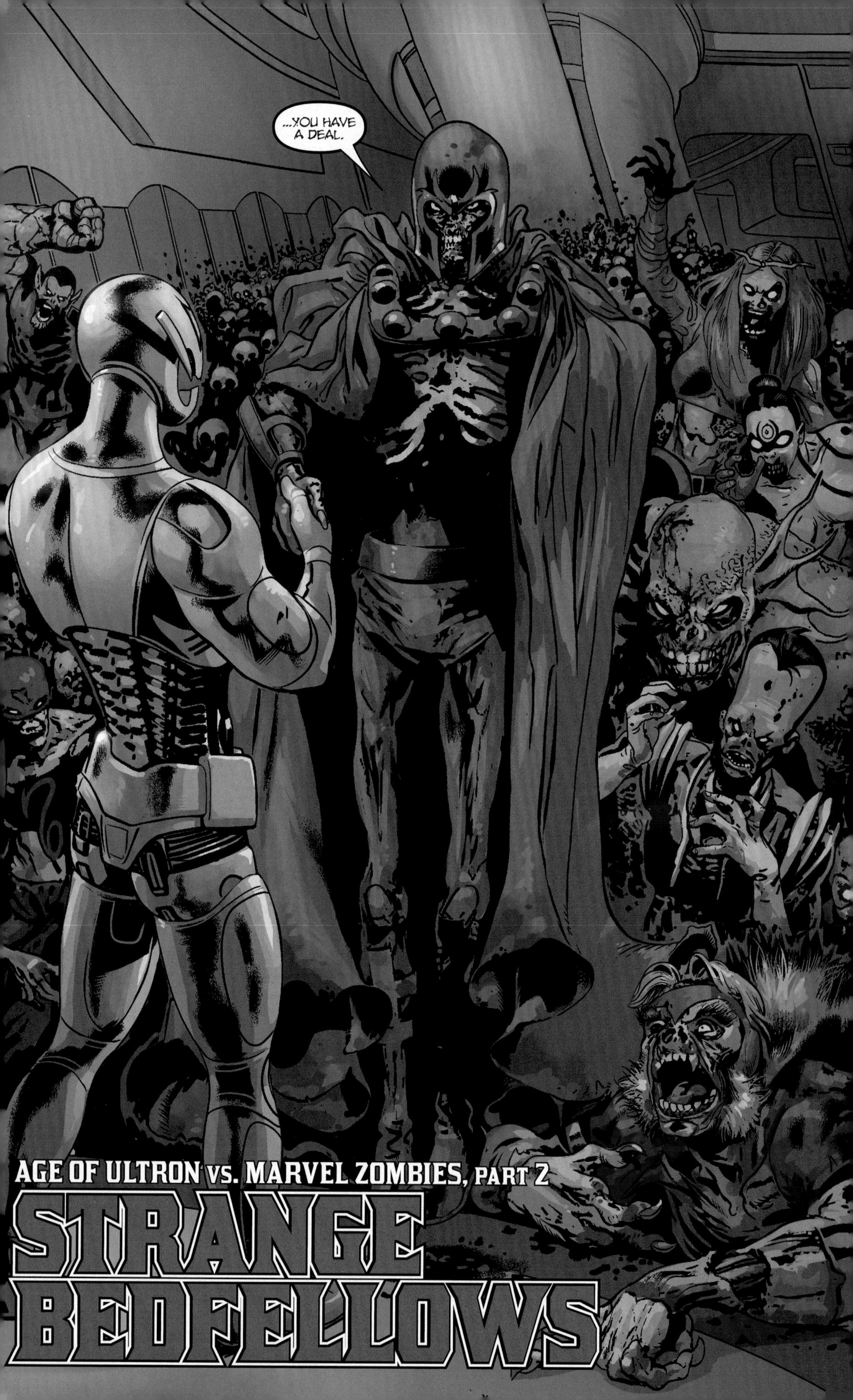

...YOU HAVE A DEAL.
AGE OF ULTRON vs. MARVEL ZOMBIES, PART 2
STRANGE BEDFELLOWS

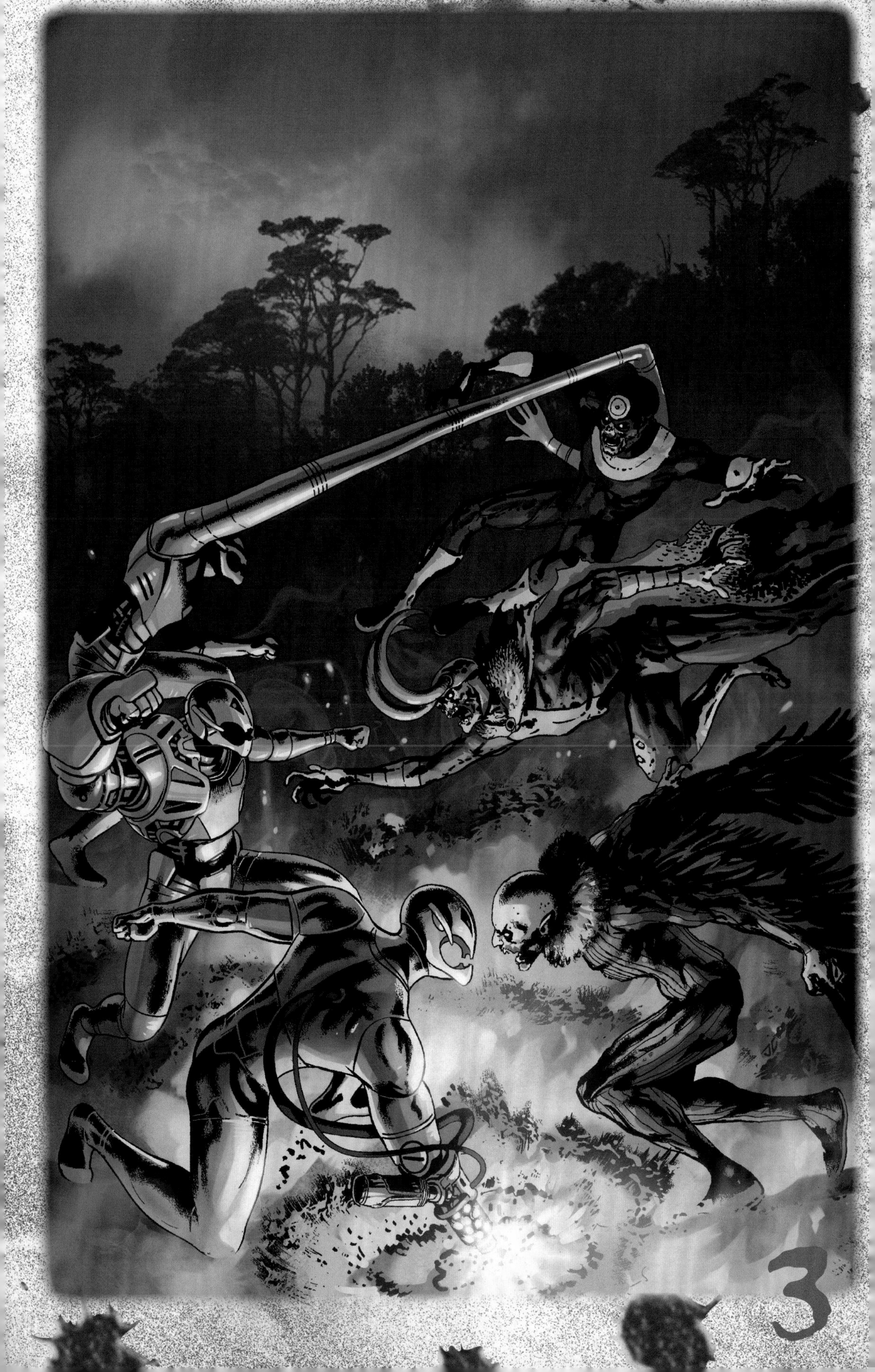

3

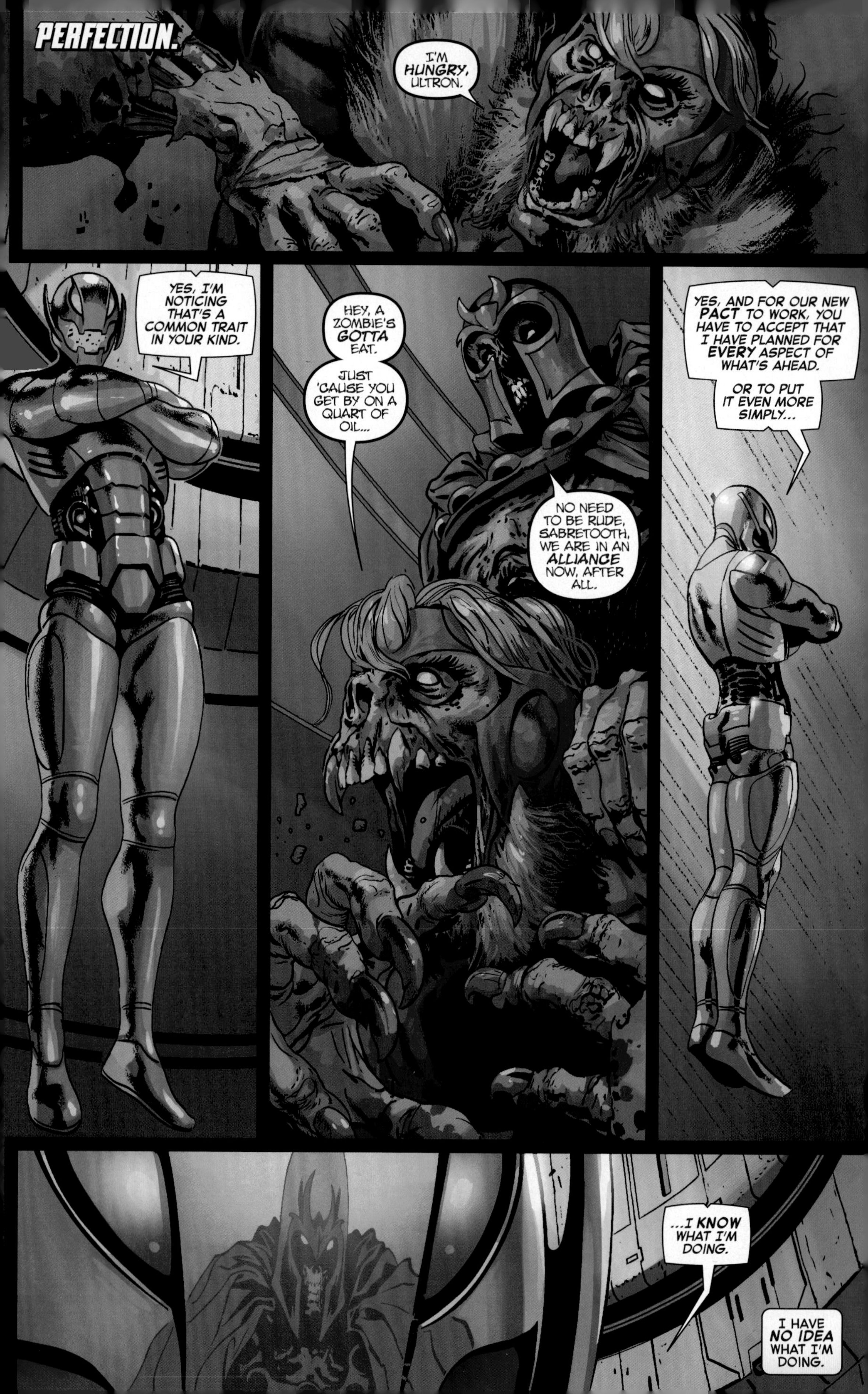
PERFECTION.
I'M HUNGRY, ULTRON.
YES, I'M NOTICING THAT'S A COMMON TRAIT IN YOUR KIND.
HEY, A ZOMBIE'S GOTTA EAT.
JUST 'CAUSE YOU GET BY ON A QUART OF OIL...
NO NEED TO BE RUDE, SABRETOOTH, WE ARE IN AN ALLIANCE NOW, AFTER ALL.
YES, AND FOR OUR NEW PACT TO WORK, YOU HAVE TO ACCEPT THAT I HAVE PLANNED FOR EVERY ASPECT OF WHAT'S AHEAD.
OR TO PUT IT EVEN MORE SIMPLY...
...I KNOW WHAT I'M DOING.
I HAVE NO IDEA WHAT I'M DOING.

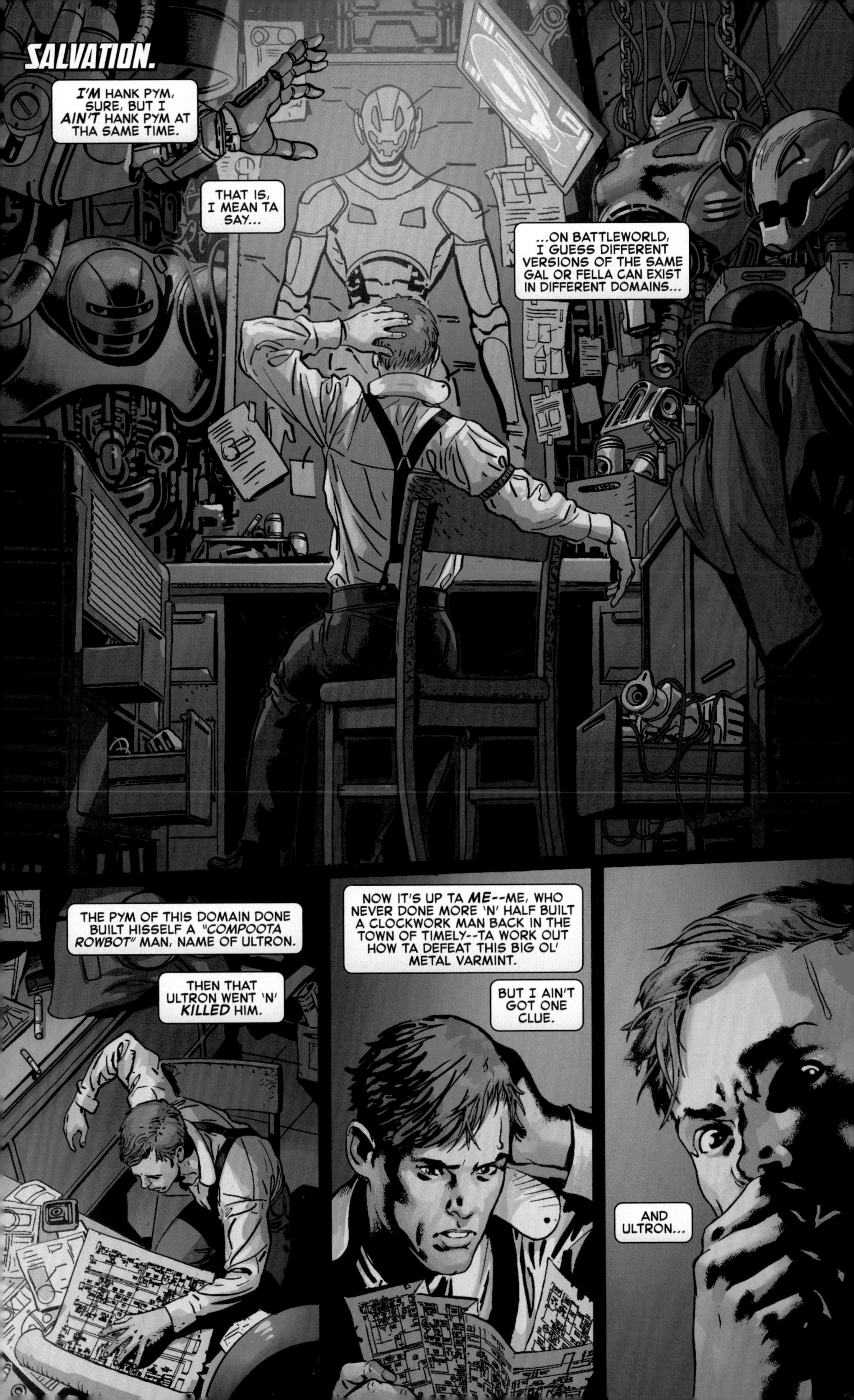
SALVATION.
I'M HANK PYM, SURE, BUT I AIN'T HANK PYM AT THA SAME TIME.
THAT IS, I MEAN TA SAY...
...ON BATTLEWORLD, I GUESS DIFFERENT VERSIONS OF THE SAME GAL OR FELLA CAN EXIST IN DIFFERENT DOMAINS...
THE PYM OF THIS DOMAIN DONE BUILT HISSELF A "COMPOOTA ROWBOT" MAN, NAME OF ULTRON.
THEN THAT ULTRON WENT 'N' KILLED HIM.
NOW IT'S UP TA ME--ME, WHO NEVER DONE MORE 'N' HALF BUILT A CLOCKWORK MAN BACK IN THE TOWN OF TIMELY--TA WORK OUT HOW TA DEFEAT THIS BIG OL' METAL VARMINT.
BUT I AIN'T GOT ONE CLUE.
AND ULTRON...

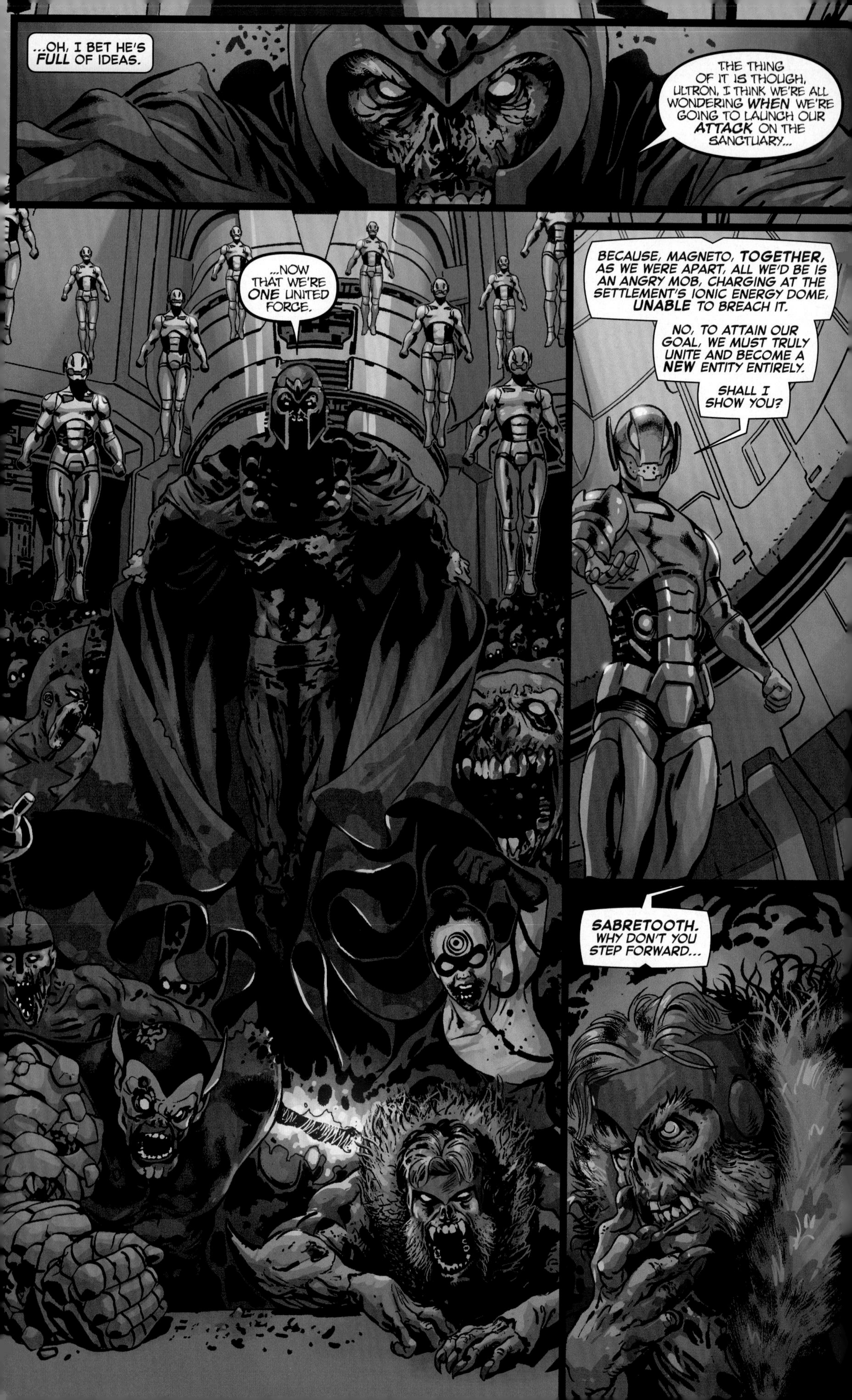
...OH, I BET HE'S FULL OF IDEAS.
THE THING OF IT IS THOUGH, ULTRON, I THINK WE'RE ALL WONDERING WHEN WE'RE GOING TO LAUNCH OUR ATTACK ON THE SANCTUARY...
...NOW THAT WE'RE ONE UNITED FORCE.
BECAUSE, MAGNETO, TOGETHER, AS WE WERE APART, ALL WE'D BE IS AN ANGRY MOB, CHARGING AT THE SETTLEMENT'S IONIC ENERGY DOME, UNABLE TO BREACH IT.
NO, TO ATTAIN OUR GOAL, WE MUST TRULY UNITE AND BECOME A NEW ENTITY ENTIRELY.
SHALL I SHOW YOU?
SABRETOOTH. WHY DON'T YOU STEP FORWARD...

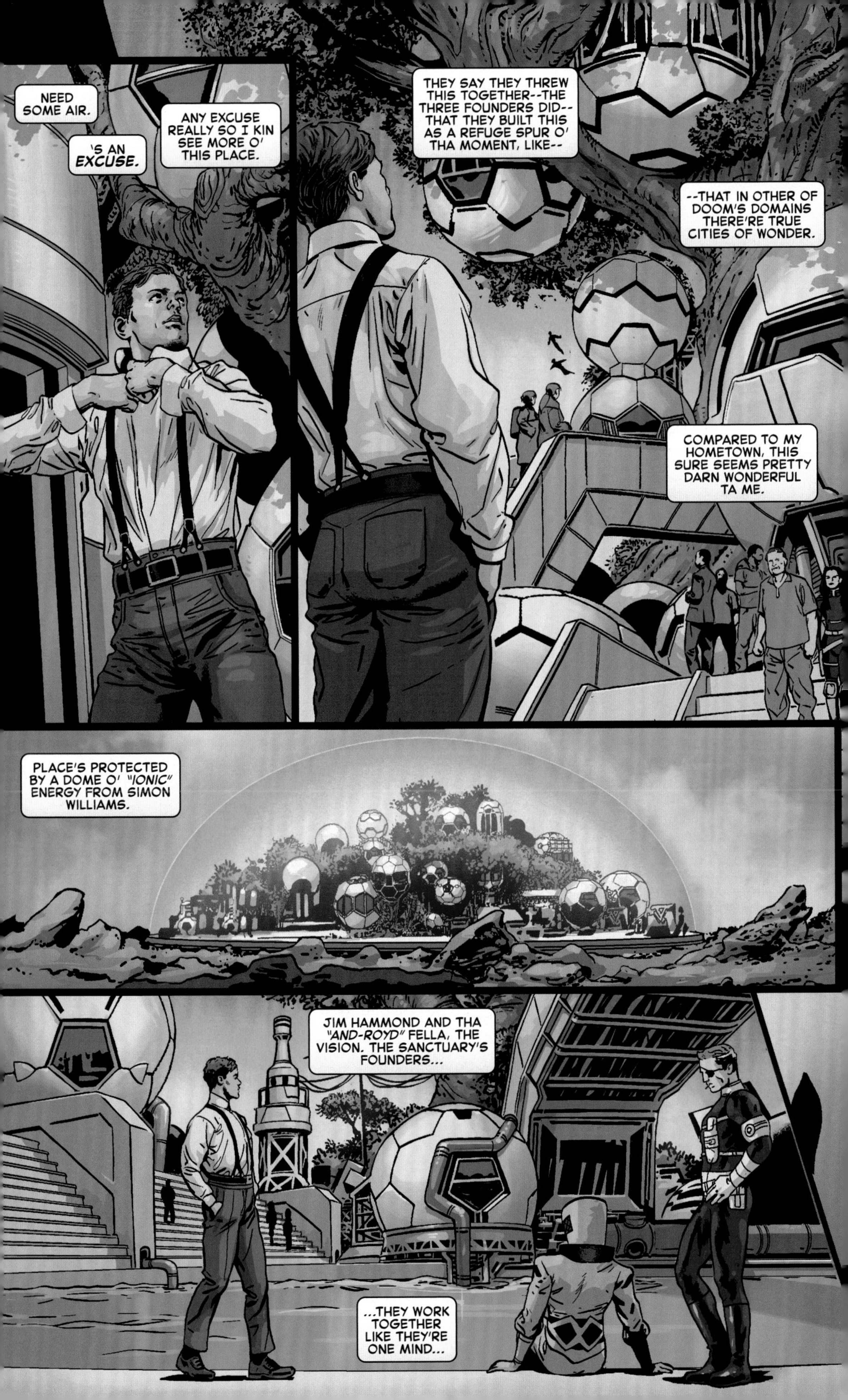
NEED SOME AIR.
'S AN *EXCUSE.*
ANY EXCUSE REALLY SO I KIN SEE MORE O' THIS PLACE.
THEY SAY THEY THREW THIS TOGETHER--THE THREE FOUNDERS DID--THAT THEY BUILT THIS AS A REFUGE SPUR O' THA MOMENT, LIKE--
--THAT IN OTHER OF DOOM'S DOMAINS THERE'RE TRUE CITIES OF WONDER.
COMPARED TO MY HOMETOWN, THIS SURE SEEMS PRETTY DARN WONDERFUL TA ME.
PLACE'S PROTECTED BY A DOME O' *"IONIC"* ENERGY FROM SIMON WILLIAMS.
JIM HAMMOND AND THA *"AND-ROYD"* FELLA, THE VISION. THE SANCTUARY'S FOUNDERS...
...THEY WORK TOGETHER LIKE THEY'RE ONE MIND...

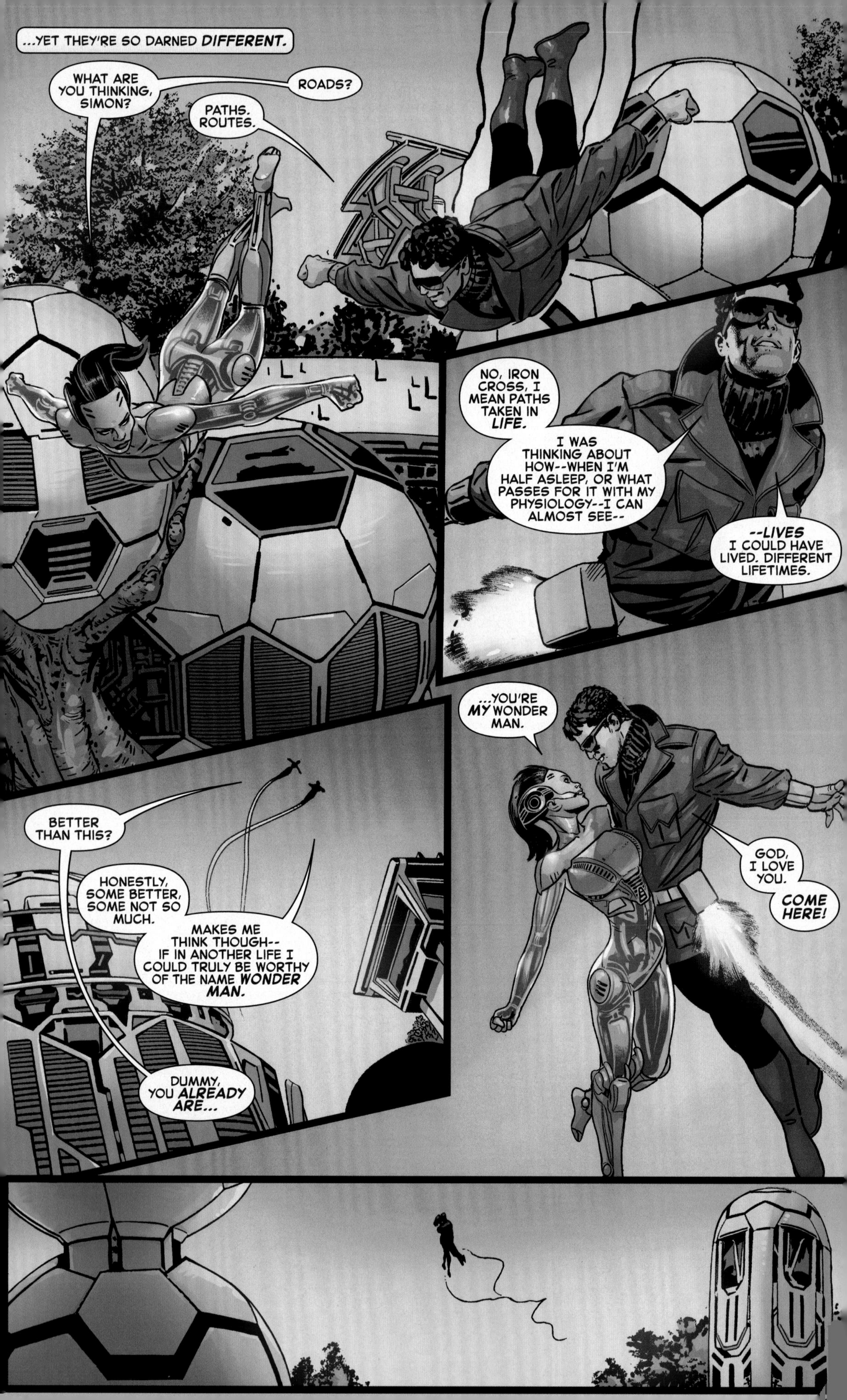
...YET THEY'RE SO DARNED DIFFERENT.
WHAT ARE YOU THINKING, SIMON?
ROADS?
PATHS. ROUTES.
NO, IRON CROSS, I MEAN PATHS TAKEN IN LIFE.
I WAS THINKING ABOUT HOW--WHEN I'M HALF ASLEEP, OR WHAT PASSES FOR IT WITH MY PHYSIOLOGY--I CAN ALMOST SEE--
--LIVES I COULD HAVE LIVED. DIFFERENT LIFETIMES.
BETTER THAN THIS?
HONESTLY, SOME BETTER, SOME NOT SO MUCH.
MAKES ME THINK THOUGH-- IF IN ANOTHER LIFE I COULD TRULY BE WORTHY OF THE NAME WONDER MAN.
DUMMY, YOU ALREADY ARE...
...YOU'RE MY WONDER MAN.
GOD, I LOVE YOU.
COME HERE!

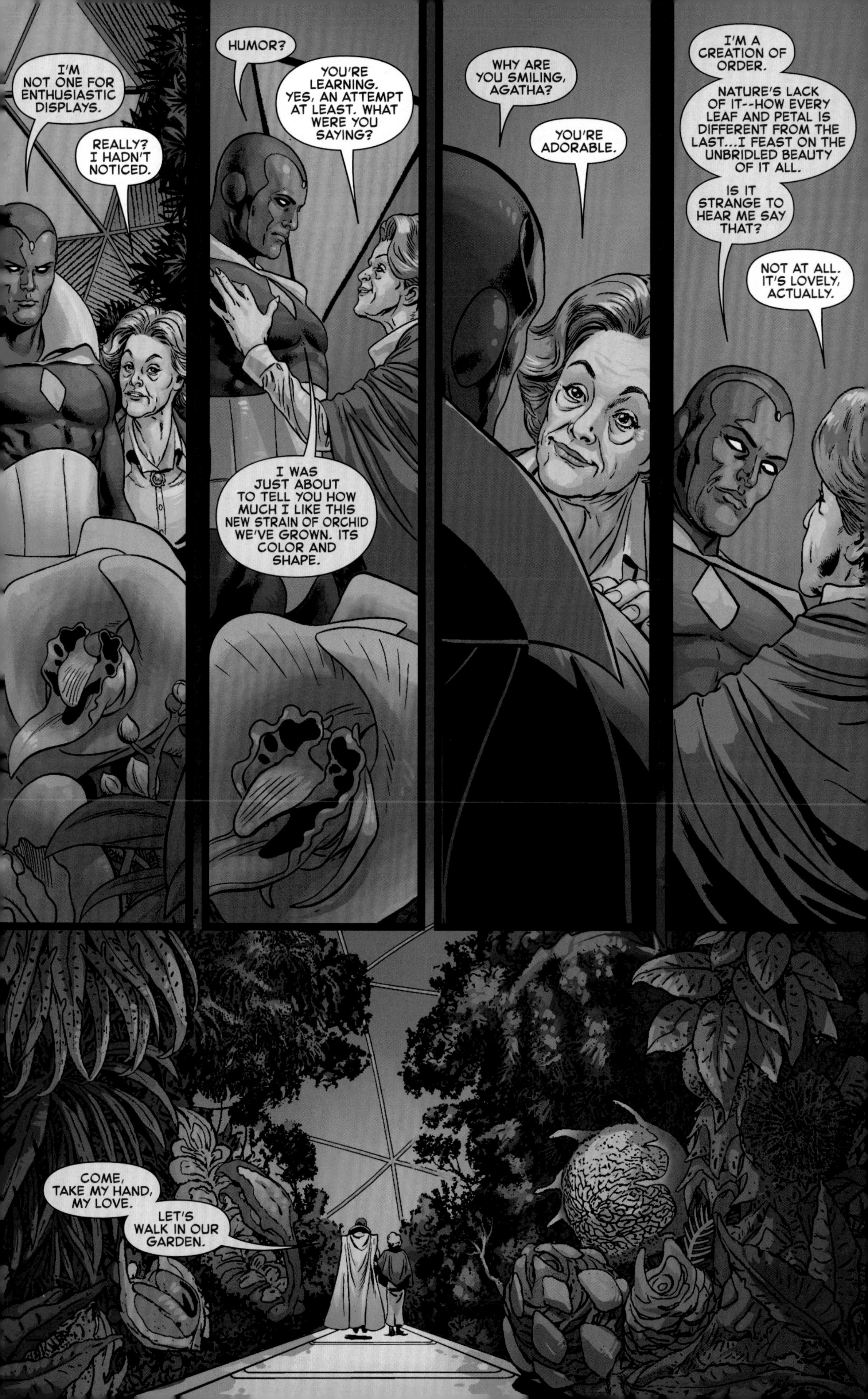

I'M NOT ONE FOR ENTHUSIASTIC DISPLAYS.
REALLY? I HADN'T NOTICED.
HUMOR?
YOU'RE LEARNING. YES, AN ATTEMPT AT LEAST. WHAT WERE YOU SAYING?
I WAS JUST ABOUT TO TELL YOU HOW MUCH I LIKE THIS NEW STRAIN OF ORCHID WE'VE GROWN. ITS COLOR AND SHAPE.
WHY ARE YOU SMILING, AGATHA?
YOU'RE ADORABLE.
I'M A CREATION OF ORDER.
NATURE'S LACK OF IT--HOW EVERY LEAF AND PETAL IS DIFFERENT FROM THE LAST...I FEAST ON THE UNBRIDLED BEAUTY OF IT ALL.
IS IT STRANGE TO HEAR ME SAY THAT?
NOT AT ALL. IT'S LOVELY, ACTUALLY.
COME, TAKE MY HAND, MY LOVE.
LET'S WALK IN OUR GARDEN.

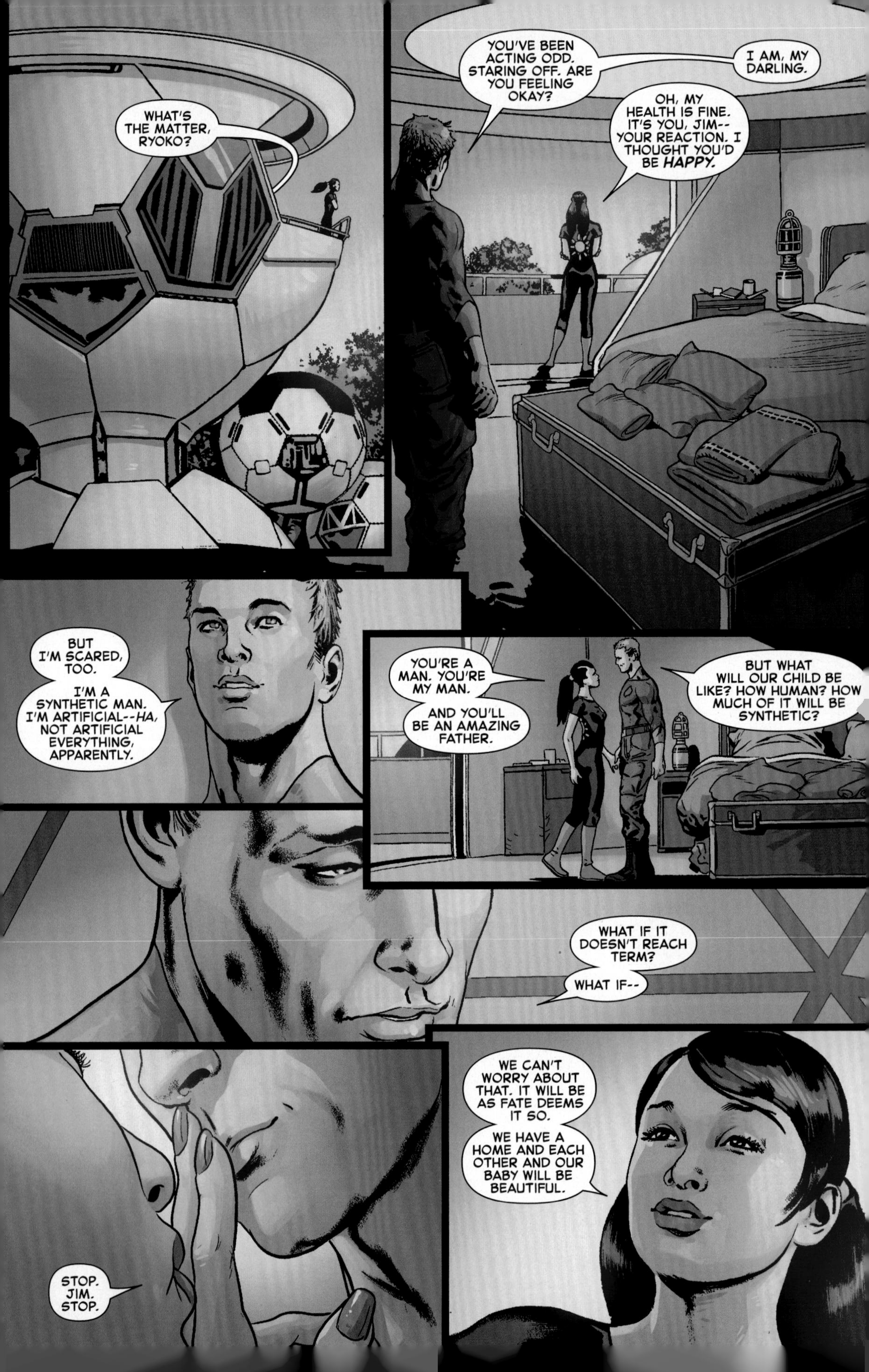
WHAT'S THE MATTER, RYOKO?
YOU'VE BEEN ACTING ODD. STARING OFF. ARE YOU FEELING OKAY?
I AM, MY DARLING.
OH, MY HEALTH IS FINE. IT'S YOU, JIM-- YOUR REACTION. I THOUGHT YOU'D BE HAPPY.
BUT I'M SCARED, TOO.
I'M A SYNTHETIC MAN. I'M ARTIFICIAL--HA, NOT ARTIFICIAL EVERYTHING, APPARENTLY.
YOU'RE A MAN. YOU'RE MY MAN.
AND YOU'LL BE AN AMAZING FATHER.
BUT WHAT WILL OUR CHILD BE LIKE? HOW HUMAN? HOW MUCH OF IT WILL BE SYNTHETIC?
WHAT IF IT DOESN'T REACH TERM?
WHAT IF--
STOP. JIM. STOP.
WE CAN'T WORRY ABOUT THAT. IT WILL BE AS FATE DEEMS IT SO.
WE HAVE A HOME AND EACH OTHER AND OUR BABY WILL BE BEAUTIFUL.

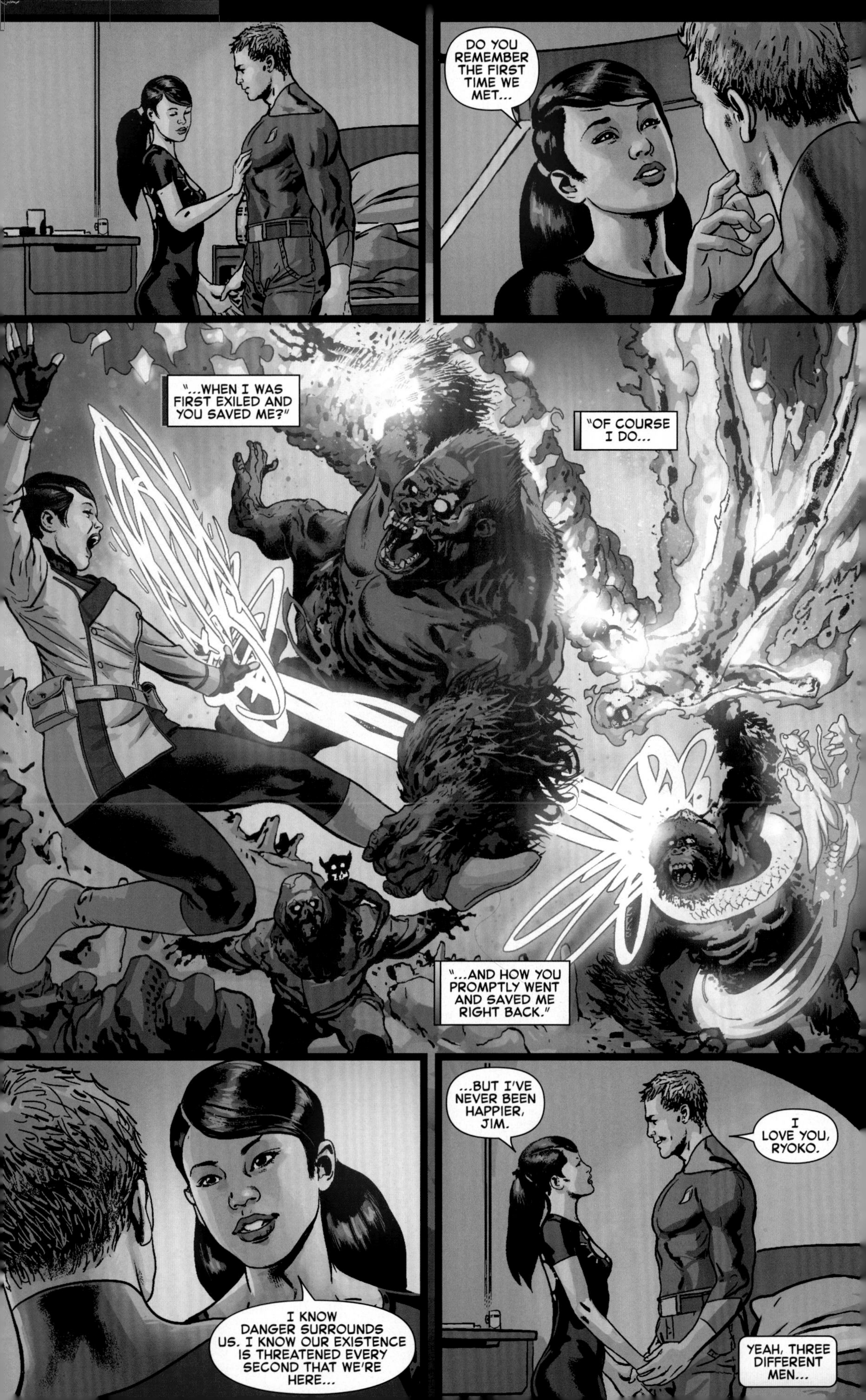
DO YOU REMEMBER THE FIRST TIME WE MET...
"...WHEN I WAS FIRST EXILED AND YOU SAVED ME?"
"OF COURSE I DO...
"...AND HOW YOU PROMPTLY WENT AND SAVED ME RIGHT BACK."
I KNOW DANGER SURROUNDS US. I KNOW OUR EXISTENCE IS THREATENED EVERY SECOND THAT WE'RE HERE...
...BUT I'VE NEVER BEEN HAPPIER, JIM.
I LOVE YOU, RYOKO.
YEAH, THREE DIFFERENT MEN...

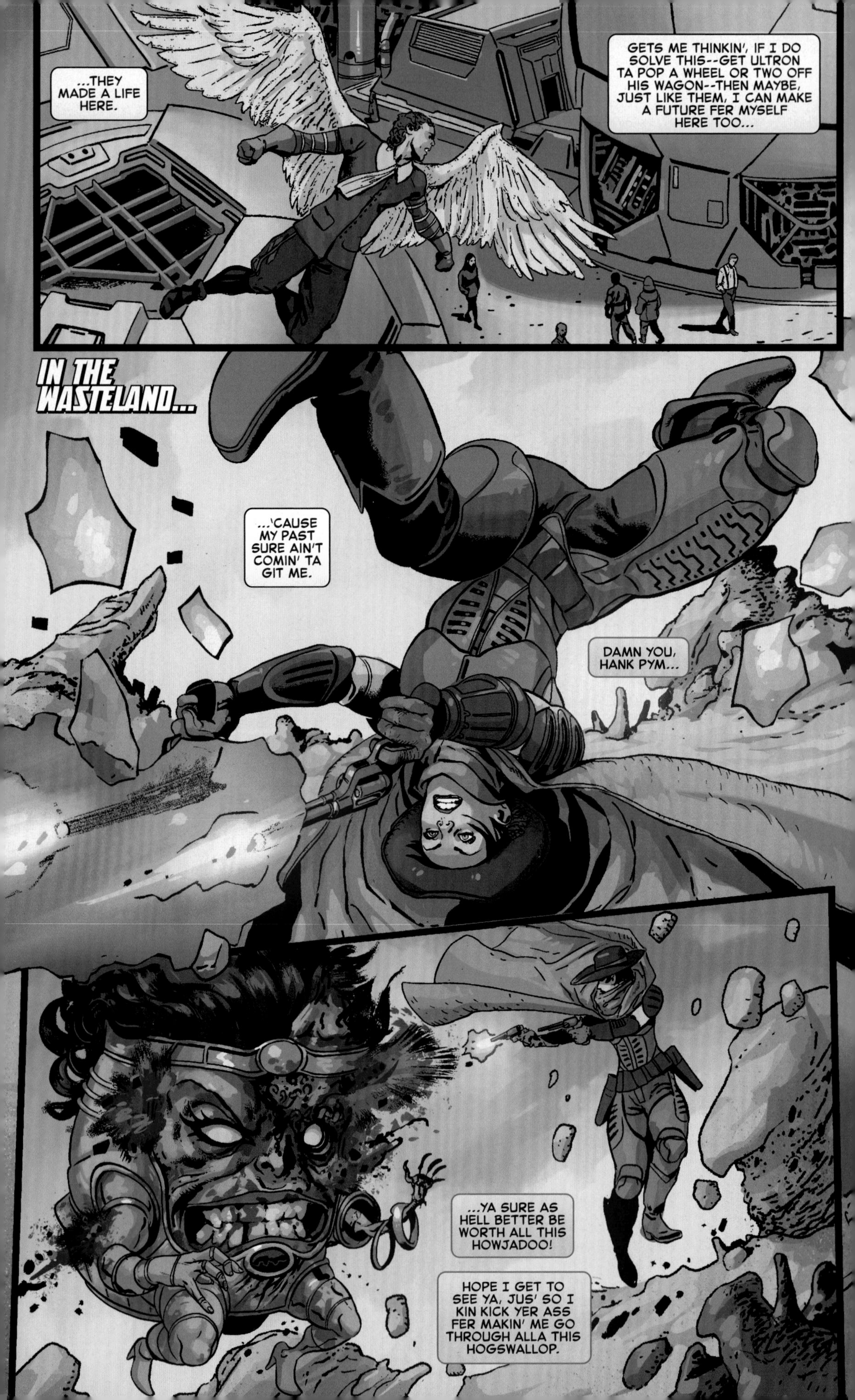
...THEY MADE A LIFE HERE.
GETS ME THINKIN', IF I DO SOLVE THIS--GET ULTRON TA POP A WHEEL OR TWO OFF HIS WAGON--THEN MAYBE, JUST LIKE THEM, I CAN MAKE A FUTURE FER MYSELF HERE TOO...
IN THE WASTELAND...
...'CAUSE MY PAST SURE AIN'T COMIN' TA GIT ME.
DAMN YOU, HANK PYM...
...YA SURE AS HELL BETTER BE WORTH ALL THIS HOWJADOO!
HOPE I GET TO SEE YA, JUS' SO I KIN KICK YER ASS FER MAKIN' ME GO THROUGH ALLA THIS HOGSWALLOP.

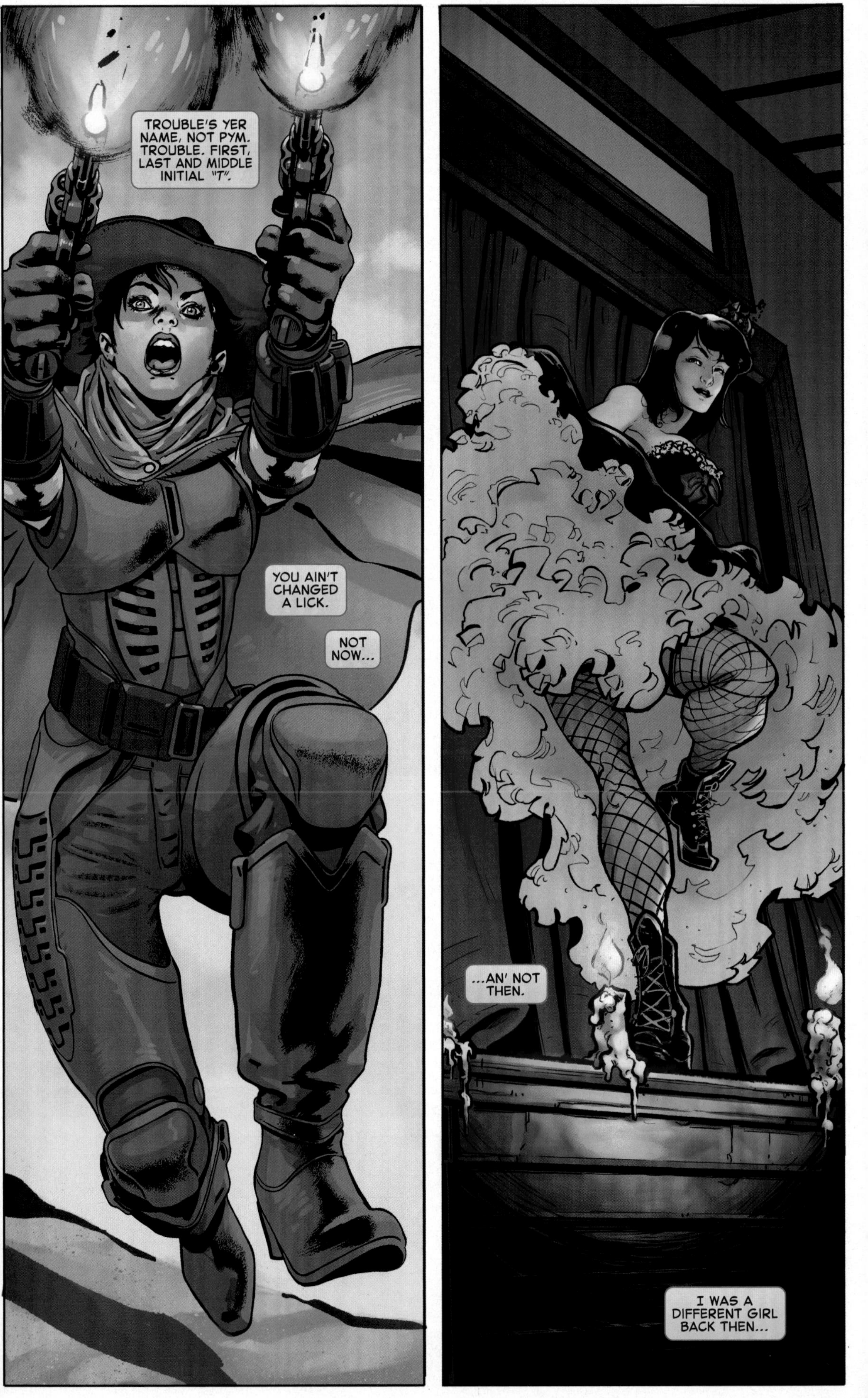
TROUBLE'S YER NAME, NOT PYM. TROUBLE. FIRST, LAST AND MIDDLE INITIAL "T".
YOU AIN'T CHANGED A LICK.
NOT NOW...
...AN' NOT THEN.
I WAS A DIFFERENT GIRL BACK THEN...

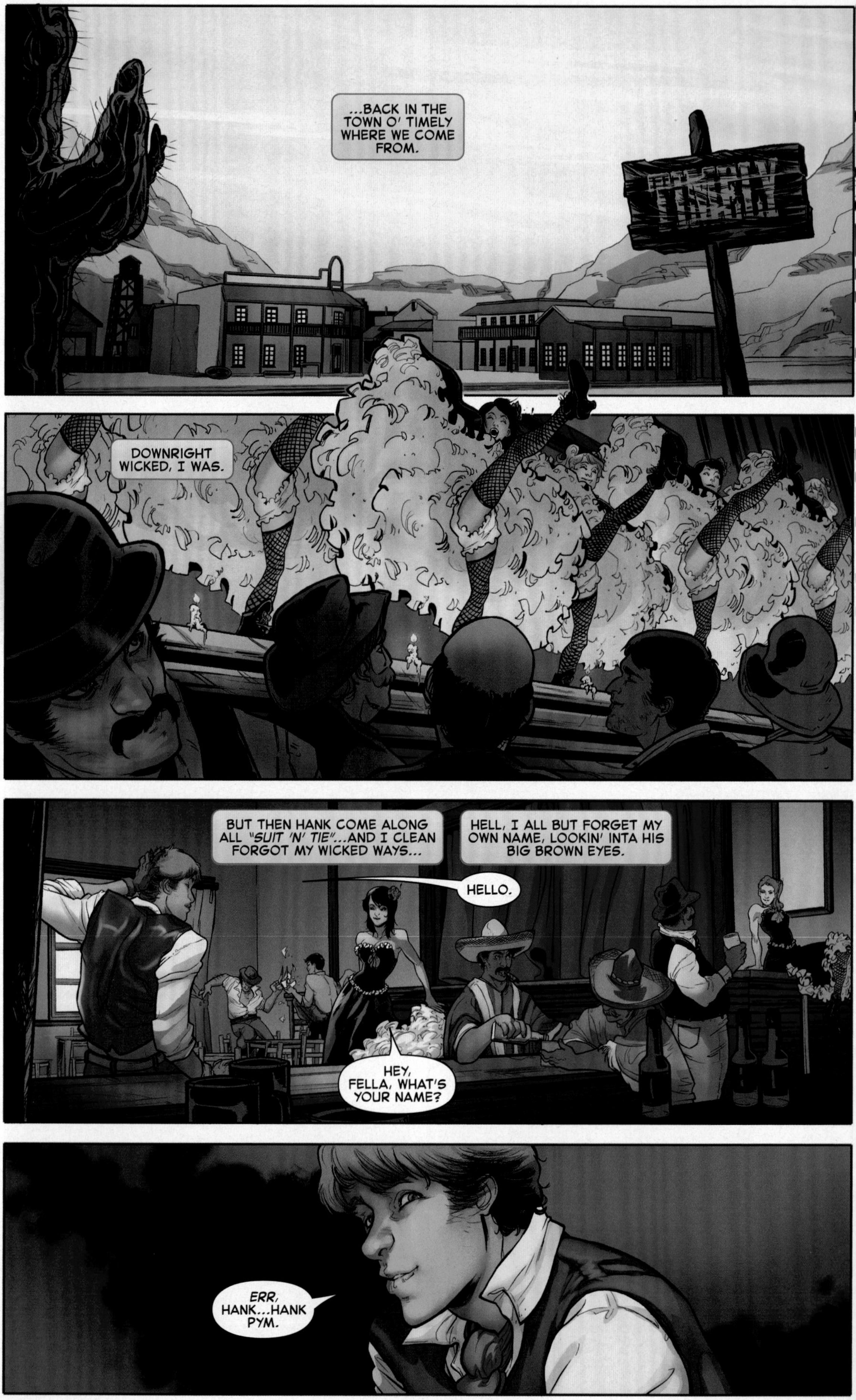
...BACK IN THE TOWN O' TIMELY WHERE WE COME FROM.
DOWNRIGHT WICKED, I WAS.
BUT THEN HANK COME ALONG ALL "SUIT 'N' TIE"...AND I CLEAN FORGOT MY WICKED WAYS...
HELL, I ALL BUT FORGET MY OWN NAME, LOOKIN' INTA HIS BIG BROWN EYES.
HELLO.
HEY, FELLA, WHAT'S YOUR NAME?
ERR, HANK...HANK PYM.

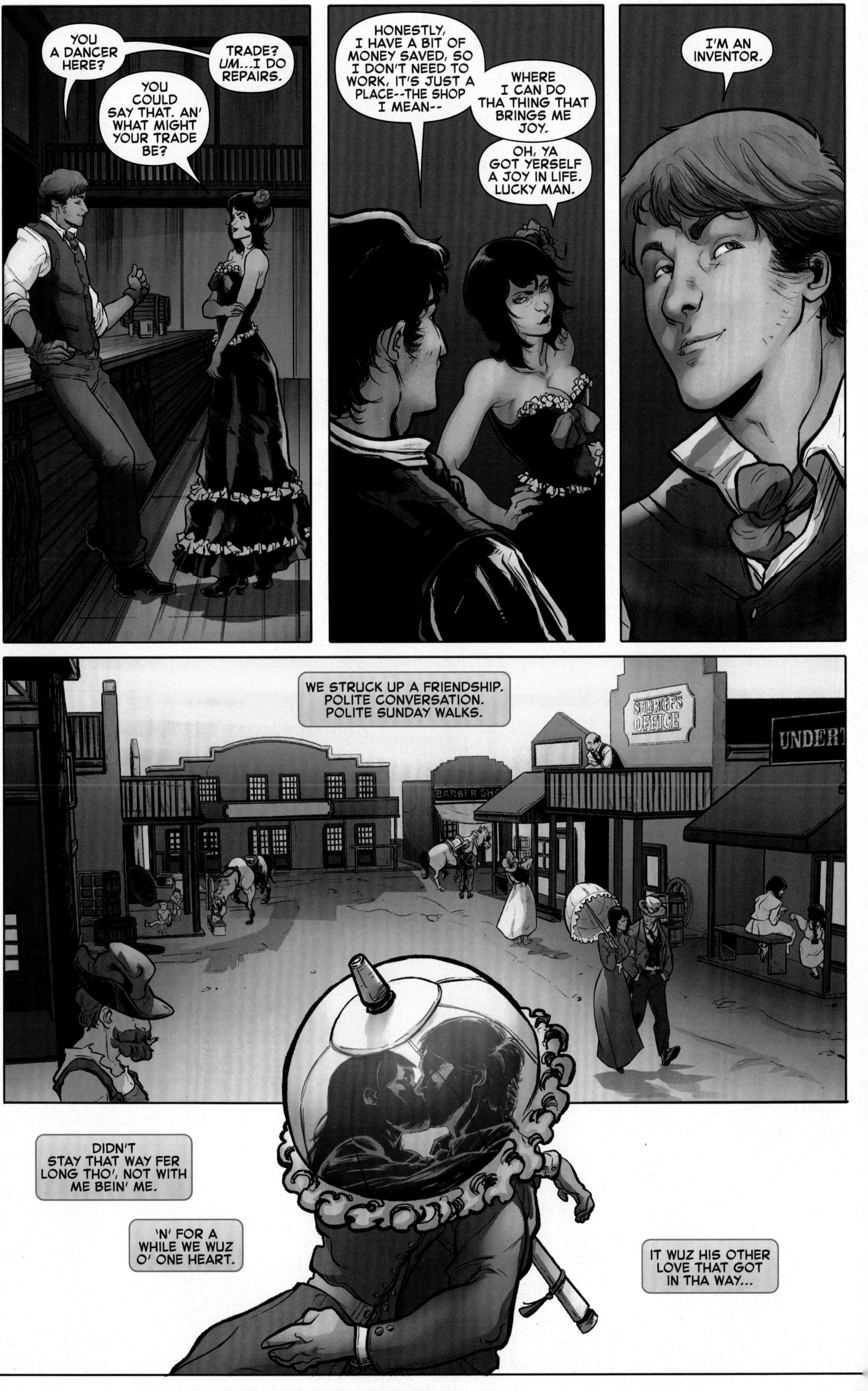
YOU A DANCER HERE?
YOU COULD SAY THAT. AN' WHAT MIGHT YOUR TRADE BE?
TRADE? *UM*...I DO REPAIRS.
HONESTLY, I HAVE A BIT OF MONEY SAVED, SO I DON'T NEED TO WORK, IT'S JUST A PLACE--THE SHOP I MEAN--
WHERE I CAN DO THA THING THAT BRINGS ME JOY.
OH, YA GOT YERSELF A JOY IN LIFE. LUCKY MAN.
I'M AN INVENTOR.
WE STRUCK UP A FRIENDSHIP. POLITE CONVERSATION. POLITE SUNDAY WALKS.
SHERIFF'S OFFICE
UNDERT
BARBER SHO
DIDN'T STAY THAT WAY FER LONG THO', NOT WITH ME BEIN' ME.
'N' FOR A WHILE WE WUZ O' ONE HEART.
IT WUZ HIS OTHER LOVE THAT GOT IN THA WAY...

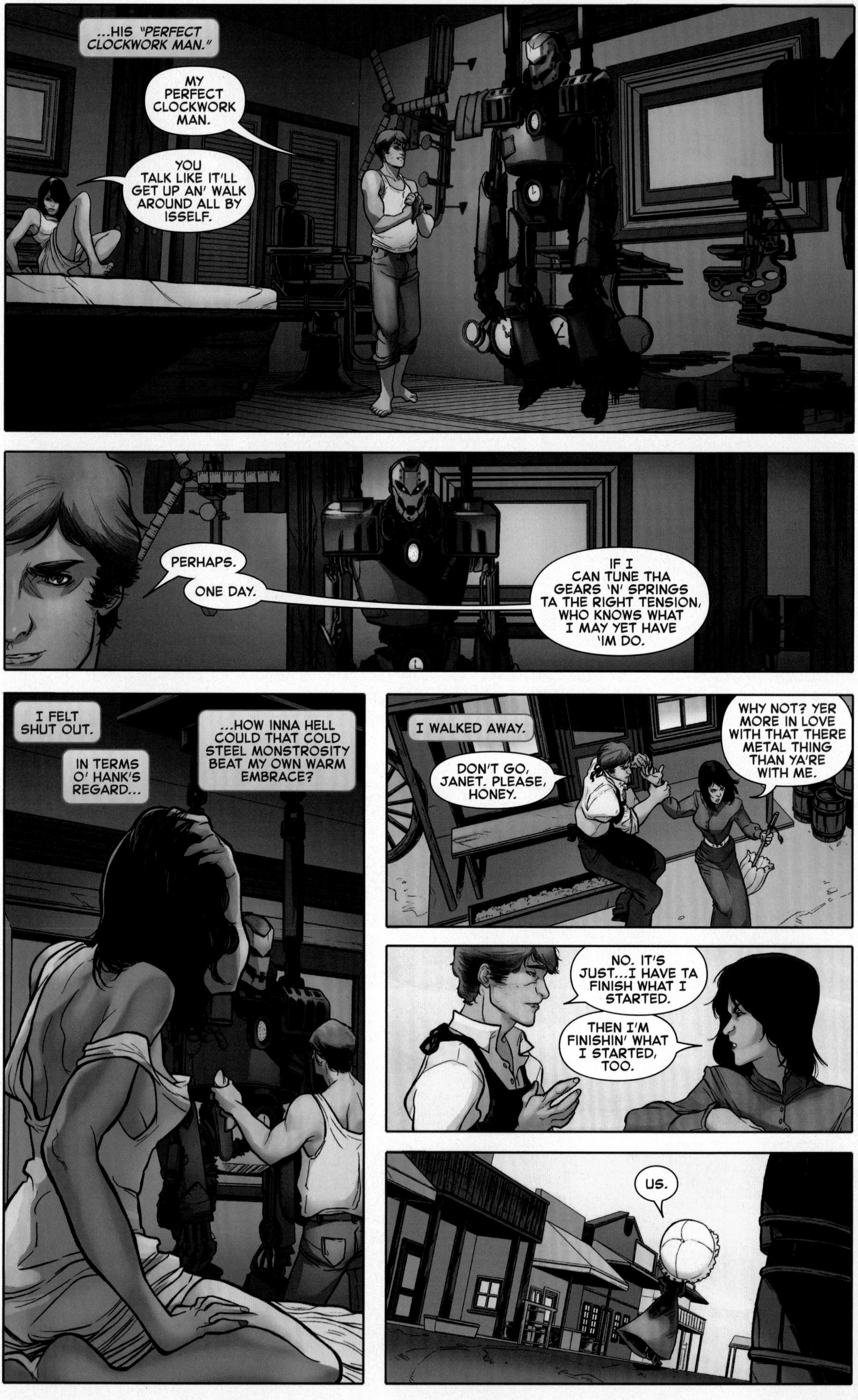
...HIS "PERFECT CLOCKWORK MAN."
MY PERFECT CLOCKWORK MAN.
YOU TALK LIKE IT'LL GET UP AN' WALK AROUND ALL BY ISSELF.
PERHAPS.
ONE DAY.
IF I CAN TUNE THA GEARS 'N' SPRINGS TA THE RIGHT TENSION, WHO KNOWS WHAT I MAY YET HAVE 'IM DO.
I FELT SHUT OUT.
IN TERMS O' HANK'S REGARD...
...HOW INNA HELL COULD THAT COLD STEEL MONSTROSITY BEAT MY OWN WARM EMBRACE?
I WALKED AWAY.
DON'T GO, JANET. PLEASE, HONEY.
WHY NOT? YER MORE IN LOVE WITH THAT THERE METAL THING THAN YA'RE WITH ME.
NO. IT'S JUST...I HAVE TA FINISH WHAT I STARTED.
THEN I'M FINISHIN' WHAT I STARTED, TOO.
US.

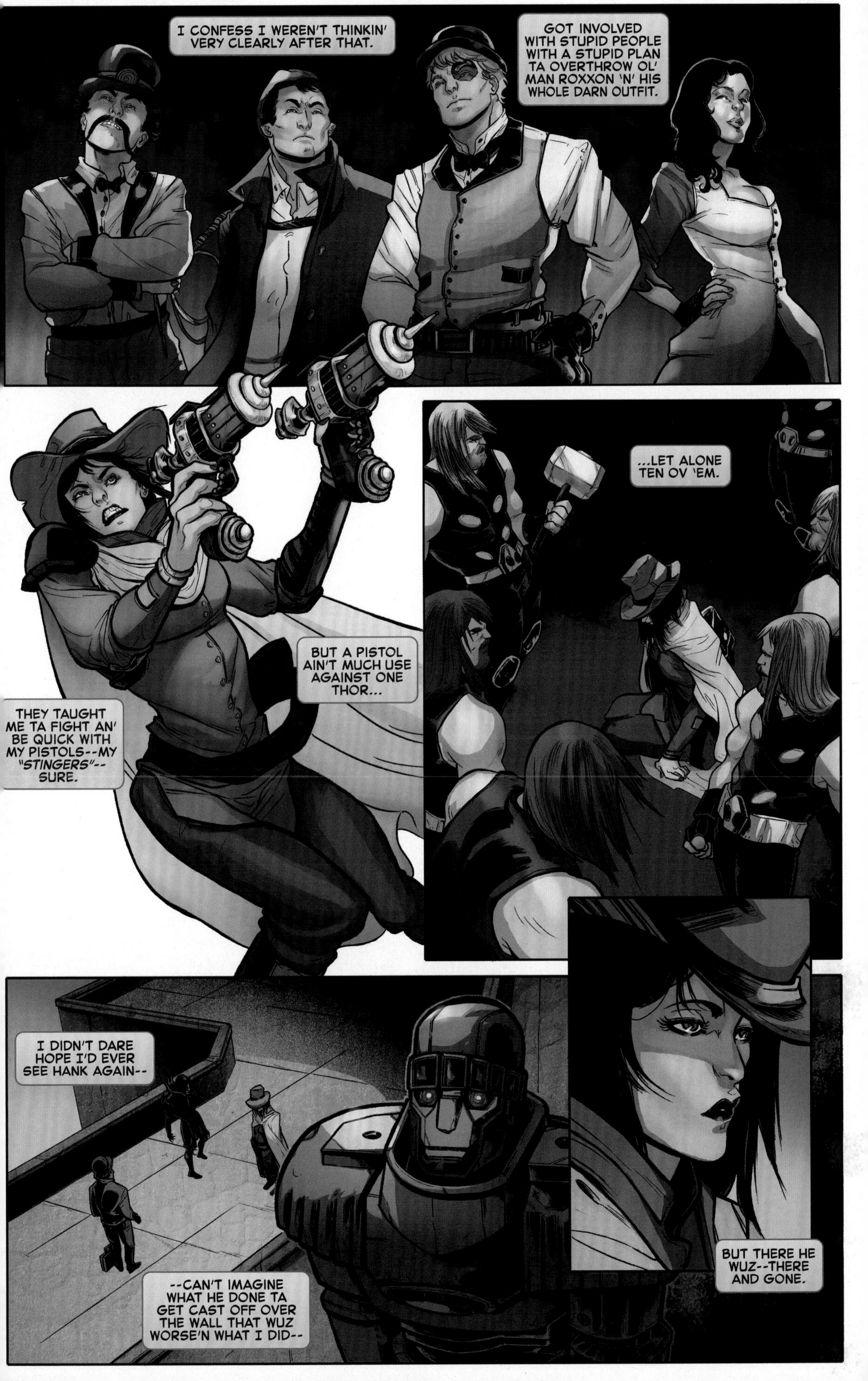
I CONFESS I WEREN'T THINKIN' VERY CLEARLY AFTER THAT.
GOT INVOLVED WITH STUPID PEOPLE WITH A STUPID PLAN TA OVERTHROW OL' MAN ROXXON 'N' HIS WHOLE DARN OUTFIT.
THEY TAUGHT ME TA FIGHT AN' BE QUICK WITH MY PISTOLS--MY "STINGERS"-- SURE.
BUT A PISTOL AIN'T MUCH USE AGAINST ONE THOR...
...LET ALONE TEN OV 'EM.
I DIDN'T DARE HOPE I'D EVER SEE HANK AGAIN--
--CAN'T IMAGINE WHAT HE DONE TA GET CAST OFF OVER THE WALL THAT WUZ WORSE'N WHAT I DID--
BUT THERE HE WUZ--THERE AND GONE.

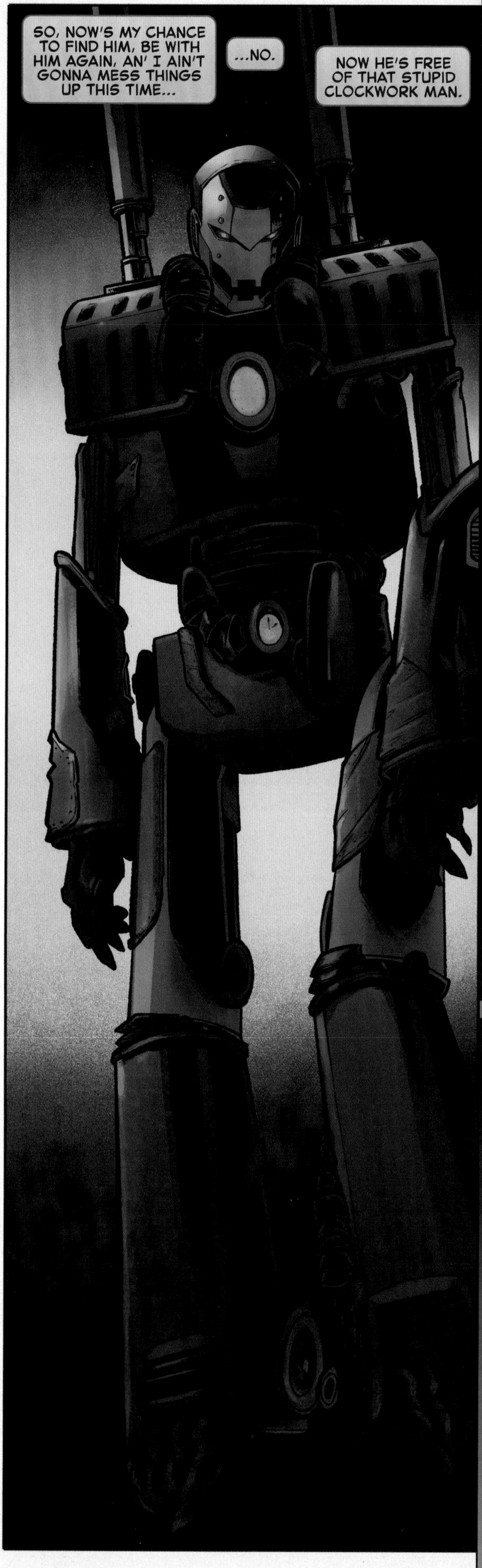
SO, NOW'S MY CHANCE TO FIND HIM, BE WITH HIM AGAIN, AN' I AIN'T GONNA MESS THINGS UP THIS TIME...
...NO.
NOW HE'S FREE OF THAT STUPID CLOCKWORK MAN.

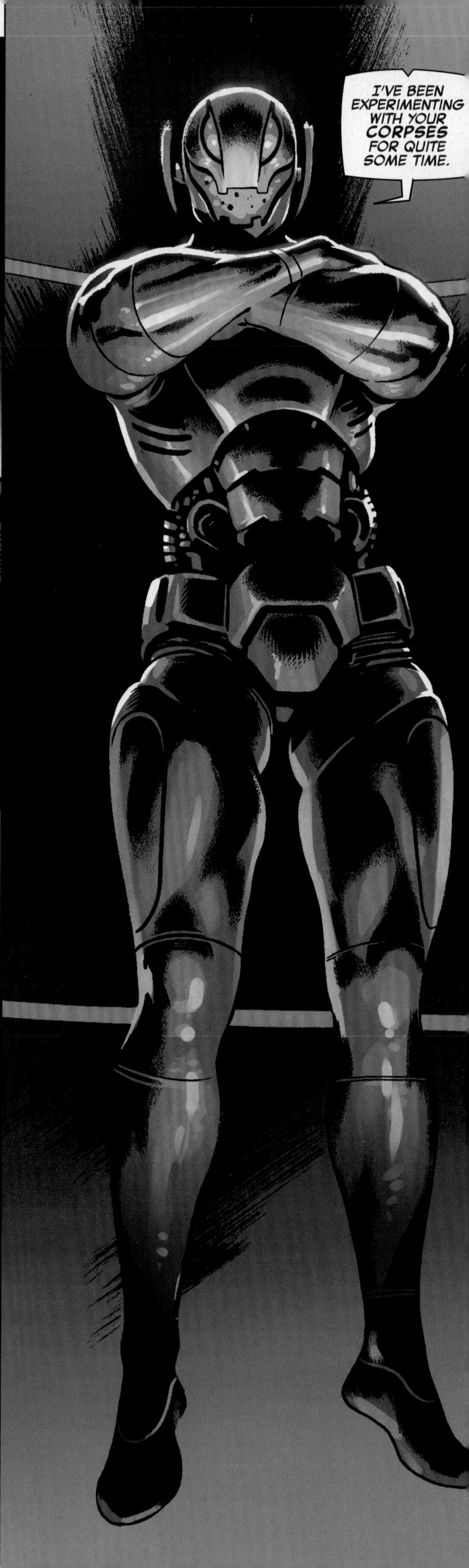
I'VE BEEN EXPERIMENTING WITH YOUR CORPSES FOR QUITE SOME TIME.

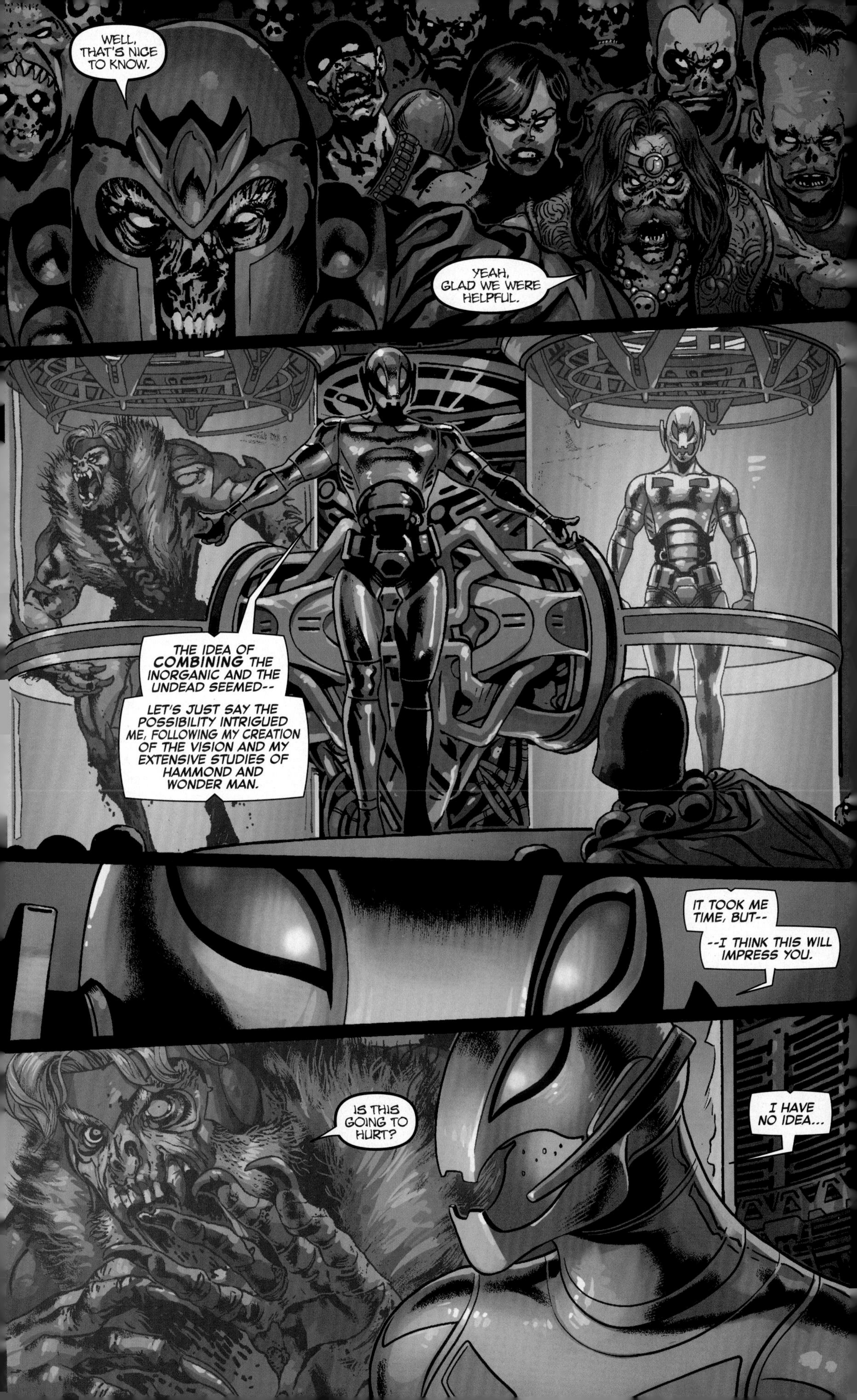
WELL, THAT'S NICE TO KNOW.
YEAH, GLAD WE WERE HELPFUL.
THE IDEA OF COMBINING THE INORGANIC AND THE UNDEAD SEEMED--
LET'S JUST SAY THE POSSIBILITY INTRIGUED ME, FOLLOWING MY CREATION OF THE VISION AND MY EXTENSIVE STUDIES OF HAMMOND AND WONDER MAN.
IT TOOK ME TIME, BUT--
--I THINK THIS WILL IMPRESS YOU.
IS THIS GOING TO HURT?
I HAVE NO IDEA...

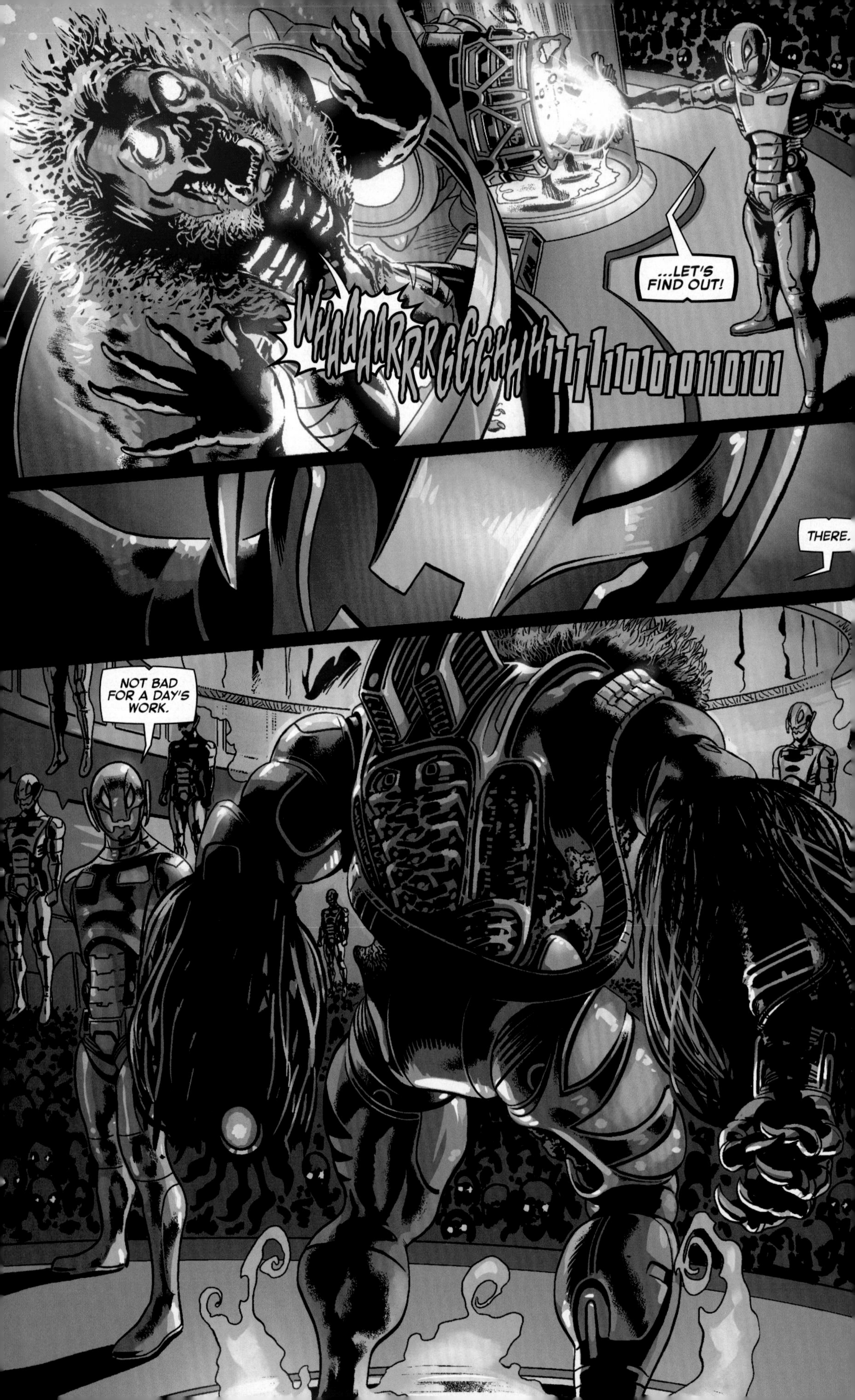
...LET'S FIND OUT!
WHAAAARRRGGGHHH1111110101010110101
THERE.
NOT BAD FOR A DAY'S WORK.

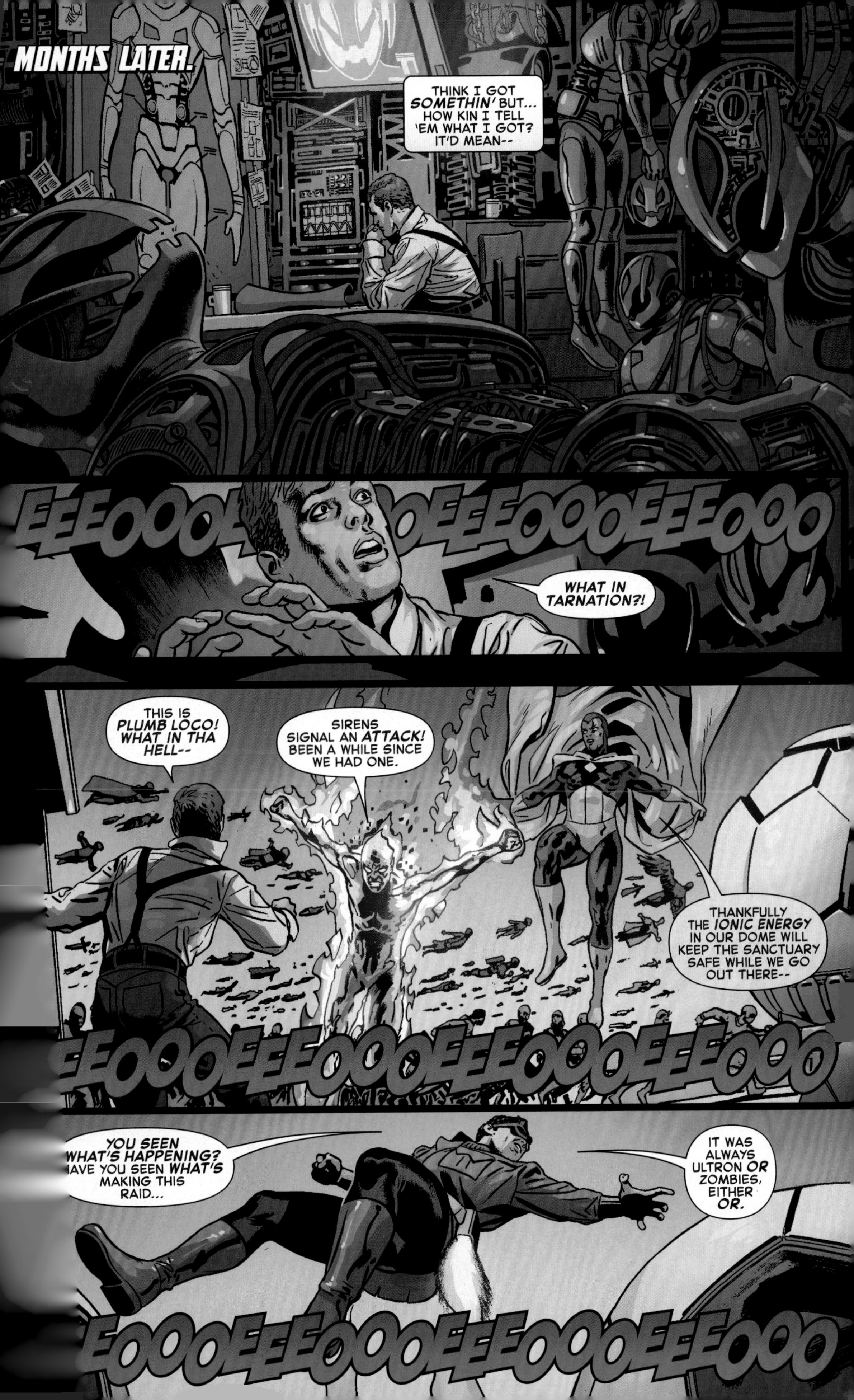
MONTHS LATER.
THINK I GOT SOMETHIN' BUT... HOW KIN I TELL 'EM WHAT I GOT? IT'D MEAN--
EEEOOOEEEOOOEEEOOOEEEOOO
WHAT IN TARNATION?!
THIS IS PLUMB LOCO! WHAT IN THA HELL--
SIRENS SIGNAL AN ATTACK! BEEN A WHILE SINCE WE HAD ONE.
THANKFULLY THE IONIC ENERGY IN OUR DOME WILL KEEP THE SANCTUARY SAFE WHILE WE GO OUT THERE--
EEOOOEEEOOOEEEOOOEEEOOO
YOU SEEN WHAT'S HAPPENING? HAVE YOU SEEN WHAT'S MAKING THIS RAID...
IT WAS ALWAYS ULTRON OR ZOMBIES, EITHER OR.
EOOOEEEOOOEEEOOOEEEOOO

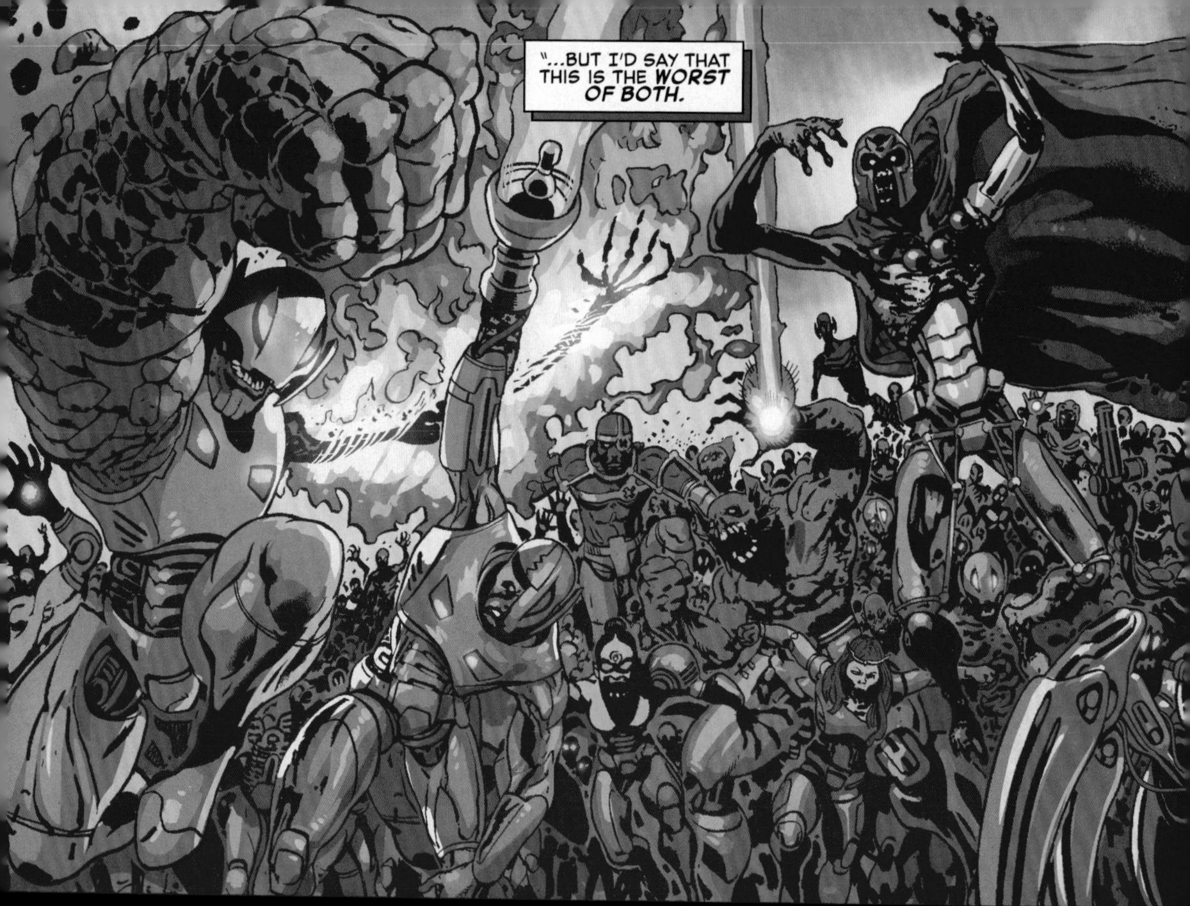
"...BUT I'D SAY THAT THIS IS THE WORST OF BOTH.
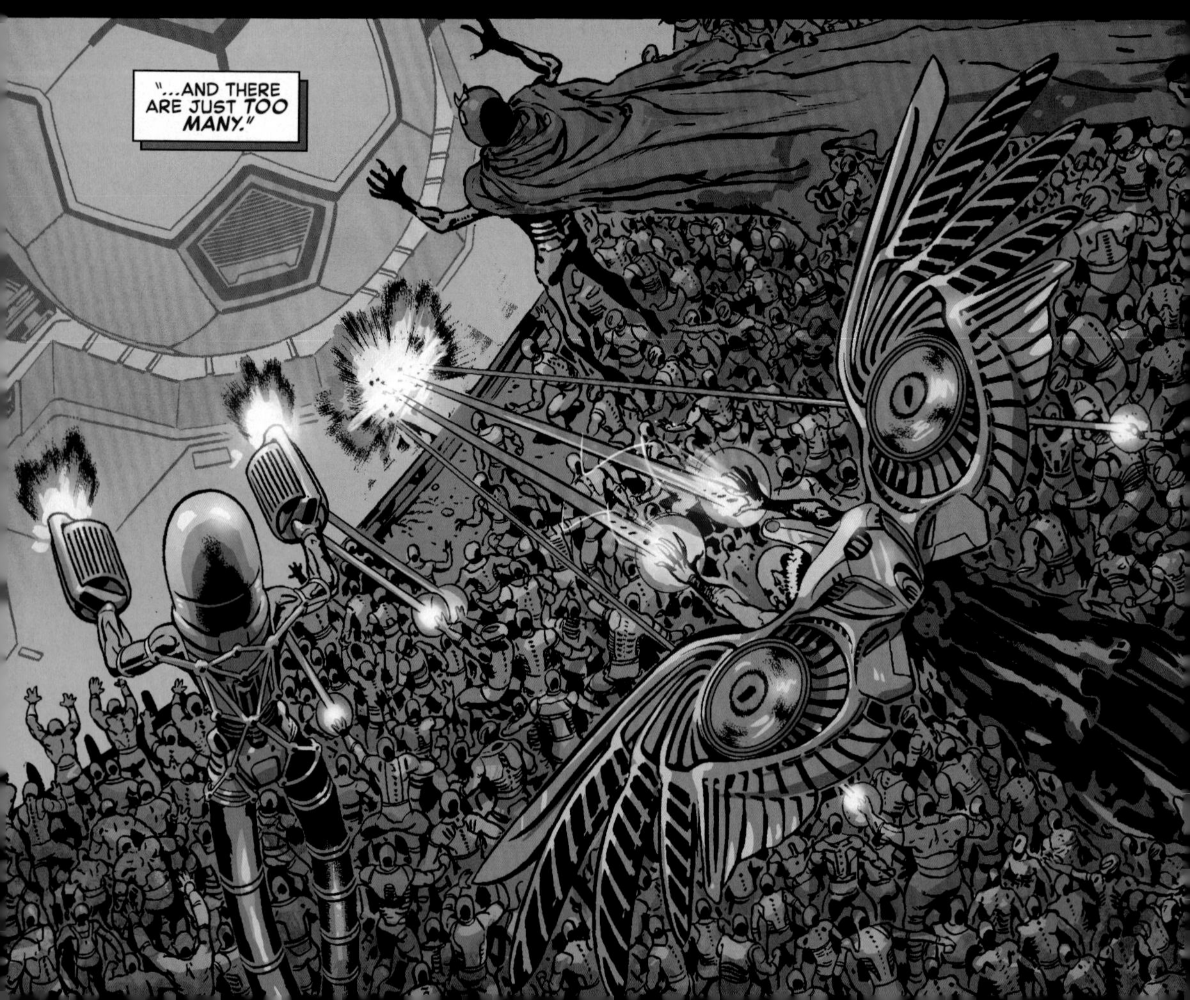
"...AND THERE ARE JUST TOO MANY."

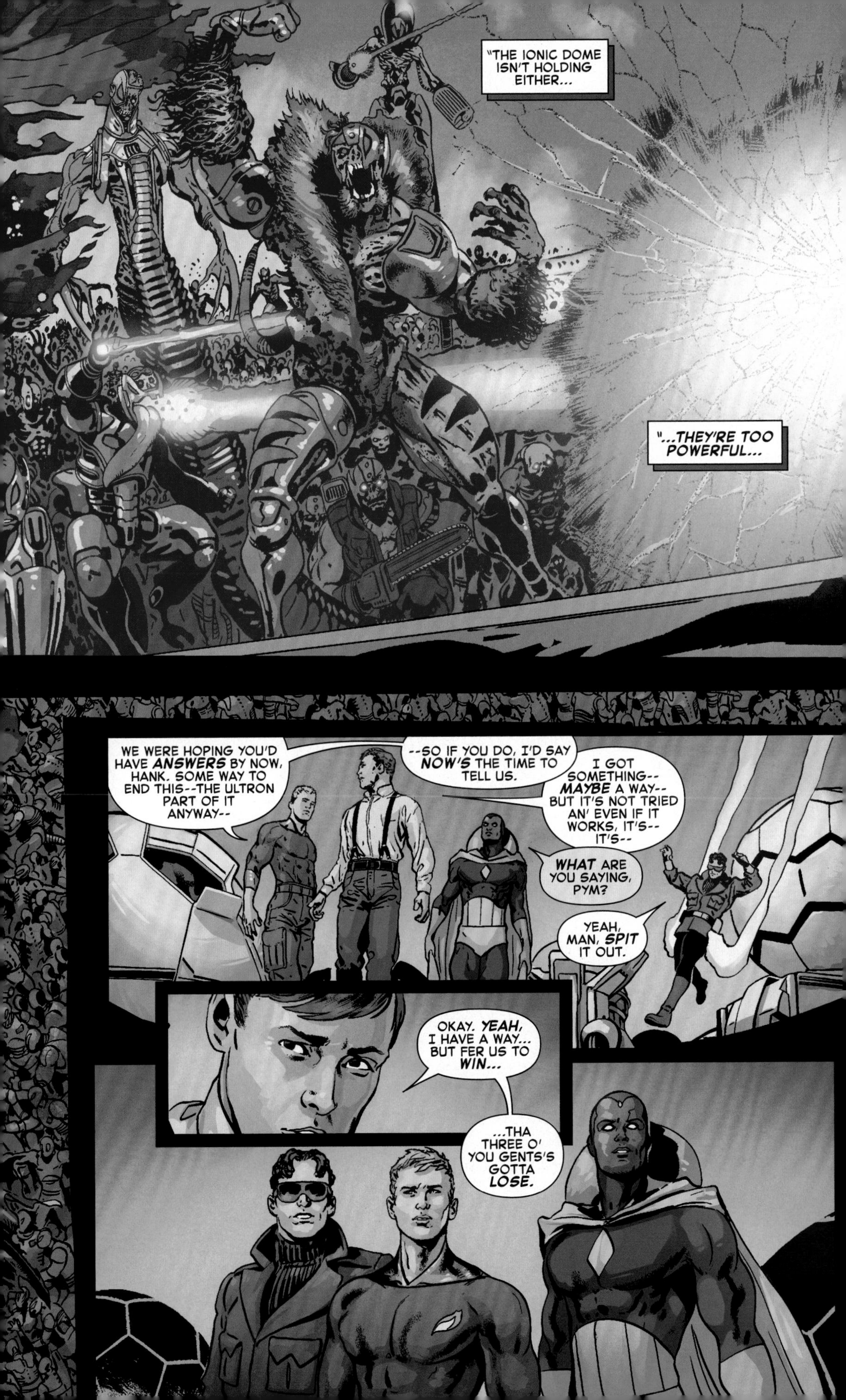
"THE IONIC DOME ISN'T HOLDING EITHER...
"...THEY'RE TOO POWERFUL...
WE WERE HOPING YOU'D HAVE ANSWERS BY NOW, HANK. SOME WAY TO END THIS--THE ULTRON PART OF IT ANYWAY--
--SO IF YOU DO, I'D SAY NOW'S THE TIME TO TELL US.
I GOT SOMETHING-- MAYBE A WAY-- BUT IT'S NOT TRIED AN' EVEN IF IT WORKS, IT'S-- IT'S--
WHAT ARE YOU SAYING, PYM?
YEAH, MAN, SPIT IT OUT.
OKAY. YEAH, I HAVE A WAY... BUT FER US TO WIN...
...THA THREE O' YOU GENTS'S GOTTA LOSE.

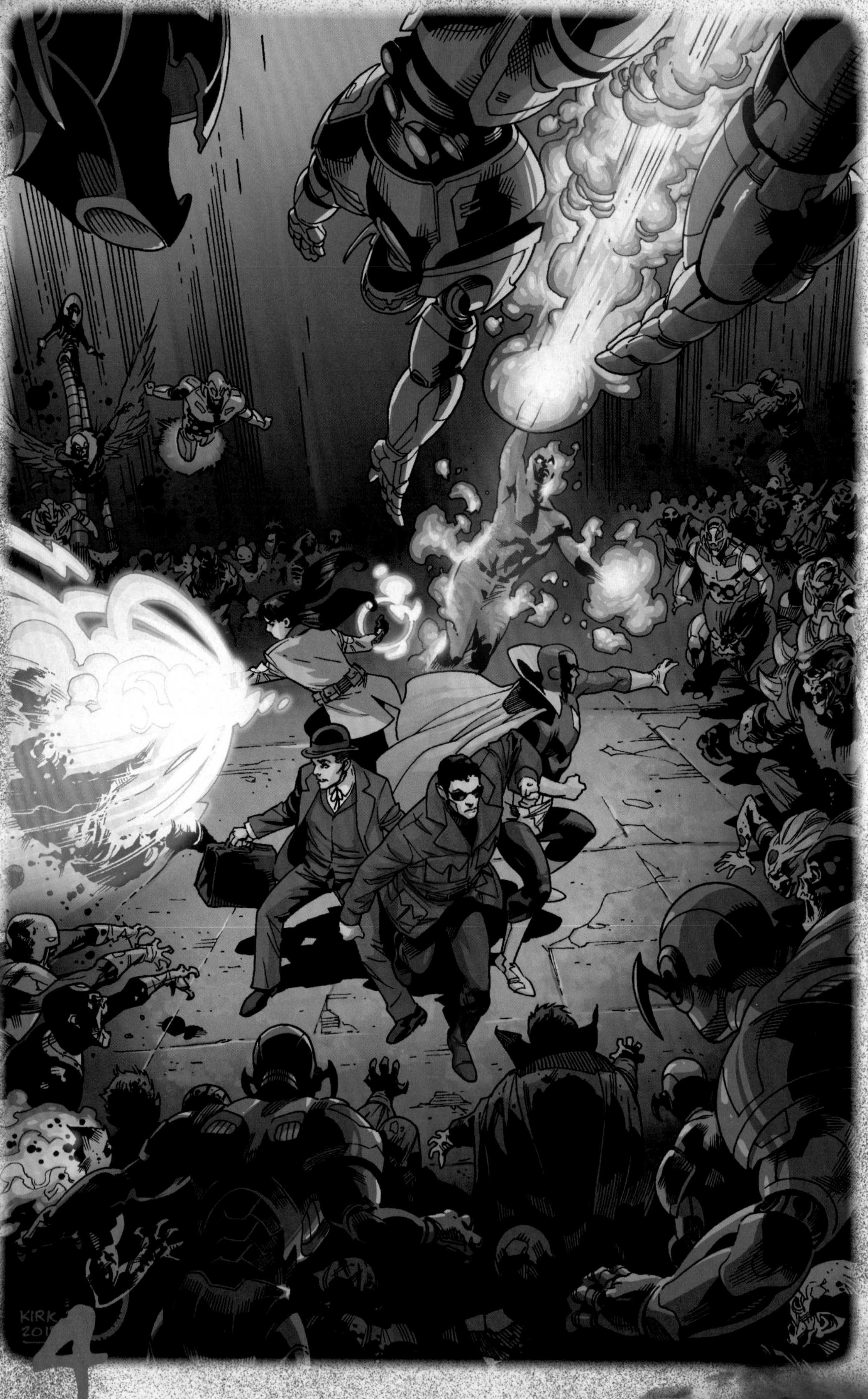
KIRK

4

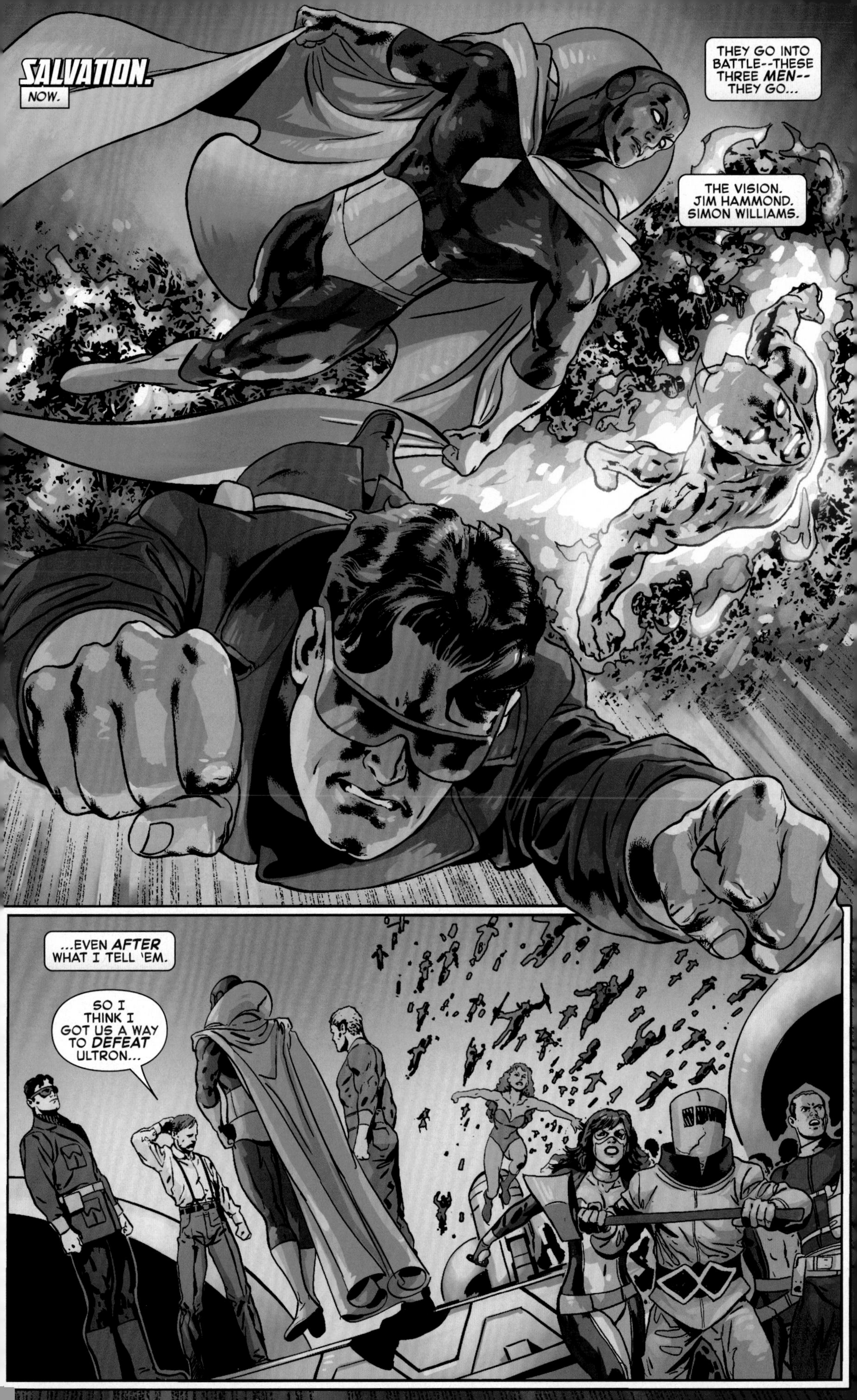
SALVATION.
NOW.
THEY GO INTO BATTLE--THESE THREE *MEN*--THEY GO...
THE VISION. JIM HAMMOND. SIMON WILLIAMS.
...EVEN *AFTER* WHAT I TELL 'EM.
SO I THINK I GOT US A WAY TO *DEFEAT* ULTRON...

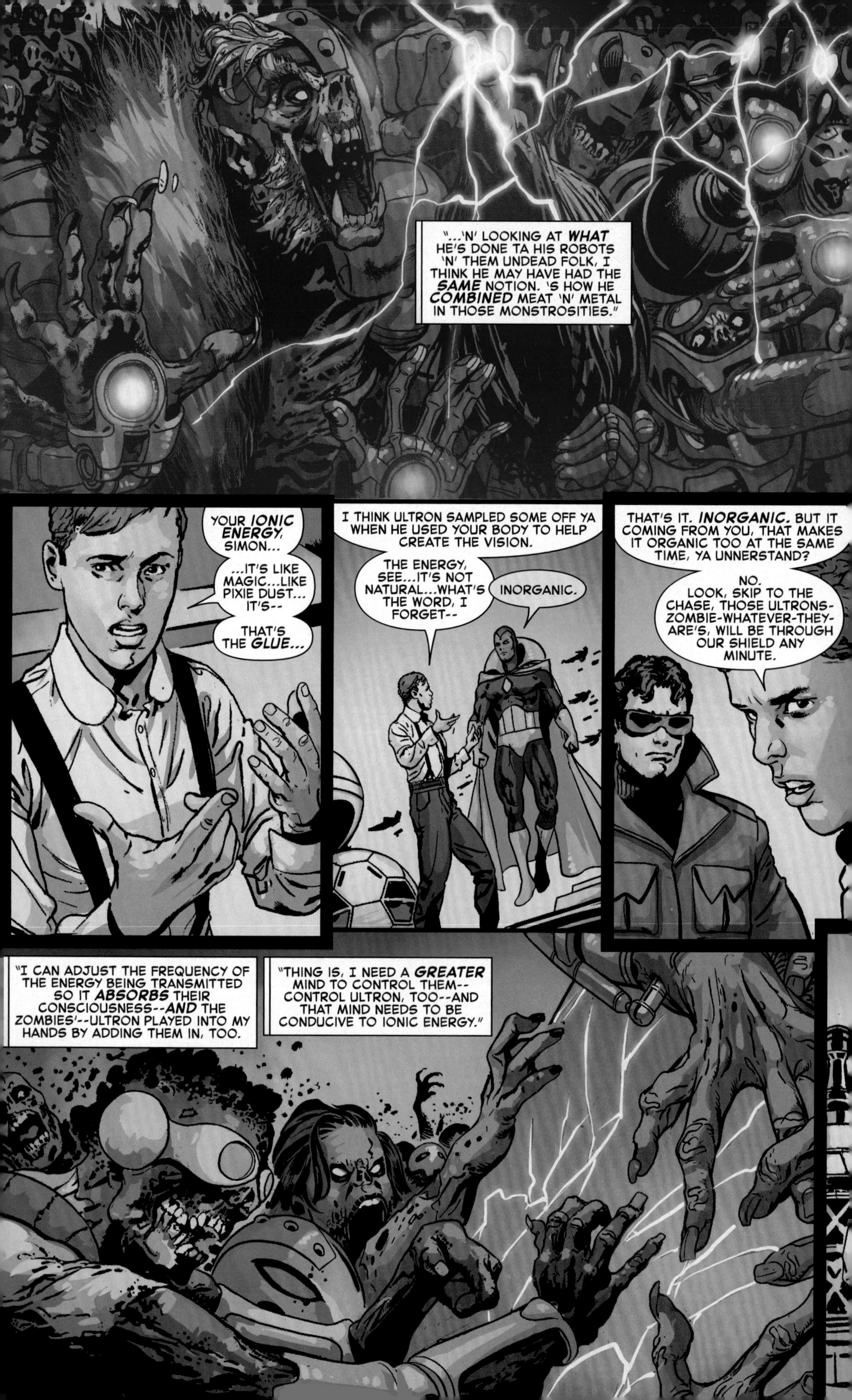
"...'N' LOOKING AT WHAT HE'S DONE TA HIS ROBOTS 'N' THEM UNDEAD FOLK, I THINK HE MAY HAVE HAD THE SAME NOTION. 'S HOW HE COMBINED MEAT 'N' METAL IN THOSE MONSTROSITIES."
YOUR IONIC ENERGY, SIMON...
...IT'S LIKE MAGIC...LIKE PIXIE DUST... IT'S--
THAT'S THE GLUE...
I THINK ULTRON SAMPLED SOME OFF YA WHEN HE USED YOUR BODY TO HELP CREATE THE VISION.
THE ENERGY, SEE...IT'S NOT NATURAL...WHAT'S THE WORD, I FORGET--
INORGANIC.
THAT'S IT. INORGANIC. BUT IT COMING FROM YOU, THAT MAKES IT ORGANIC TOO AT THE SAME TIME, YA UNNERSTAND?
NO. LOOK, SKIP TO THE CHASE, THOSE ULTRONS-ZOMBIE-WHATEVER-THEY-ARE'S, WILL BE THROUGH OUR SHIELD ANY MINUTE.
"I CAN ADJUST THE FREQUENCY OF THE ENERGY BEING TRANSMITTED SO IT ABSORBS THEIR CONSCIOUSNESS--AND THE ZOMBIES'--ULTRON PLAYED INTO MY HANDS BY ADDING THEM IN, TOO.
"THING IS, I NEED A GREATER MIND TO CONTROL THEM--CONTROL ULTRON, TOO--AND THAT MIND NEEDS TO BE CONDUCIVE TO IONIC ENERGY."

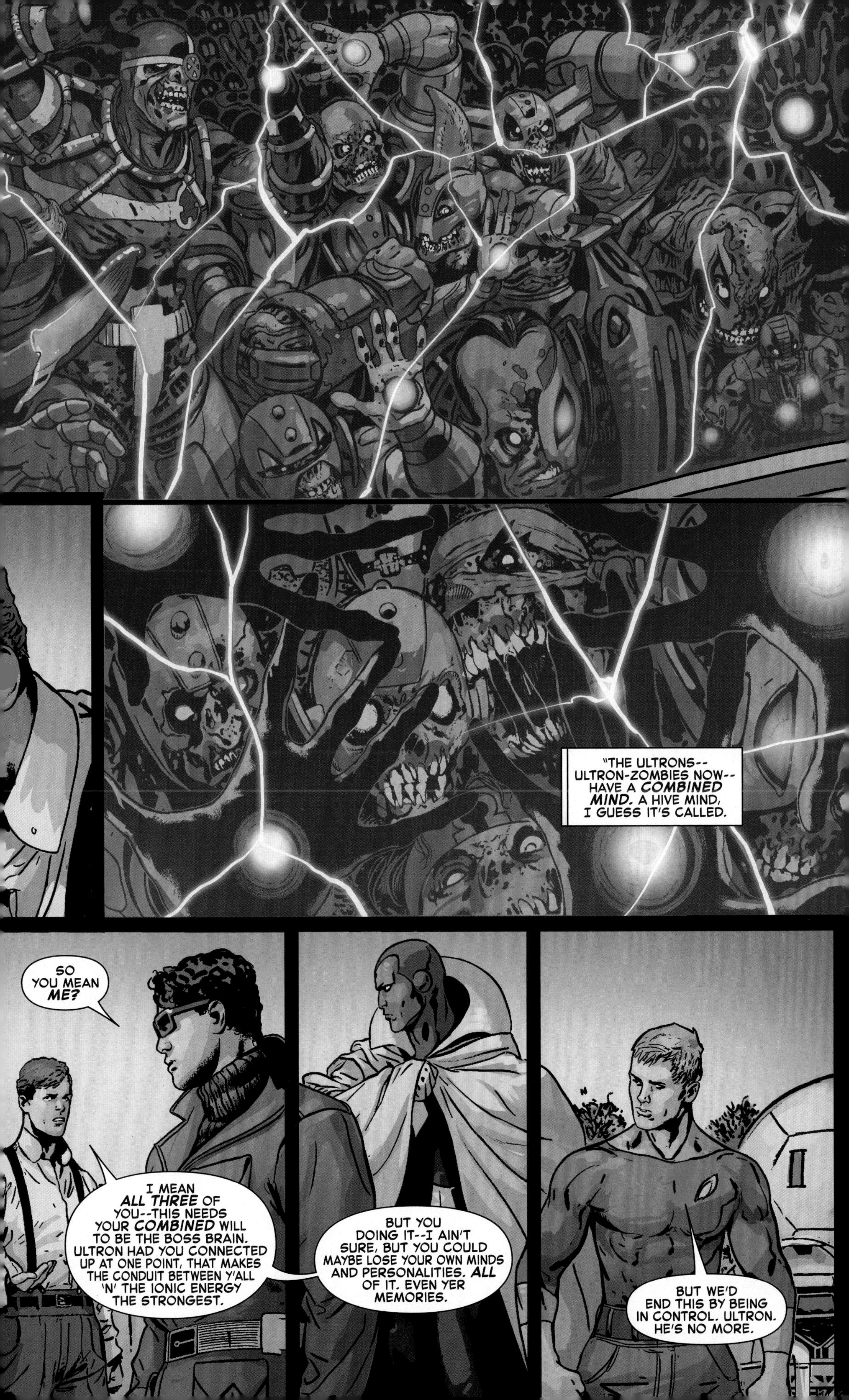
"THE ULTRONS--ULTRON-ZOMBIES NOW--HAVE A COMBINED MIND. A HIVE MIND, I GUESS IT'S CALLED.
SO YOU MEAN ME?
I MEAN ALL THREE OF YOU--THIS NEEDS YOUR COMBINED WILL TO BE THE BOSS BRAIN. ULTRON HAD YOU CONNECTED UP AT ONE POINT, THAT MAKES THE CONDUIT BETWEEN Y'ALL 'N' THE IONIC ENERGY THE STRONGEST.
BUT YOU DOING IT--I AIN'T SURE, BUT YOU COULD MAYBE LOSE YOUR OWN MINDS AND PERSONALITIES. ALL OF IT. EVEN YER MEMORIES.
BUT WE'D END THIS BY BEING IN CONTROL. ULTRON. HE'S NO MORE.

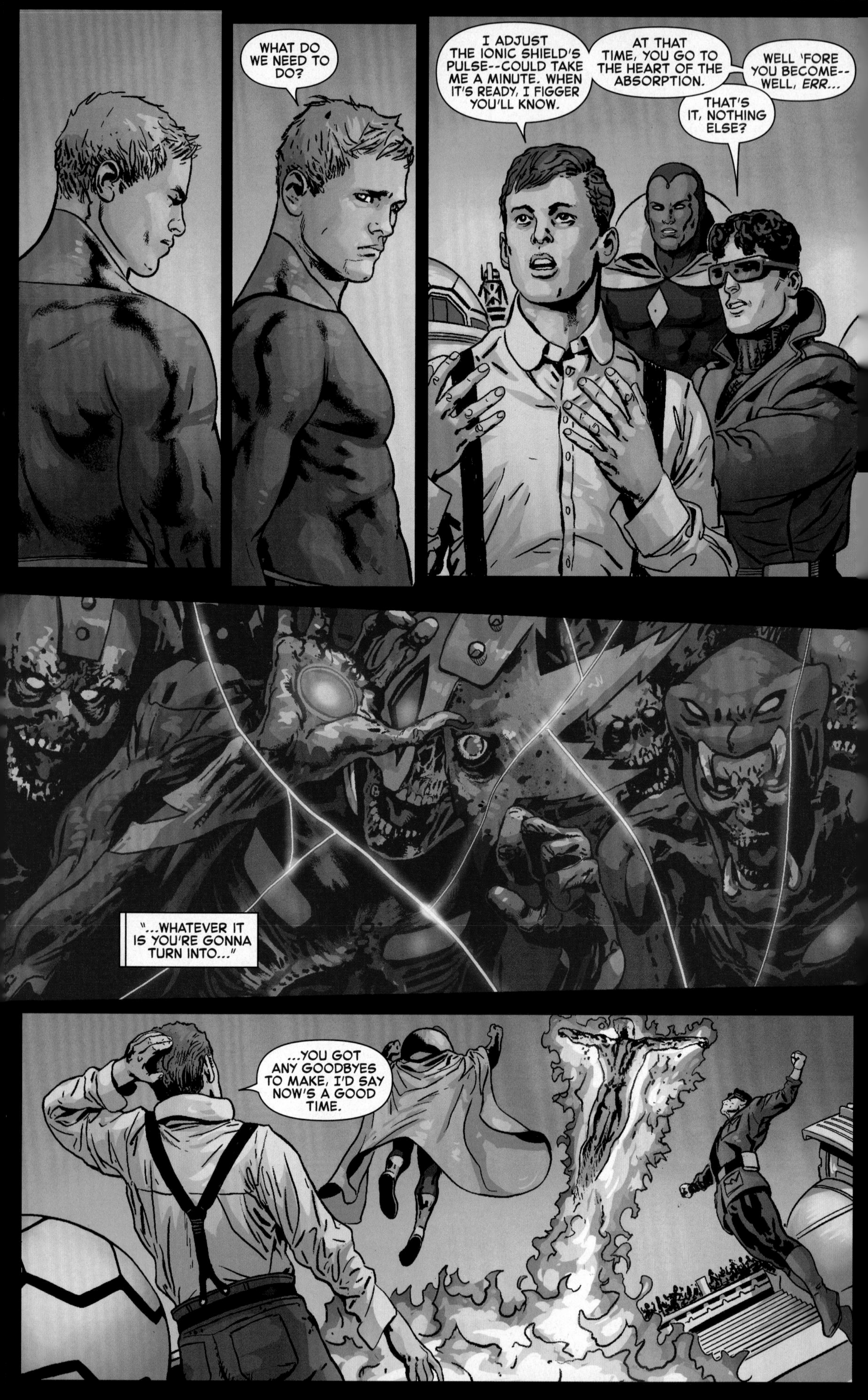
WHAT DO WE NEED TO DO?
I ADJUST THE IONIC SHIELD'S PULSE--COULD TAKE ME A MINUTE. WHEN IT'S READY, I FIGGER YOU'LL KNOW.
AT THAT TIME, YOU GO TO THE HEART OF THE ABSORPTION.
THAT'S IT, NOTHING ELSE?
WELL 'FORE YOU BECOME-- WELL, *ERR...*
"...WHATEVER IT IS YOU'RE GONNA TURN INTO..."
...YOU GOT ANY GOODBYES TO MAKE, I'D SAY NOW'S A GOOD TIME.

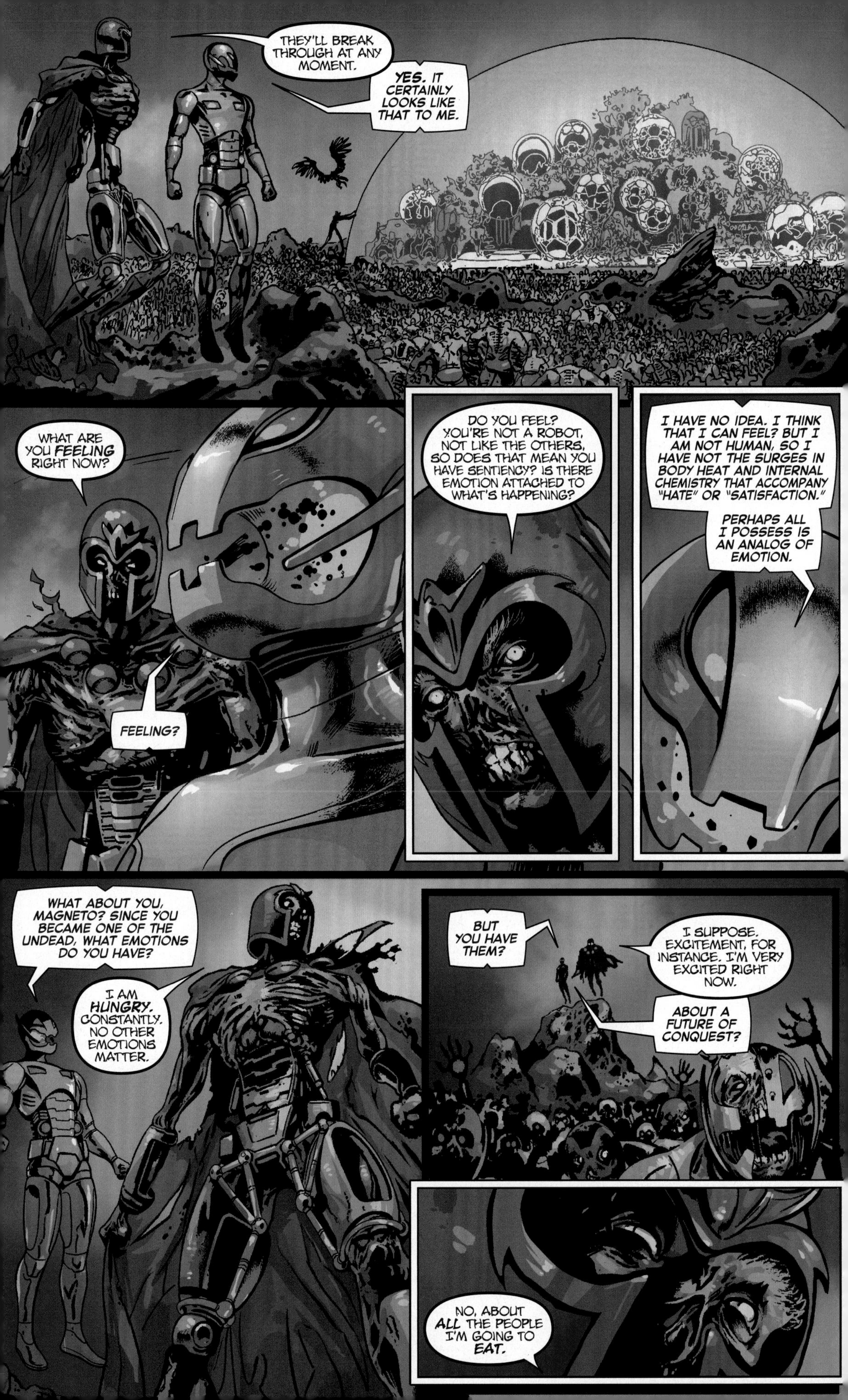
THEY'LL BREAK THROUGH AT ANY MOMENT.
YES. IT CERTAINLY LOOKS LIKE THAT TO ME.
WHAT ARE YOU FEELING RIGHT NOW?
FEELING?
DO YOU FEEL? YOU'RE NOT A ROBOT, NOT LIKE THE OTHERS, SO DOES THAT MEAN YOU HAVE SENTIENCY? IS THERE EMOTION ATTACHED TO WHAT'S HAPPENING?
I HAVE NO IDEA. I THINK THAT I CAN FEEL? BUT I AM NOT HUMAN, SO I HAVE NOT THE SURGES IN BODY HEAT AND INTERNAL CHEMISTRY THAT ACCOMPANY "HATE" OR "SATISFACTION."
PERHAPS ALL I POSSESS IS AN ANALOG OF EMOTION.
WHAT ABOUT YOU, MAGNETO? SINCE YOU BECAME ONE OF THE UNDEAD, WHAT EMOTIONS DO YOU HAVE?
I AM HUNGRY. CONSTANTLY. NO OTHER EMOTIONS MATTER.
BUT YOU HAVE THEM?
I SUPPOSE. EXCITEMENT, FOR INSTANCE. I'M VERY EXCITED RIGHT NOW.
ABOUT A FUTURE OF CONQUEST?
NO, ABOUT ALL THE PEOPLE I'M GOING TO EAT.

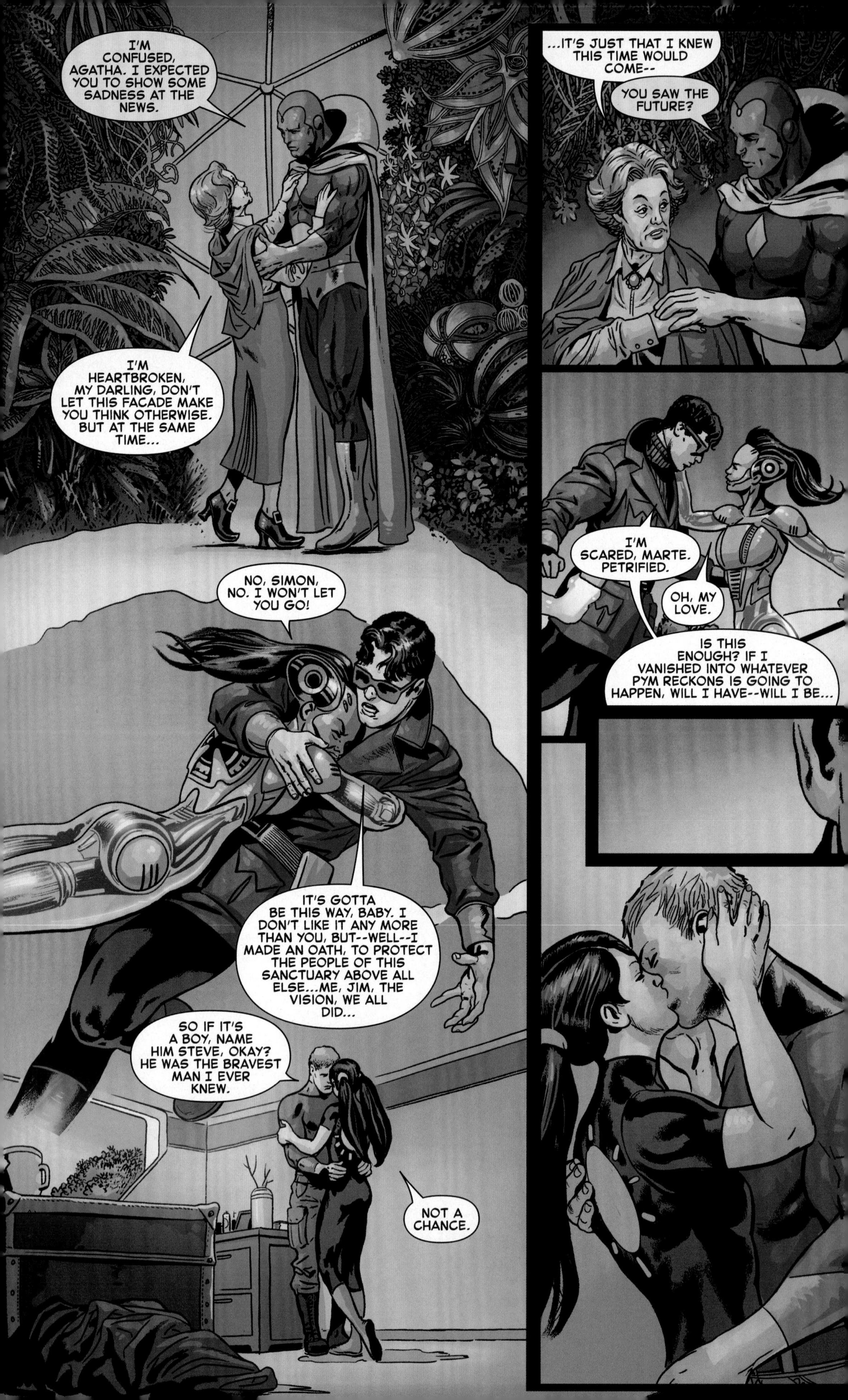
I'M CONFUSED, AGATHA. I EXPECTED YOU TO SHOW SOME SADNESS AT THE NEWS.
I'M HEARTBROKEN, MY DARLING, DON'T LET THIS FACADE MAKE YOU THINK OTHERWISE. BUT AT THE SAME TIME...
...IT'S JUST THAT I KNEW THIS TIME WOULD COME--
YOU SAW THE FUTURE?
NO, SIMON, NO. I WON'T LET YOU GO!
IT'S GOTTA BE THIS WAY, BABY. I DON'T LIKE IT ANY MORE THAN YOU, BUT--WELL--I MADE AN OATH, TO PROTECT THE PEOPLE OF THIS SANCTUARY ABOVE ALL ELSE...ME, JIM, THE VISION, WE ALL DID...
I'M SCARED, MARTE. PETRIFIED.
OH, MY LOVE.
IS THIS ENOUGH? IF I VANISHED INTO WHATEVER PYM RECKONS IS GOING TO HAPPEN, WILL I HAVE--WILL I BE...
SO IF IT'S A BOY, NAME HIM STEVE, OKAY? HE WAS THE BRAVEST MAN I EVER KNEW.
NOT A CHANCE.

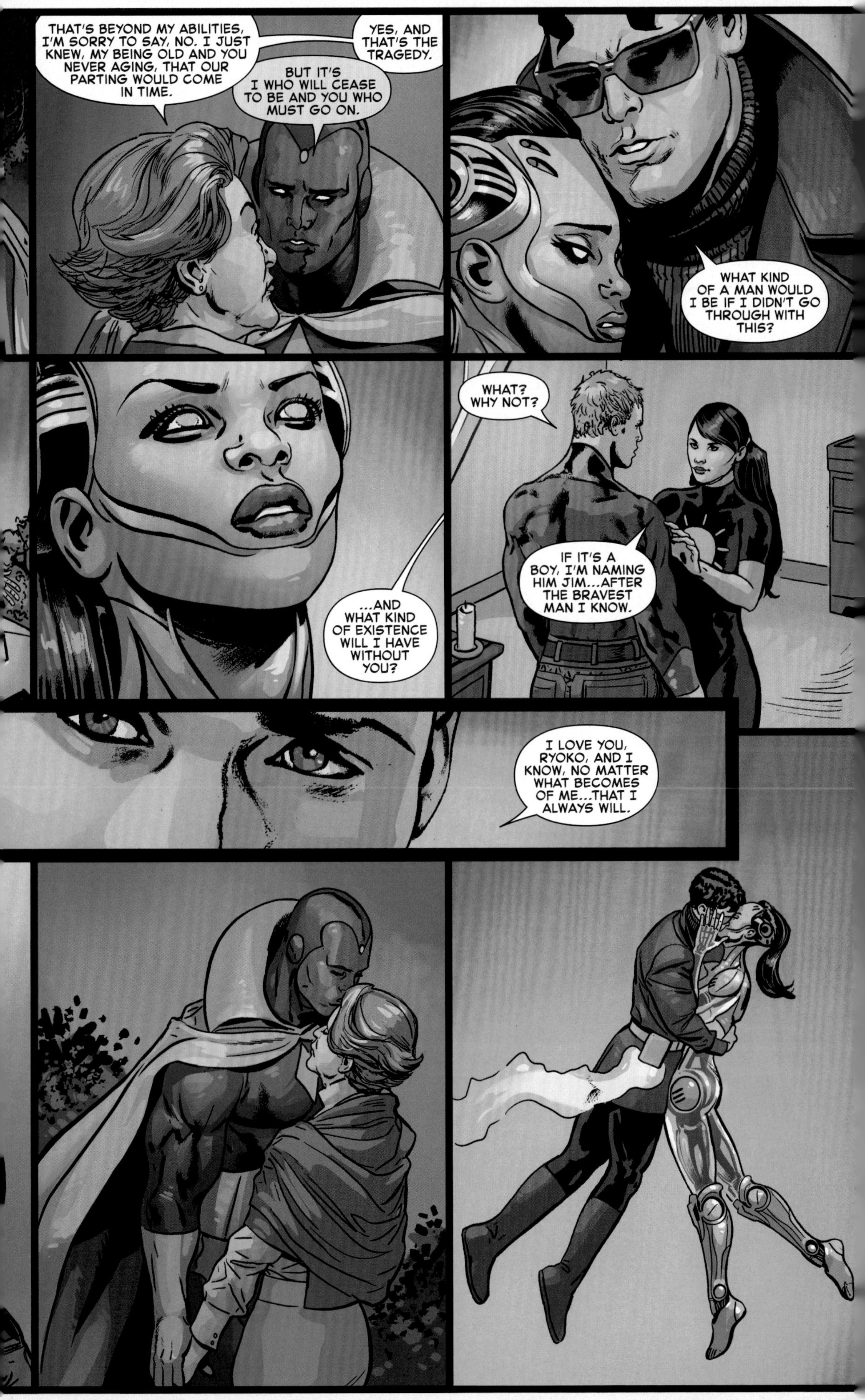
THAT'S BEYOND MY ABILITIES, I'M SORRY TO SAY, NO. I JUST KNEW, MY BEING OLD AND YOU NEVER AGING, THAT OUR PARTING WOULD COME IN TIME.
YES, AND THAT'S THE TRAGEDY.
BUT IT'S I WHO WILL CEASE TO BE AND YOU WHO MUST GO ON.
WHAT KIND OF A MAN WOULD I BE IF I DIDN'T GO THROUGH WITH THIS?
...AND WHAT KIND OF EXISTENCE WILL I HAVE WITHOUT YOU?
WHAT? WHY NOT?
IF IT'S A BOY, I'M NAMING HIM JIM...AFTER THE BRAVEST MAN I KNOW.
I LOVE YOU, RYOKO, AND I KNOW, NO MATTER WHAT BECOMES OF ME...THAT I ALWAYS WILL.

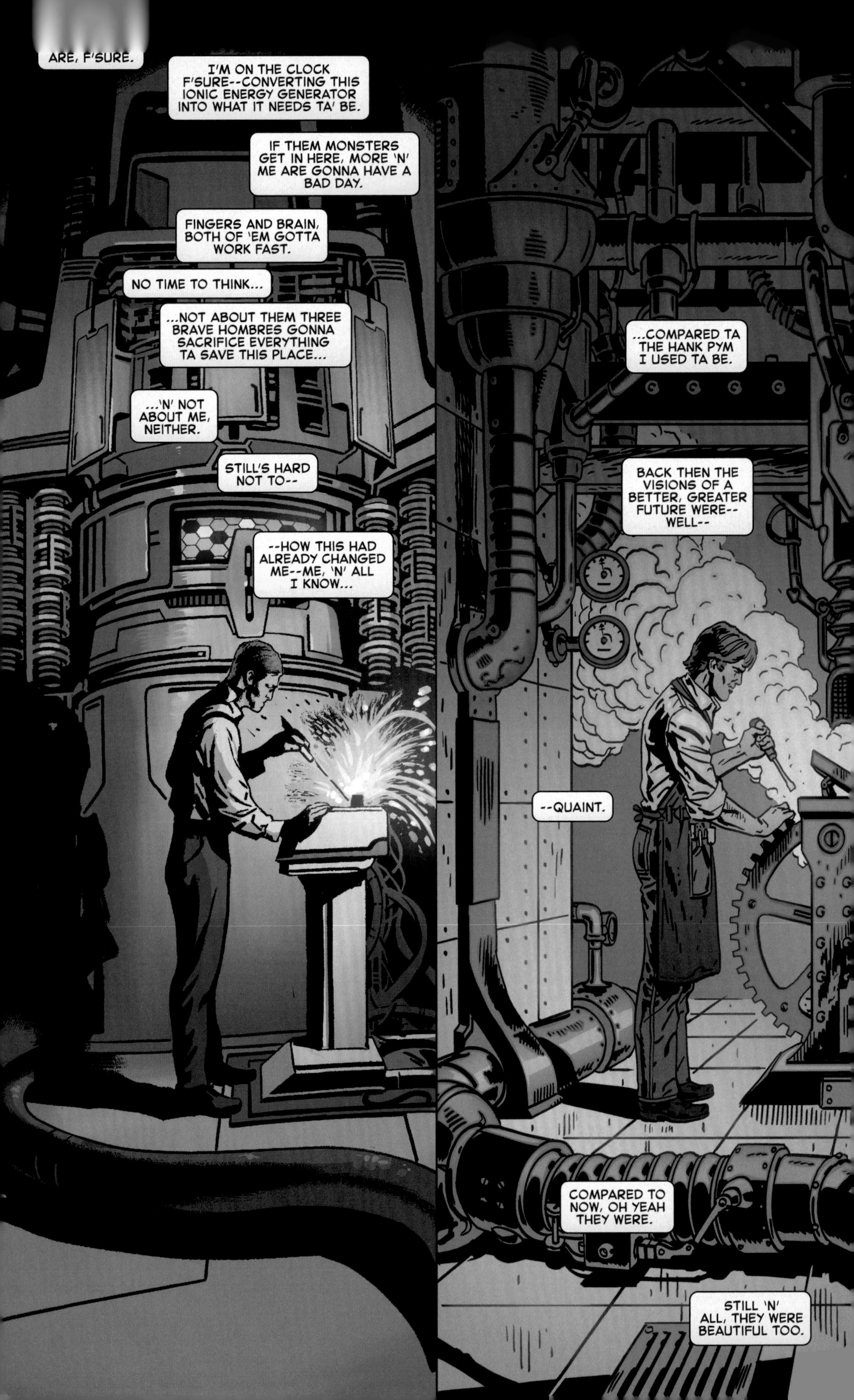
ARE, F'SURE.
I'M ON THE CLOCK F'SURE--CONVERTING THIS IONIC ENERGY GENERATOR INTO WHAT IT NEEDS TA' BE.
IF THEM MONSTERS GET IN HERE, MORE 'N' ME ARE GONNA HAVE A BAD DAY.
FINGERS AND BRAIN, BOTH OF 'EM GOTTA WORK FAST.
NO TIME TO THINK...
...NOT ABOUT THEM THREE BRAVE HOMBRES GONNA SACRIFICE EVERYTHING TA SAVE THIS PLACE...
...'N' NOT ABOUT ME, NEITHER.
STILL'S HARD NOT TO--
--HOW THIS HAD ALREADY CHANGED ME--ME, 'N' ALL I KNOW...
...COMPARED TA THE HANK PYM I USED TA BE.
BACK THEN THE VISIONS OF A BETTER, GREATER FUTURE WERE--WELL--
--QUAINT.
COMPARED TO NOW, OH YEAH THEY WERE.
STILL 'N' ALL, THEY WERE BEAUTIFUL TOO.

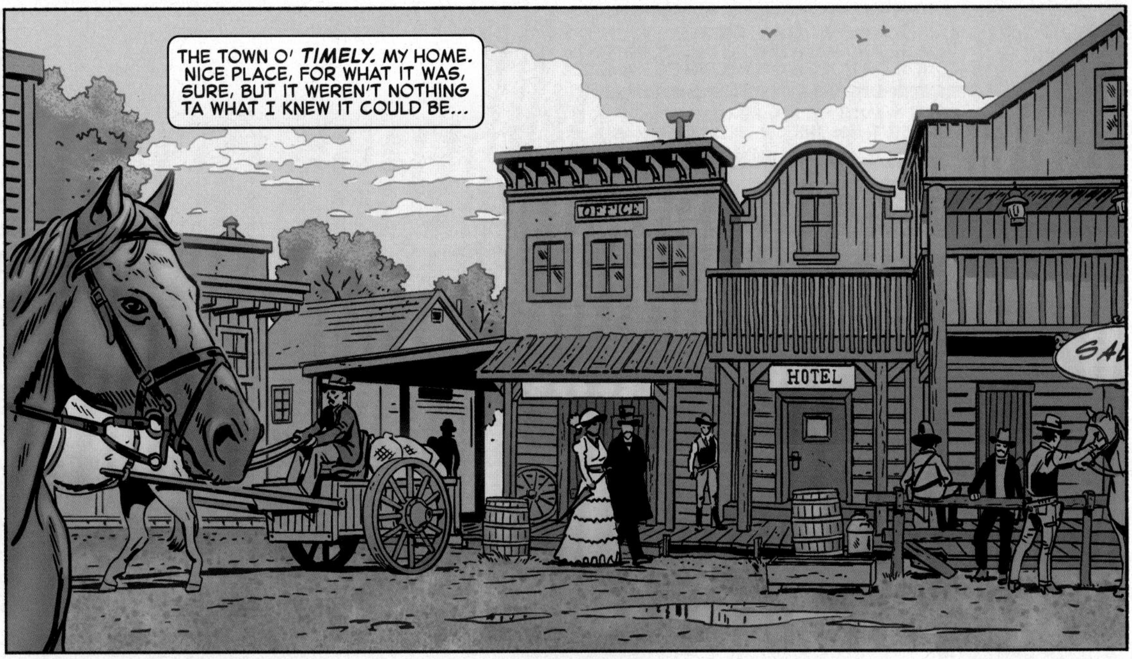
THE TOWN O' TIMELY. MY HOME. NICE PLACE, FOR WHAT IT WAS, SURE, BUT IT WEREN'T NOTHING TA WHAT I KNEW IT COULD BE...
OFFICE
HOTEL

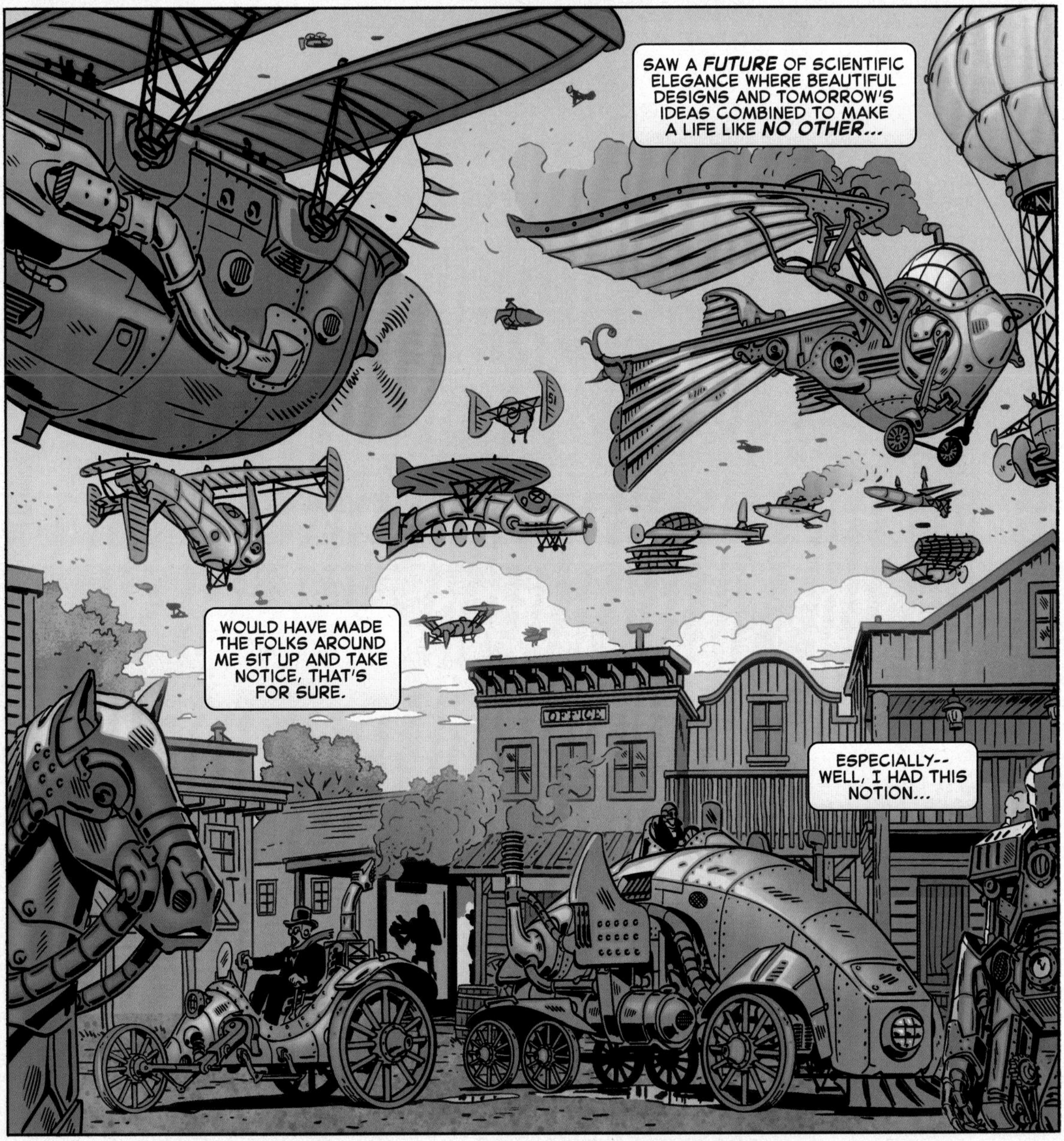
SAW A FUTURE OF SCIENTIFIC ELEGANCE WHERE BEAUTIFUL DESIGNS AND TOMORROW'S IDEAS COMBINED TO MAKE A LIFE LIKE NO OTHER...
WOULD HAVE MADE THE FOLKS AROUND ME SIT UP AND TAKE NOTICE, THAT'S FOR SURE.
OFFICE
ESPECIALLY-- WELL, I HAD THIS NOTION...

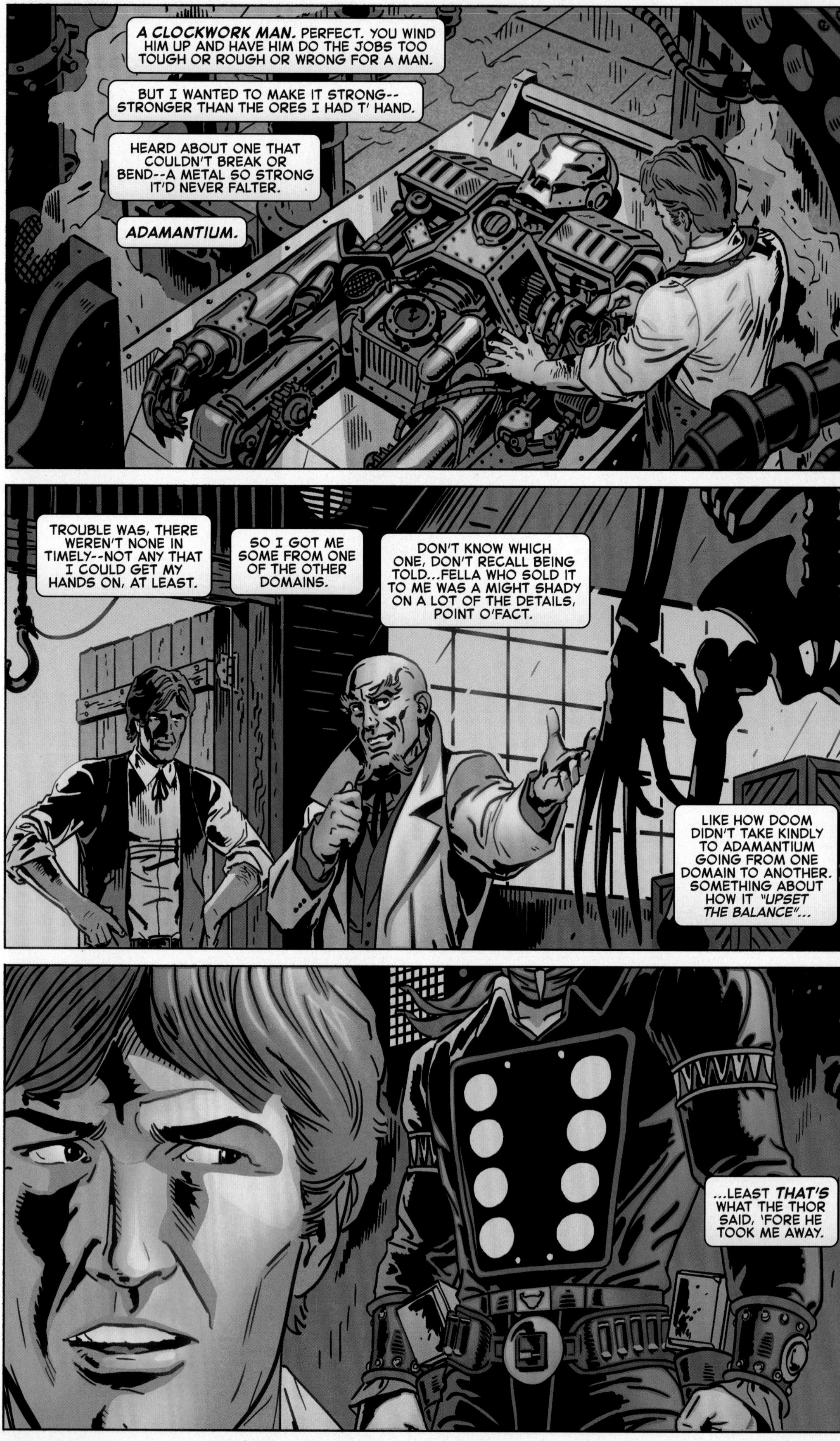
A CLOCKWORK MAN. PERFECT. YOU WIND HIM UP AND HAVE HIM DO THE JOBS TOO TOUGH OR ROUGH OR WRONG FOR A MAN.
BUT I WANTED TO MAKE IT STRONG-- STRONGER THAN THE ORES I HAD T' HAND.
HEARD ABOUT ONE THAT COULDN'T BREAK OR BEND--A METAL SO STRONG IT'D NEVER FALTER.
ADAMANTIUM.
TROUBLE WAS, THERE WEREN'T NONE IN TIMELY--NOT ANY THAT I COULD GET MY HANDS ON, AT LEAST.
SO I GOT ME SOME FROM ONE OF THE OTHER DOMAINS.
DON'T KNOW WHICH ONE, DON'T RECALL BEING TOLD...FELLA WHO SOLD IT TO ME WAS A MIGHT SHADY ON A LOT OF THE DETAILS, POINT O'FACT.
LIKE HOW DOOM DIDN'T TAKE KINDLY TO ADAMANTIUM GOING FROM ONE DOMAIN TO ANOTHER. SOMETHING ABOUT HOW IT "UPSET THE BALANCE"...
...LEAST THAT'S WHAT THE THOR SAID, 'FORE HE TOOK ME AWAY.

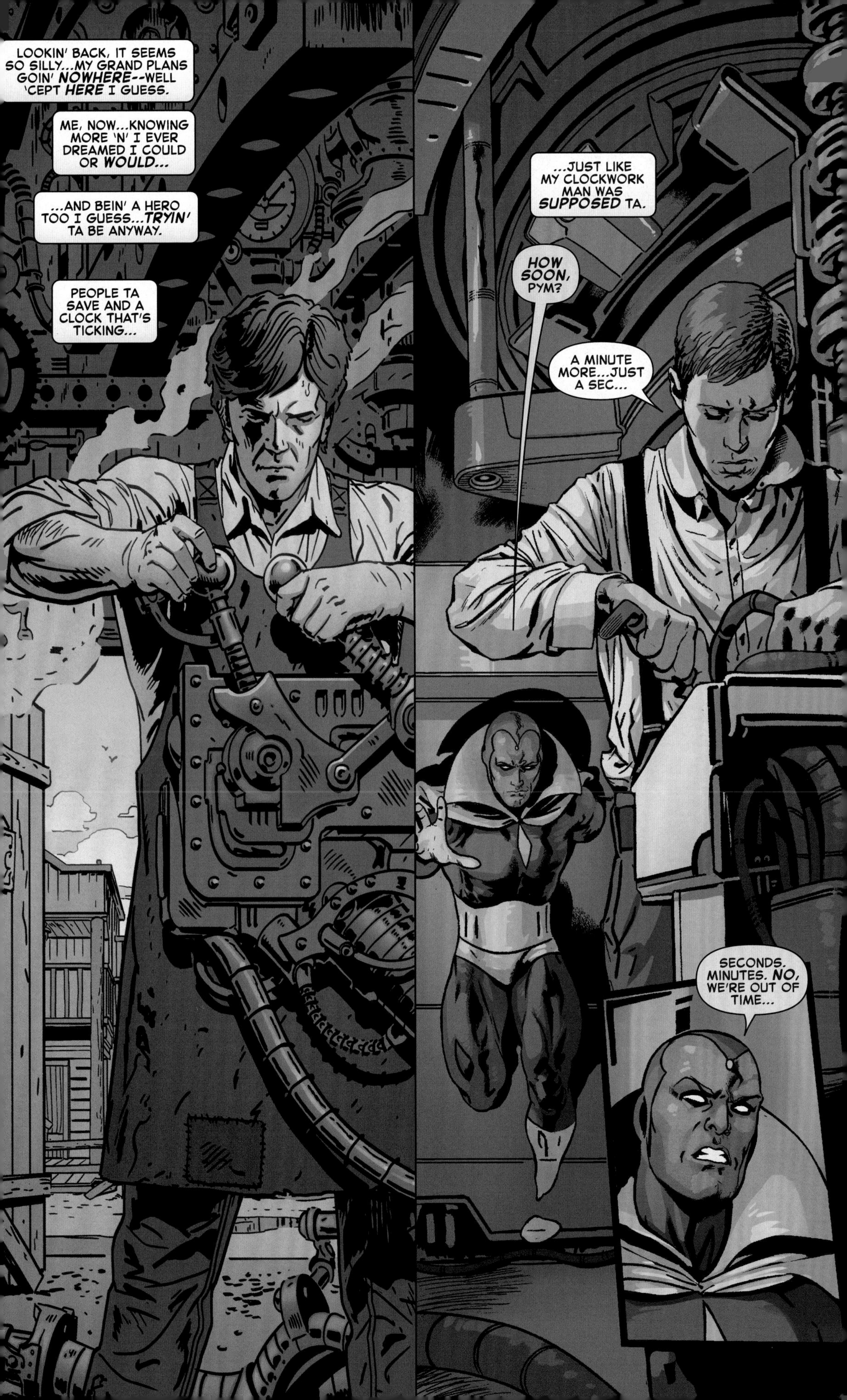
LOOKIN' BACK, IT SEEMS SO SILLY...MY GRAND PLANS GOIN' NOWHERE--WELL 'CEPT HERE I GUESS.
ME, NOW...KNOWING MORE 'N' I EVER DREAMED I COULD OR WOULD...
...AND BEIN' A HERO TOO I GUESS...TRYIN' TA BE ANYWAY.
PEOPLE TA SAVE AND A CLOCK THAT'S TICKING...
...JUST LIKE MY CLOCKWORK MAN WAS SUPPOSED TA.
HOW SOON, PYM?
A MINUTE MORE...JUST A SEC...
SECONDS. MINUTES. NO, WE'RE OUT OF TIME...

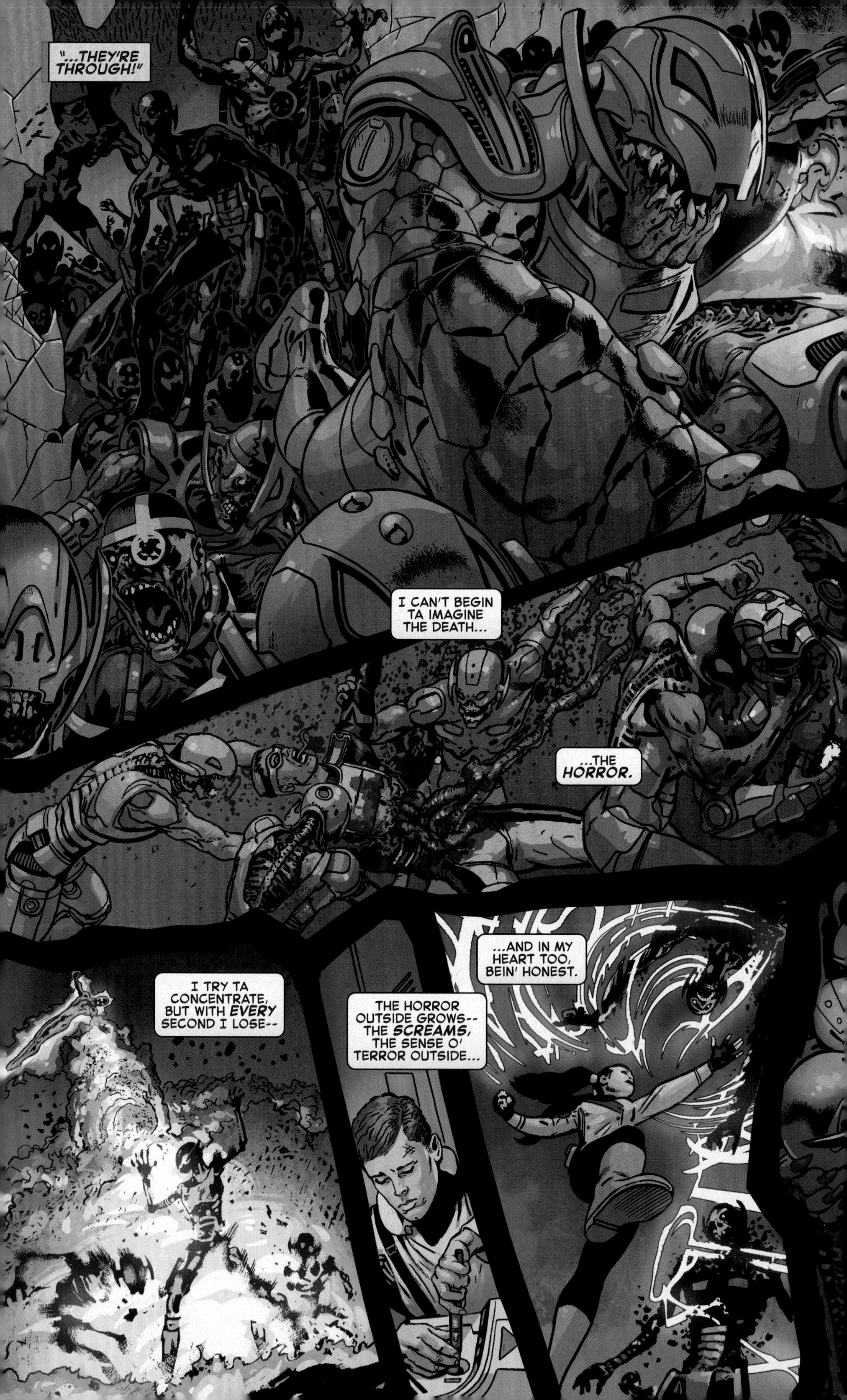
"...THEY'RE THROUGH!"
I CAN'T BEGIN TA IMAGINE THE DEATH...
...THE HORROR.
I TRY TA CONCENTRATE, BUT WITH EVERY SECOND I LOSE--
THE HORROR OUTSIDE GROWS-- THE SCREAMS, THE SENSE O' TERROR OUTSIDE...
...AND IN MY HEART TOO, BEIN' HONEST.

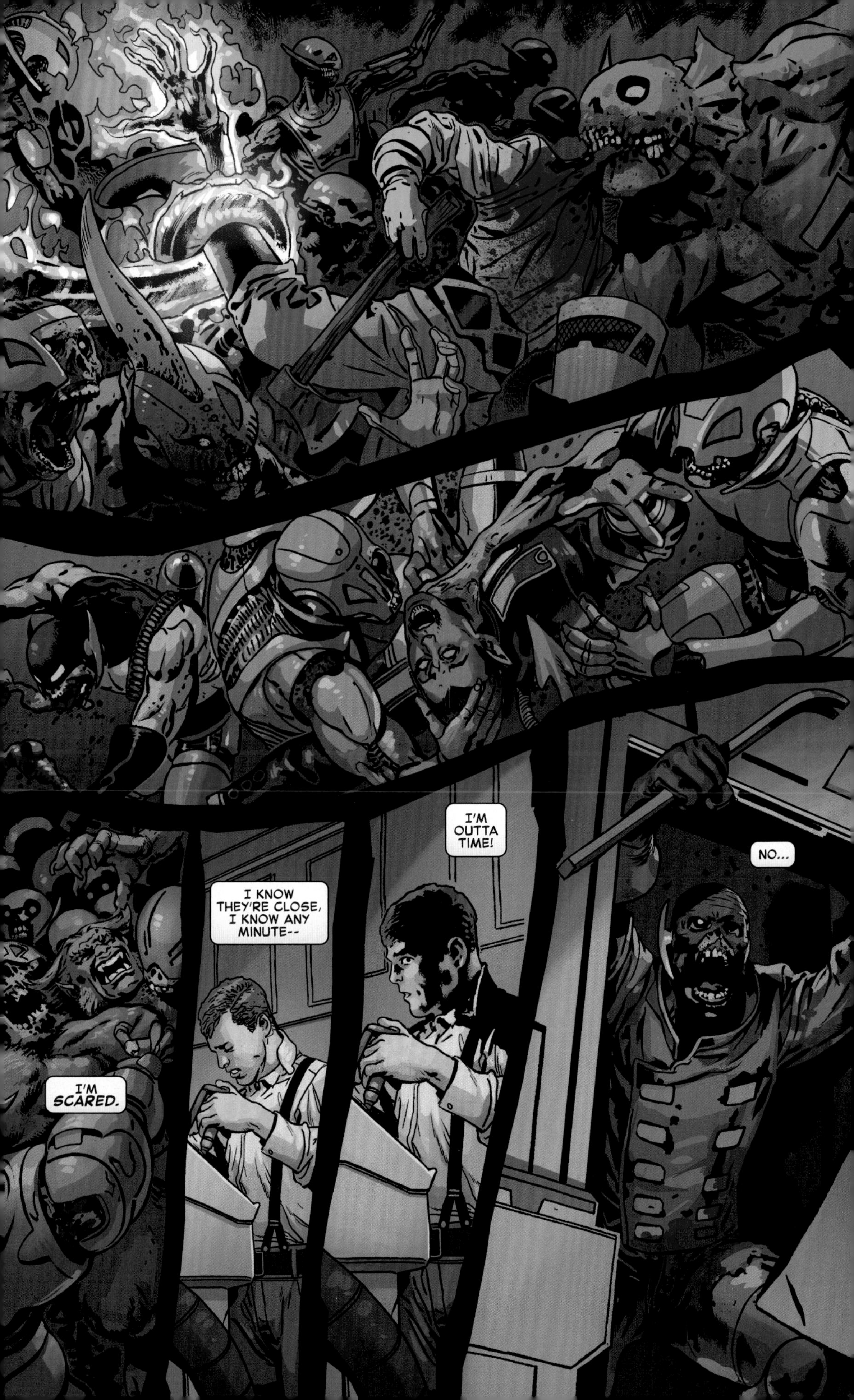
I'M SCARED.
I KNOW THEY'RE CLOSE, I KNOW ANY MINUTE--
I'M OUTTA TIME!
NO...

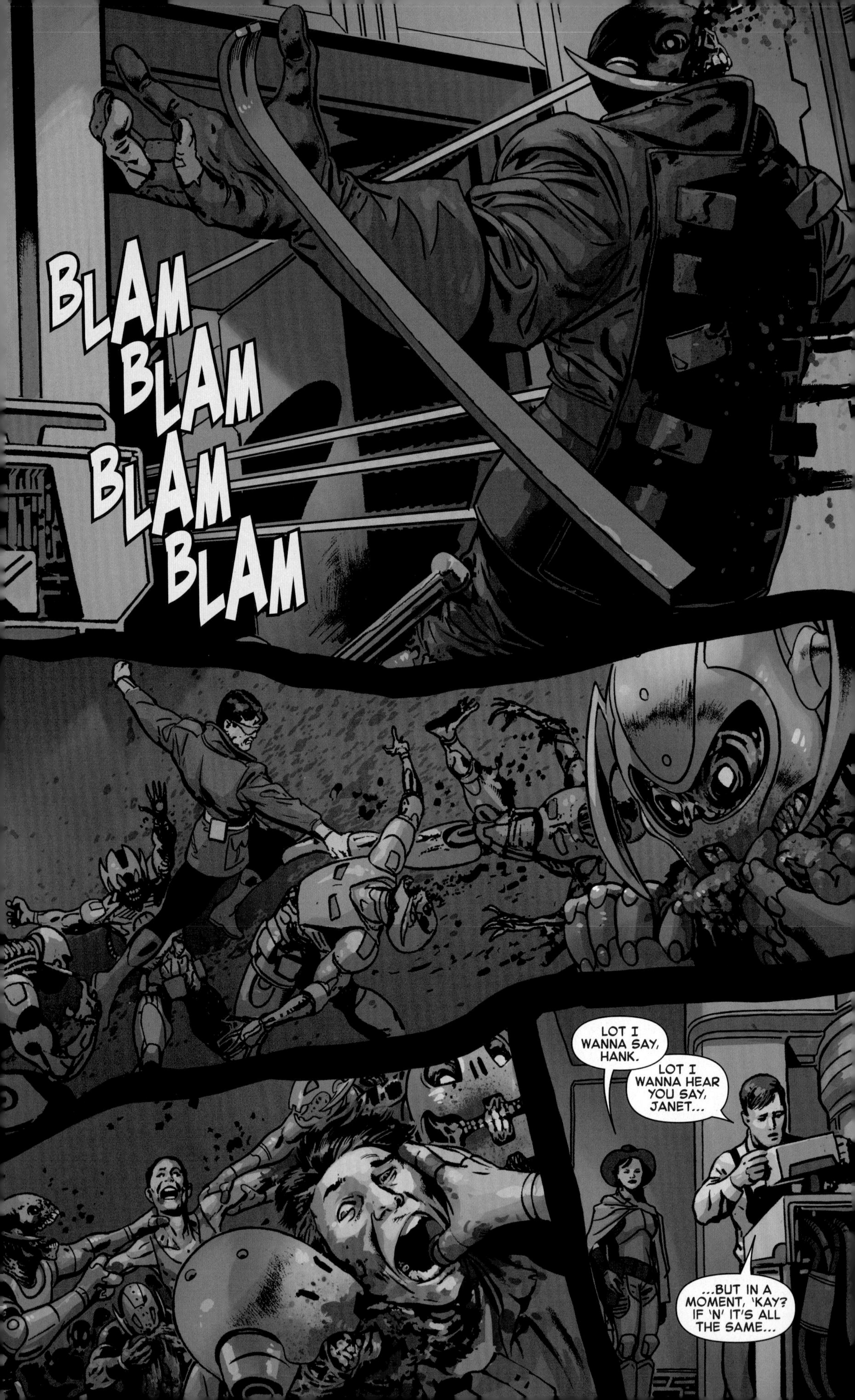

BLAM BLAM BLAM BLAM
LOT I WANNA SAY, HANK.
LOT I WANNA HEAR YOU SAY, JANET...
...BUT IN A MOMENT, 'KAY? IF 'N' IT'S ALL THE SAME...

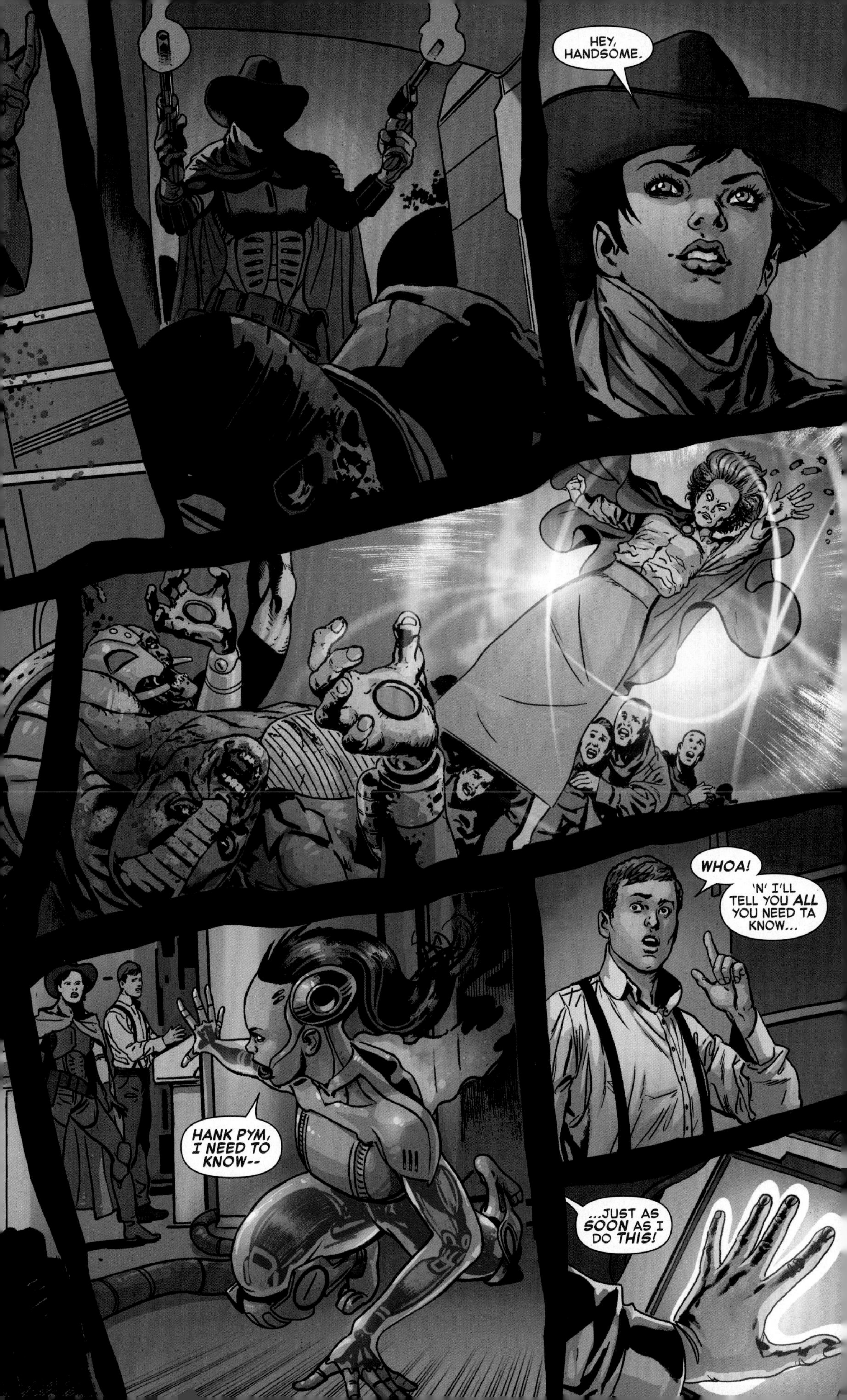
HEY, HANDSOME.
WHOA!
'N' I'LL TELL YOU ALL YOU NEED TA KNOW...
HANK PYM, I NEED TO KNOW--
...JUST AS SOON AS I DO THIS!

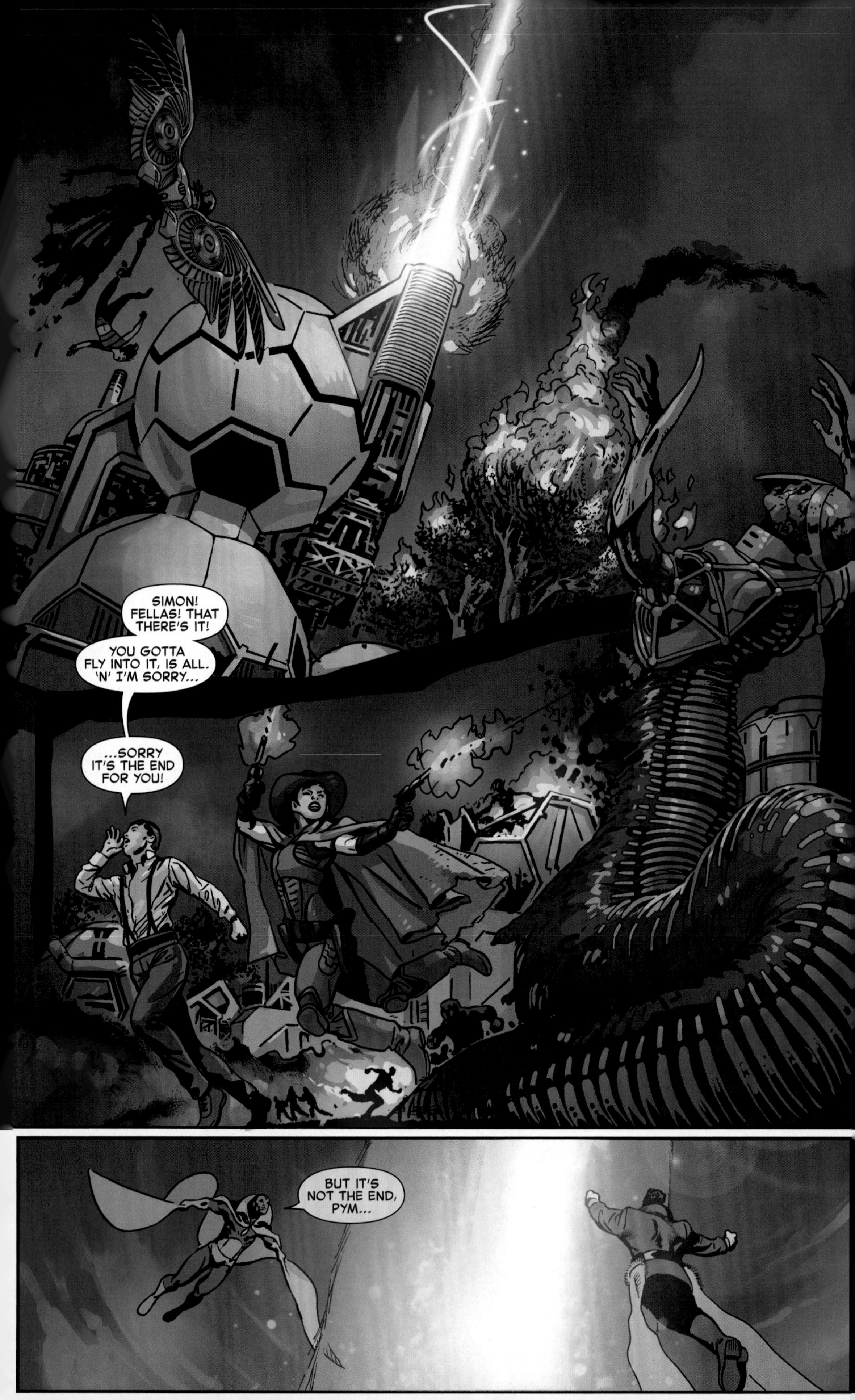
SIMON! FELLAS! THAT THERE'S IT!
YOU GOTTA FLY INTO IT, IS ALL. 'N' I'M SORRY...
...SORRY IT'S THE END FOR YOU!
BUT IT'S NOT THE END, PYM...

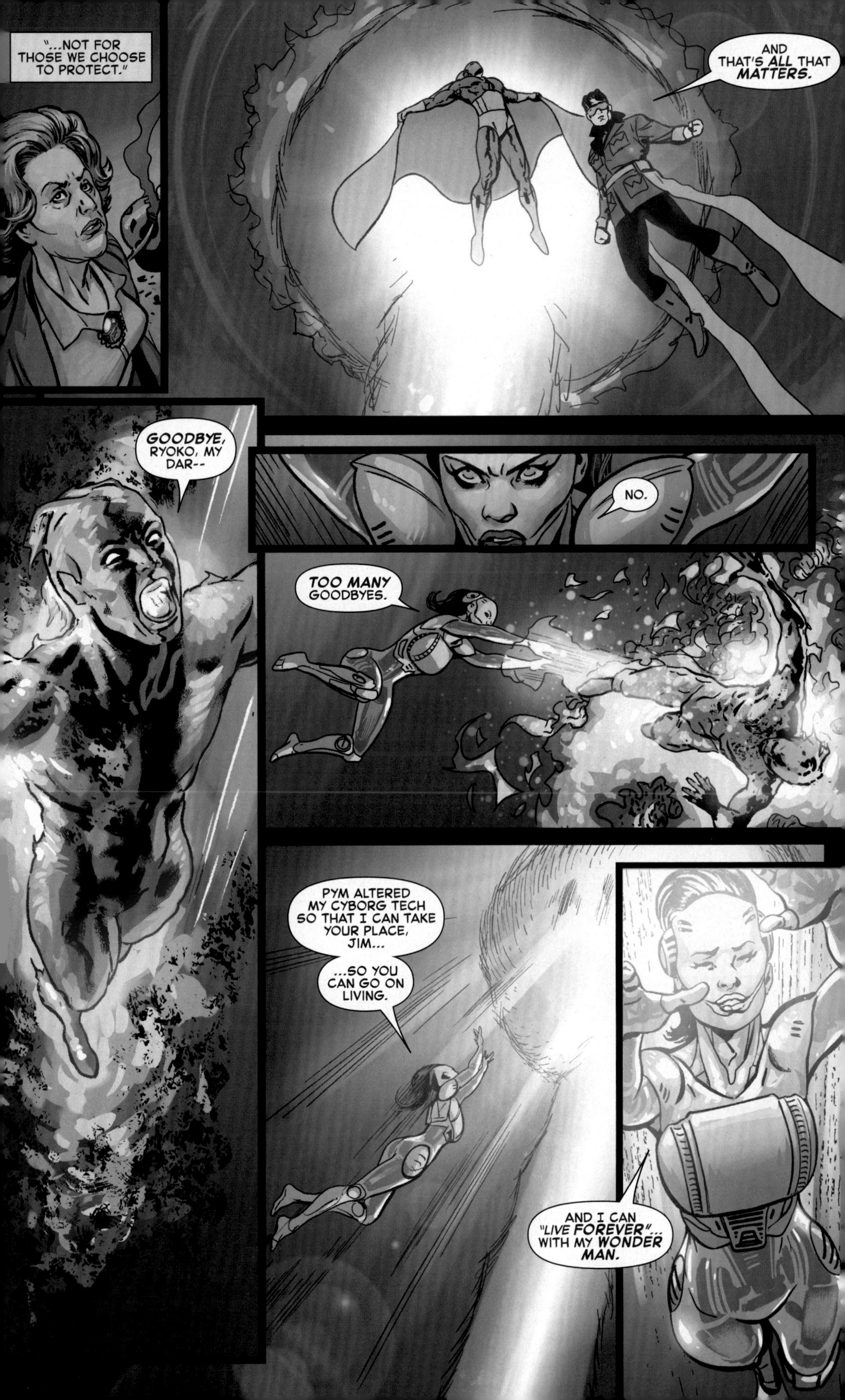
"...NOT FOR THOSE WE CHOOSE TO PROTECT."
AND THAT'S ALL THAT MATTERS.
GOODBYE, RYOKO, MY DAR--
NO.
TOO MANY GOODBYES.
PYM ALTERED MY CYBORG TECH SO THAT I CAN TAKE YOUR PLACE, JIM...
...SO YOU CAN GO ON LIVING.
AND I CAN "LIVE FOREVER"... WITH MY WONDER MAN.

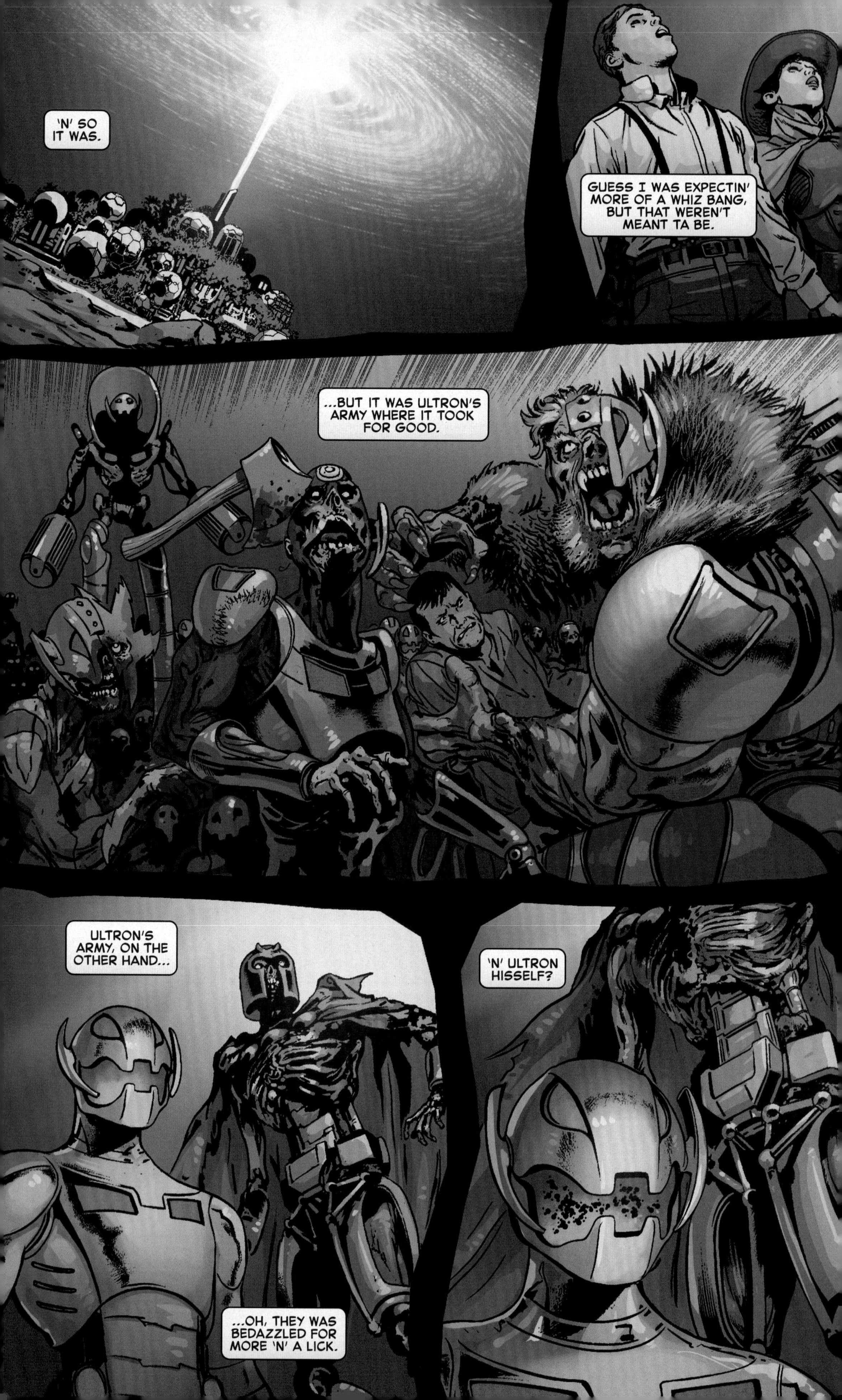
'N' SO IT WAS.
GUESS I WAS EXPECTIN' MORE OF A WHIZ BANG, BUT THAT WEREN'T MEANT TA BE.
...BUT IT WAS ULTRON'S ARMY WHERE IT TOOK FOR GOOD.
ULTRON'S ARMY, ON THE OTHER HAND...
...OH, THEY WAS BEDAZZLED FOR MORE 'N' A LICK.
'N' ULTRON HISSELF?

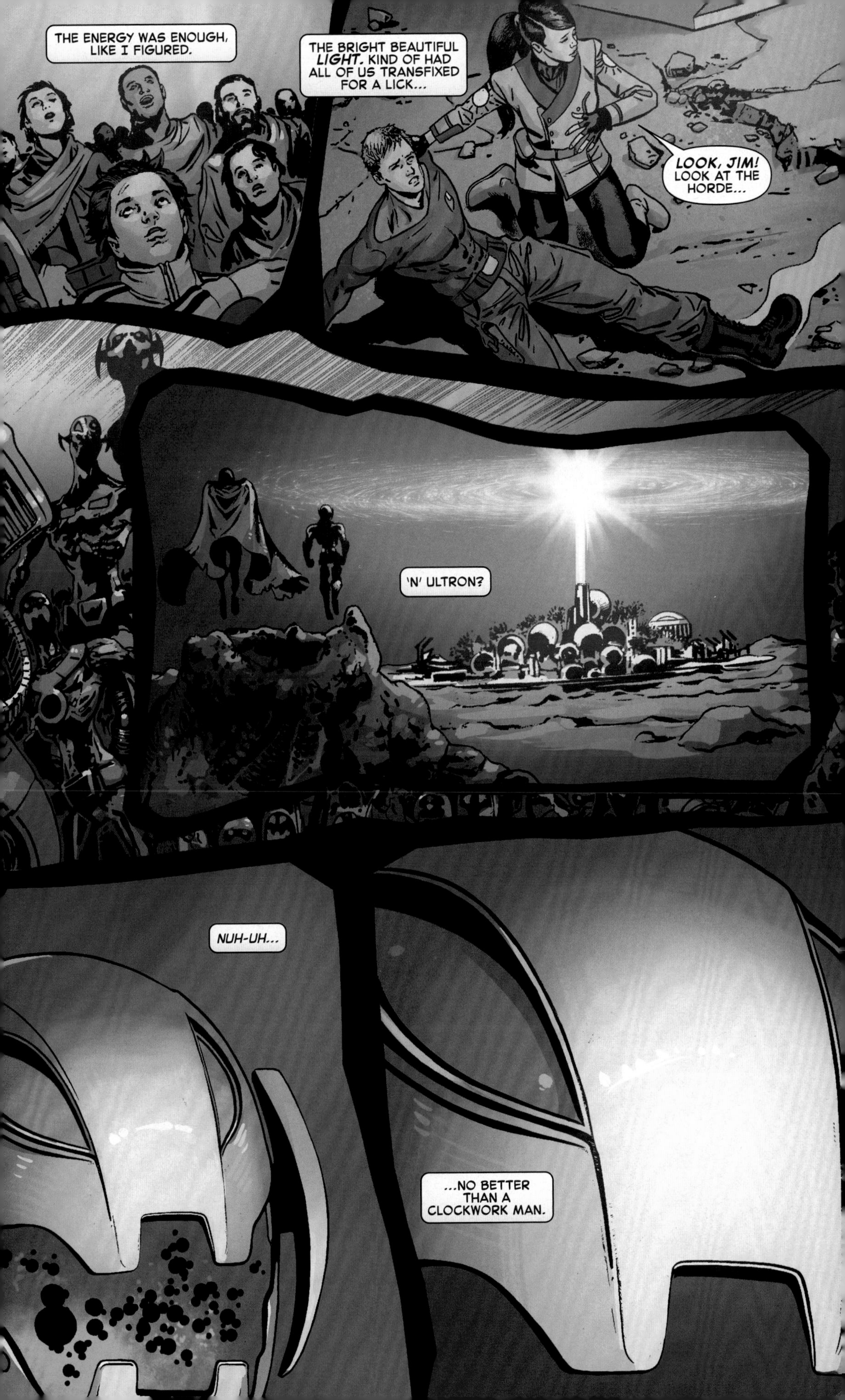
THE ENERGY WAS ENOUGH, LIKE I FIGURED.
THE BRIGHT BEAUTIFUL LIGHT. KIND OF HAD ALL OF US TRANSFIXED FOR A LICK...
LOOK, JIM! LOOK AT THE HORDE...
'N' ULTRON?
NUH-UH...
...NO BETTER THAN A CLOCKWORK MAN.

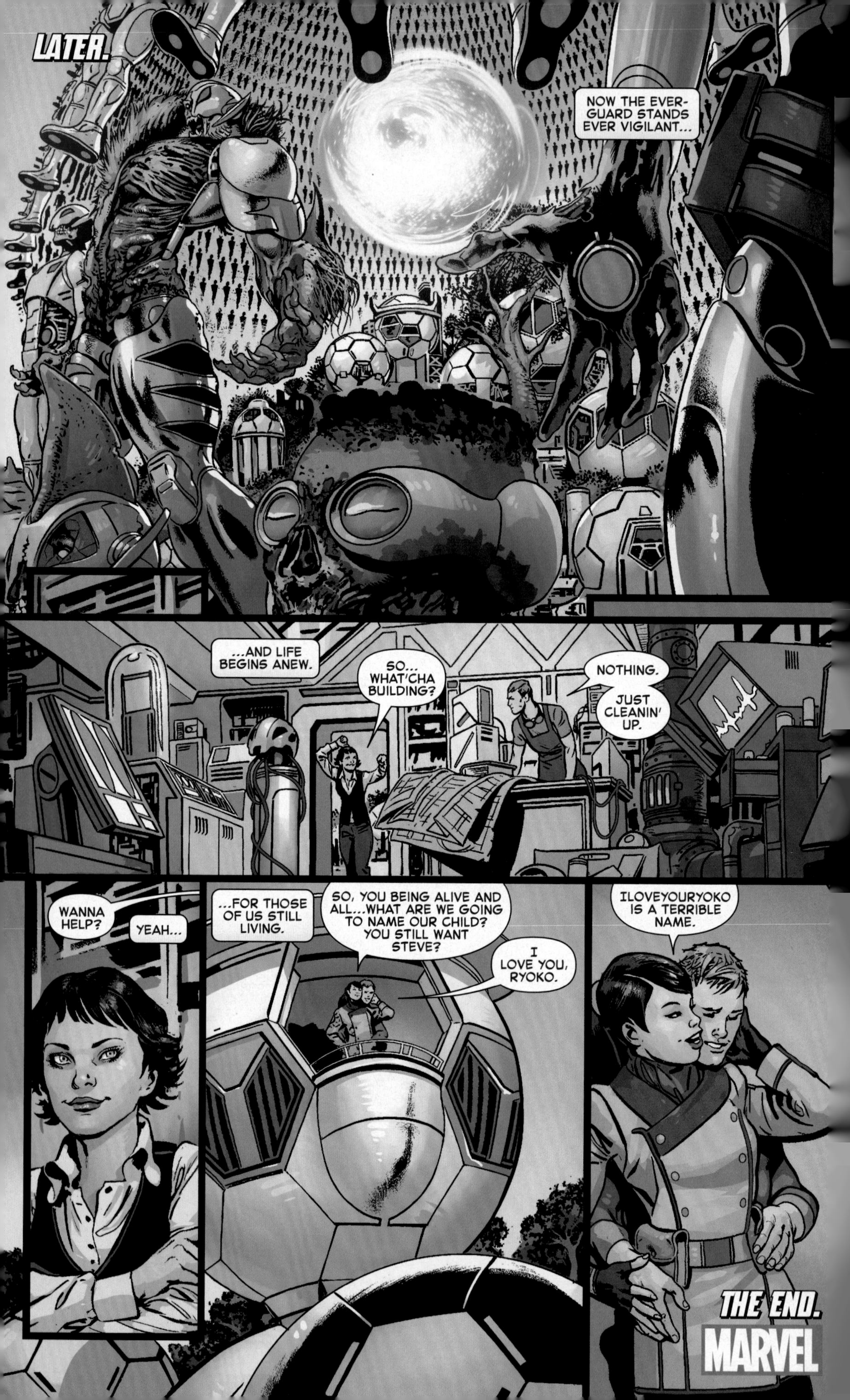
LATER.
NOW THE EVER-GUARD STANDS EVER VIGILANT...
...AND LIFE BEGINS ANEW.
SO... WHAT'CHA BUILDING?
NOTHING.
JUST CLEANIN' UP.
WANNA HELP?
YEAH...
...FOR THOSE OF US STILL LIVING.
SO, YOU BEING ALIVE AND ALL...WHAT ARE WE GOING TO NAME OUR CHILD? YOU STILL WANT STEVE?
I LOVE YOU, RYOKO.
ILOVEYOURYOKO IS A TERRIBLE NAME.
THE END.
MARVEL

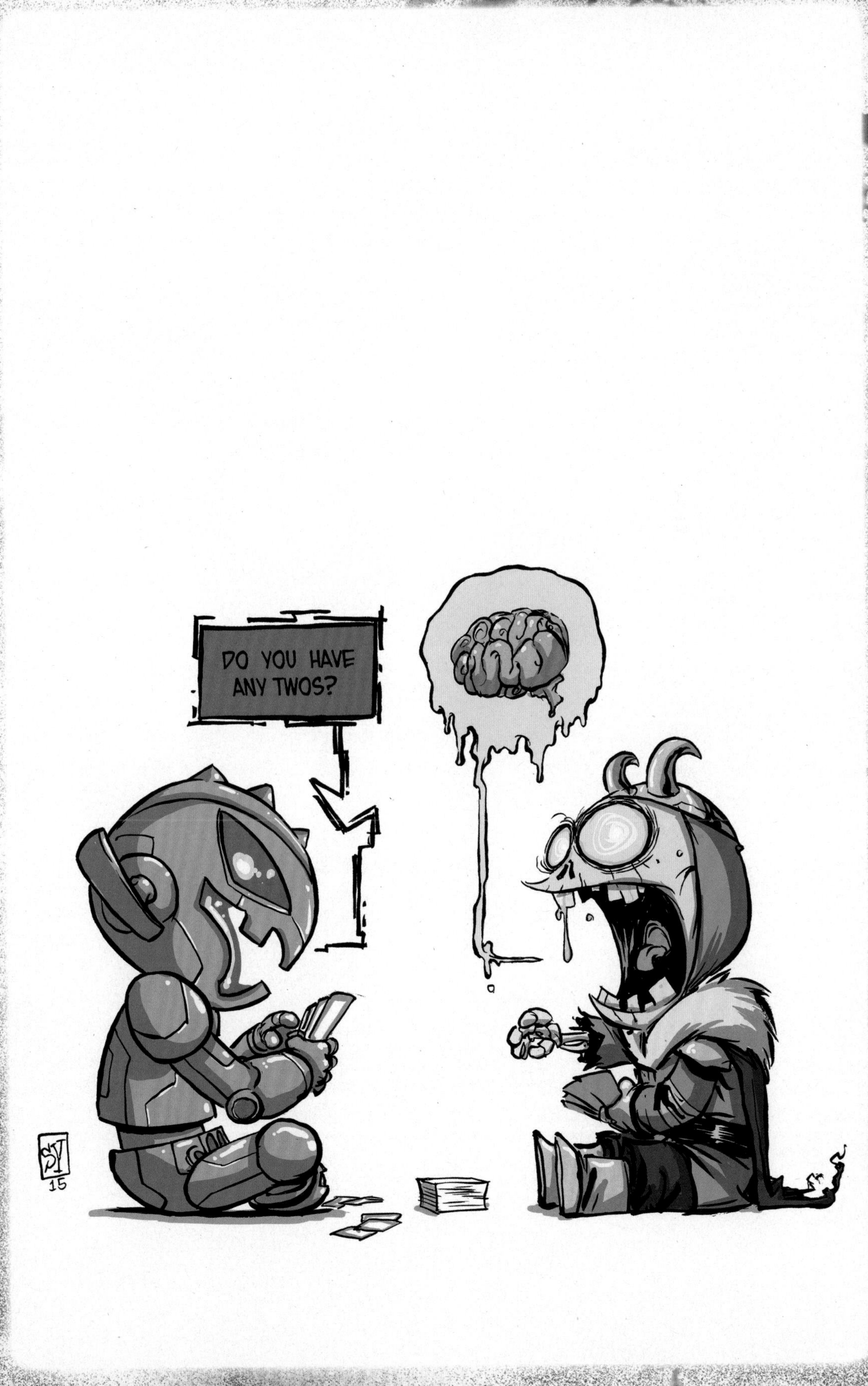
DO YOU HAVE ANY TWOS?
SY 15

#1 Variant by Skottie Young

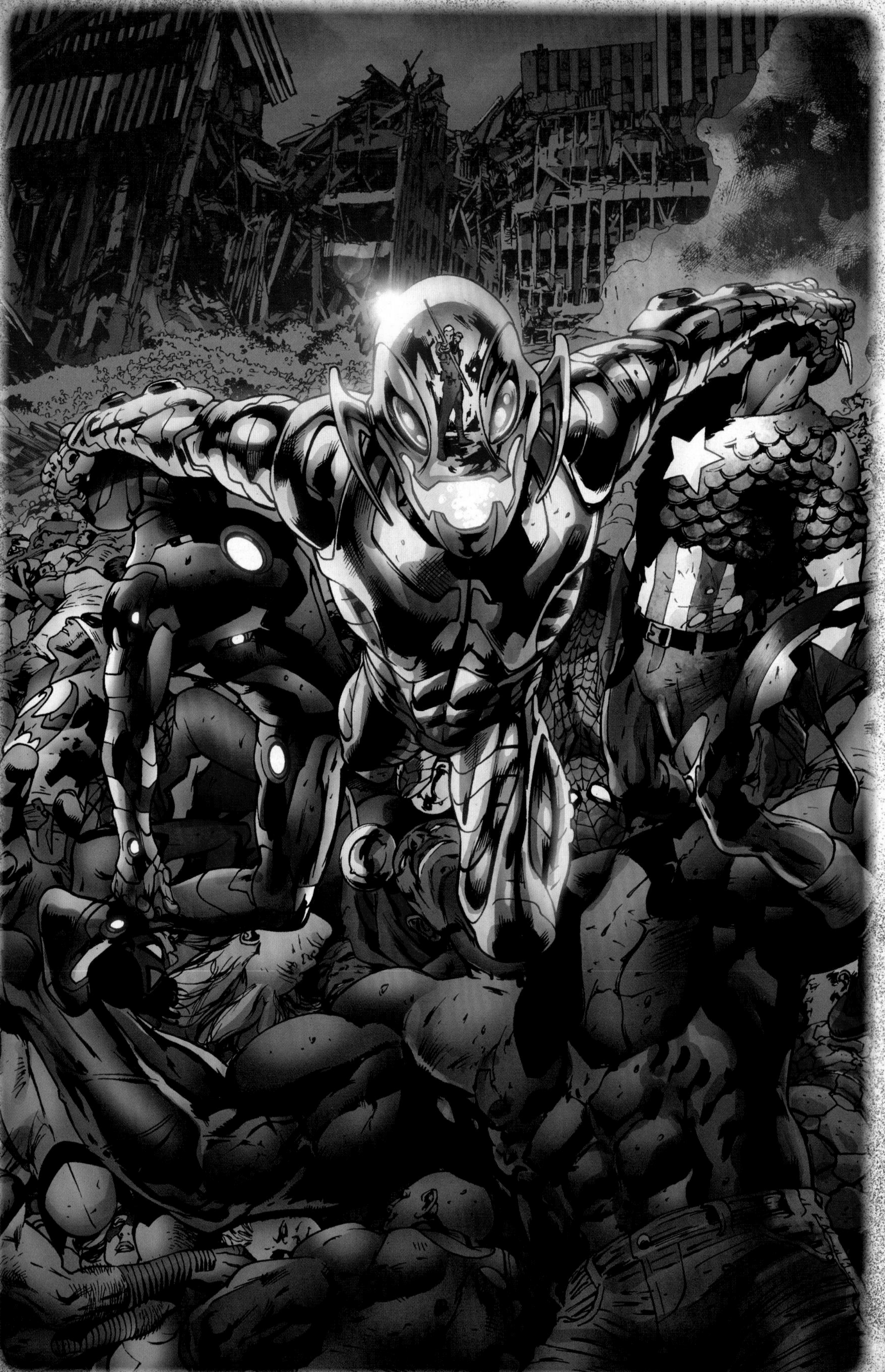

AGE OF ULTRON #1

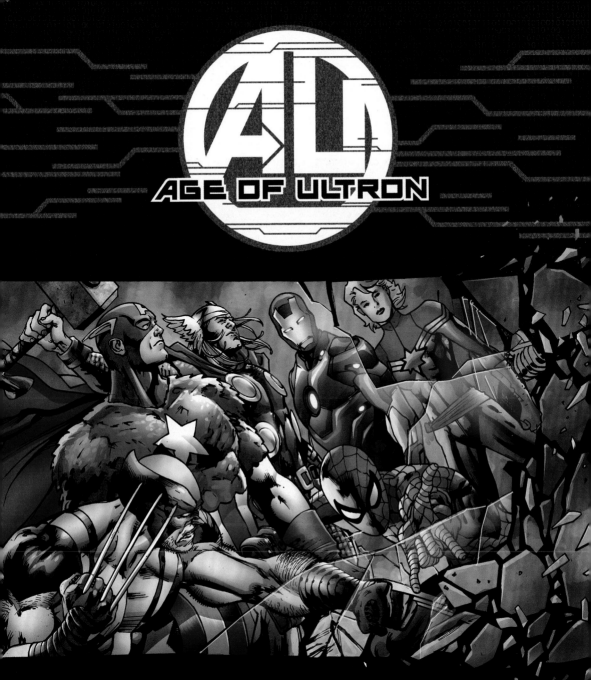

AGE OF ULTRON

HANK PYM OF THE AVENGERS CREATED THE ARTIFICIAL INTELLIGENCE KNOWN AS ULTRON.

IT HATES HUMANITY...AND IT HAS RETURNED...

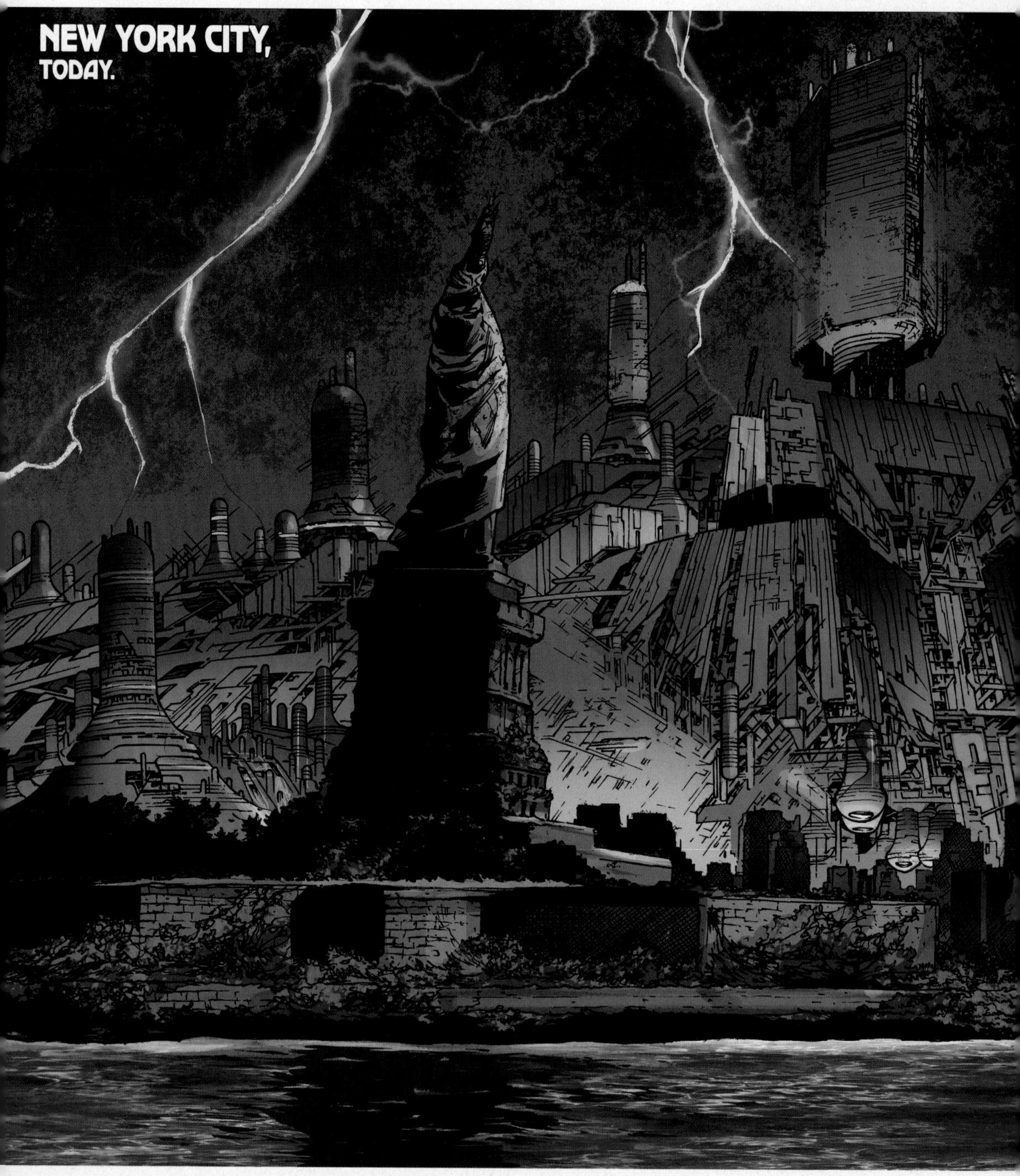
NEW YORK CITY,
TODAY.

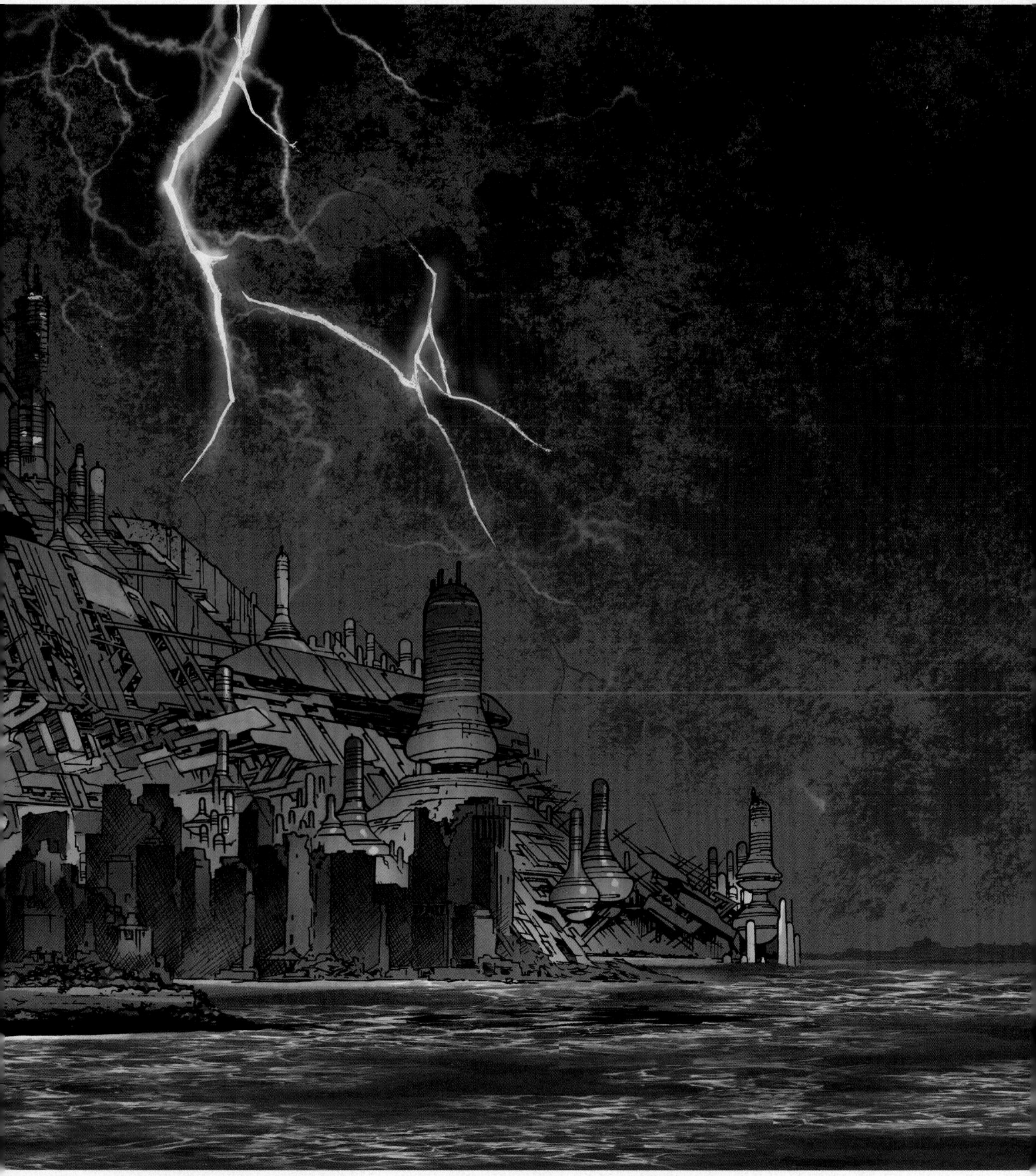

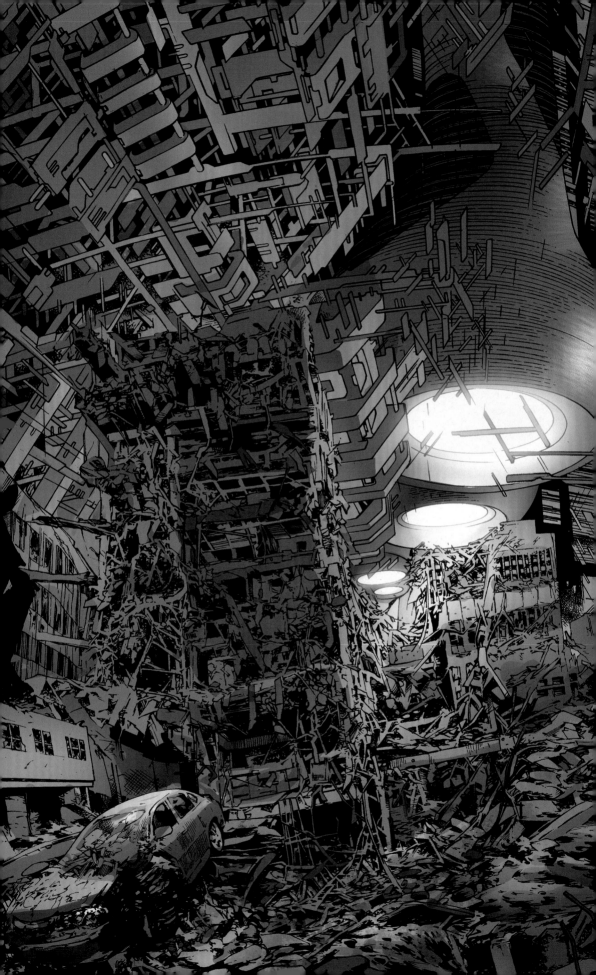

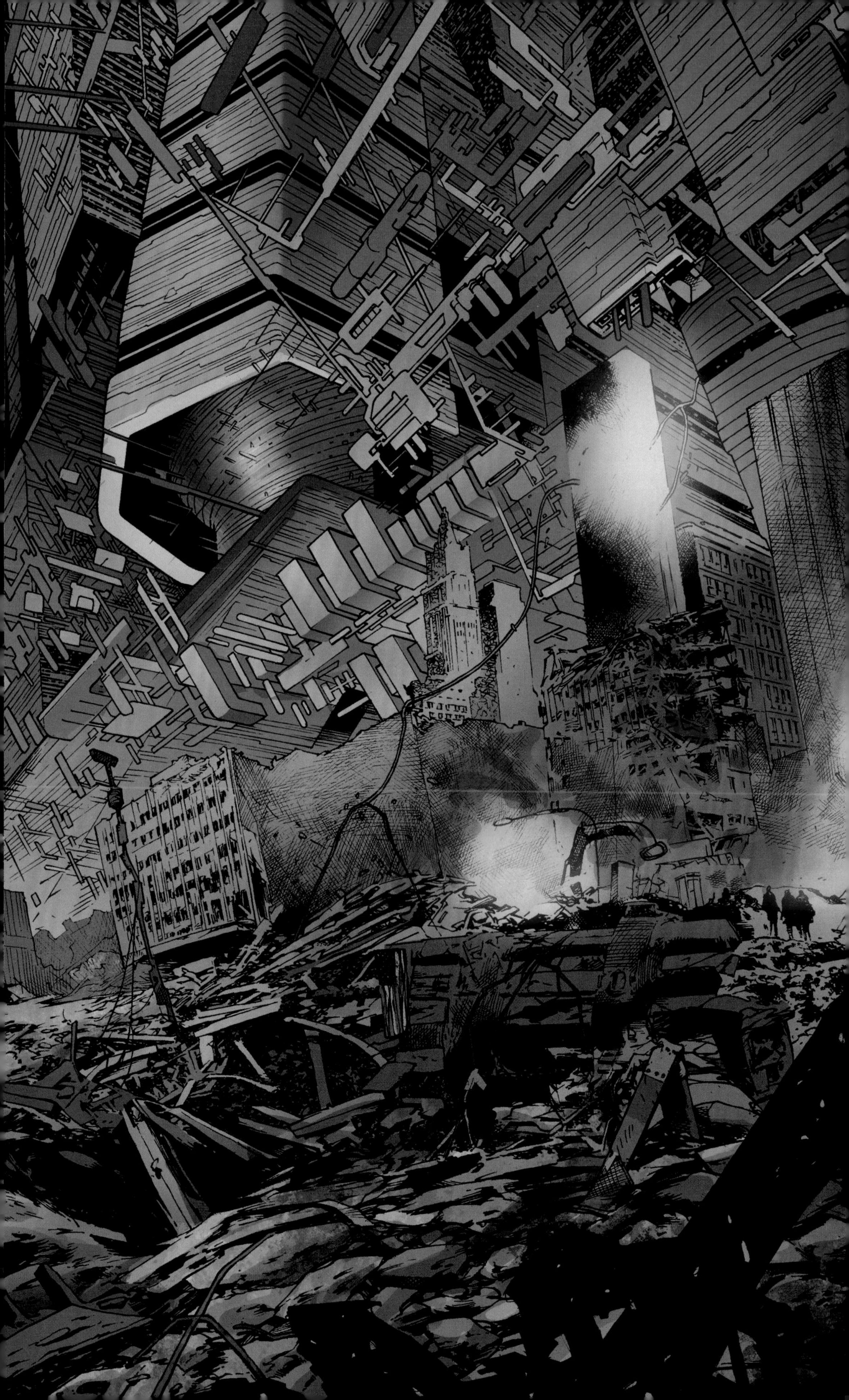

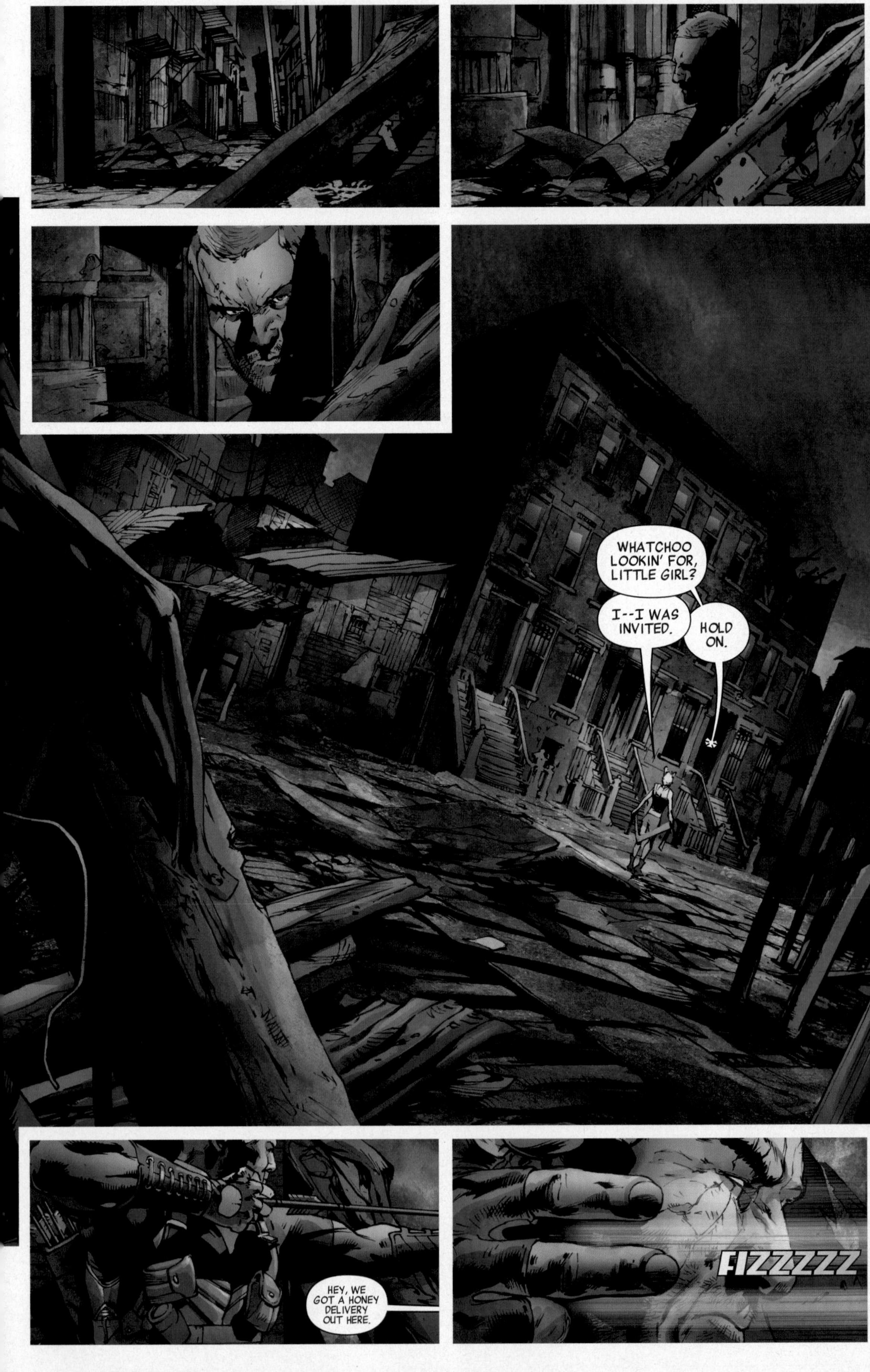
WHATCHOO LOOKIN' FOR, LITTLE GIRL?
I--I WAS INVITED.
HOLD ON.
HEY, WE GOT A HONEY DELIVERY OUT HERE.
FIZZZZZ

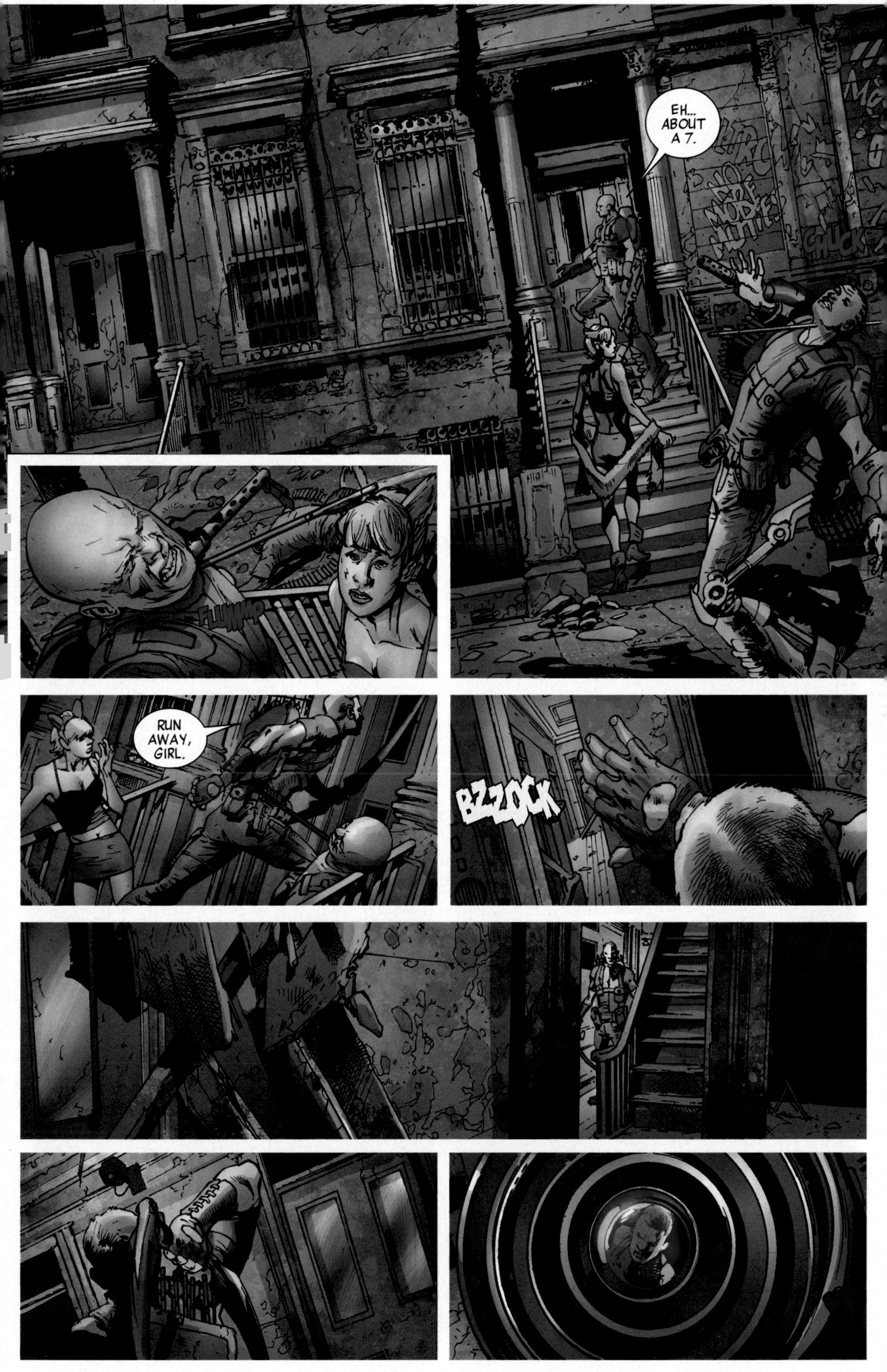
EH... ABOUT A 7.
FLUMP
RUN AWAY, GIRL.
BZZOCK

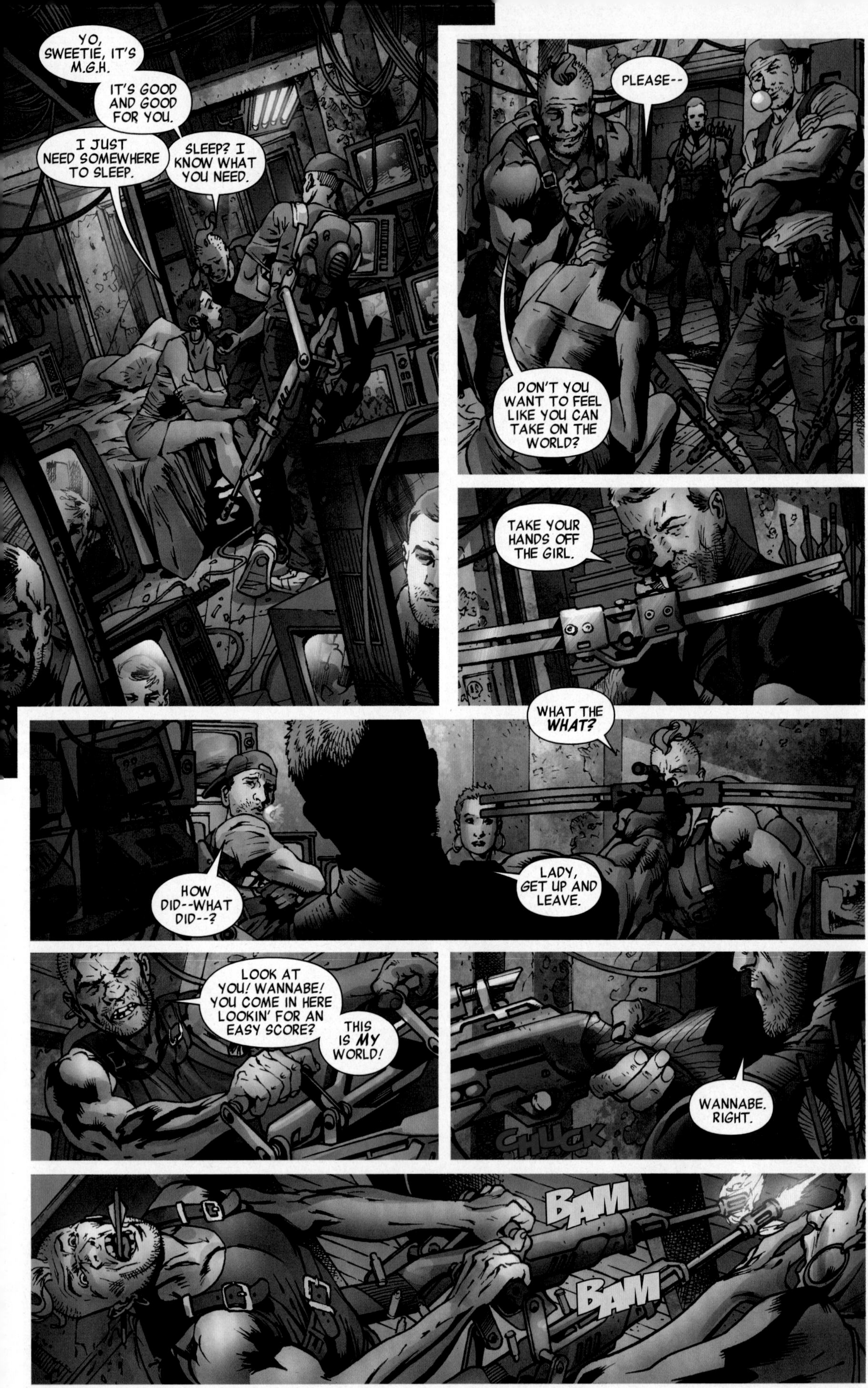
YO, SWEETIE, IT'S M.G.H.
IT'S GOOD AND GOOD FOR YOU.
I JUST NEED SOMEWHERE TO SLEEP.
SLEEP? I KNOW WHAT YOU NEED.
PLEASE--
DON'T YOU WANT TO FEEL LIKE YOU CAN TAKE ON THE WORLD?
TAKE YOUR HANDS OFF THE GIRL.
WHAT THE WHAT?
HOW DID--WHAT DID--?
LADY, GET UP AND LEAVE.
LOOK AT YOU! WANNABE! YOU COME IN HERE LOOKIN' FOR AN EASY SCORE?
THIS IS MY WORLD!
CHUCK
WANNABE. RIGHT.
BAM
BAM

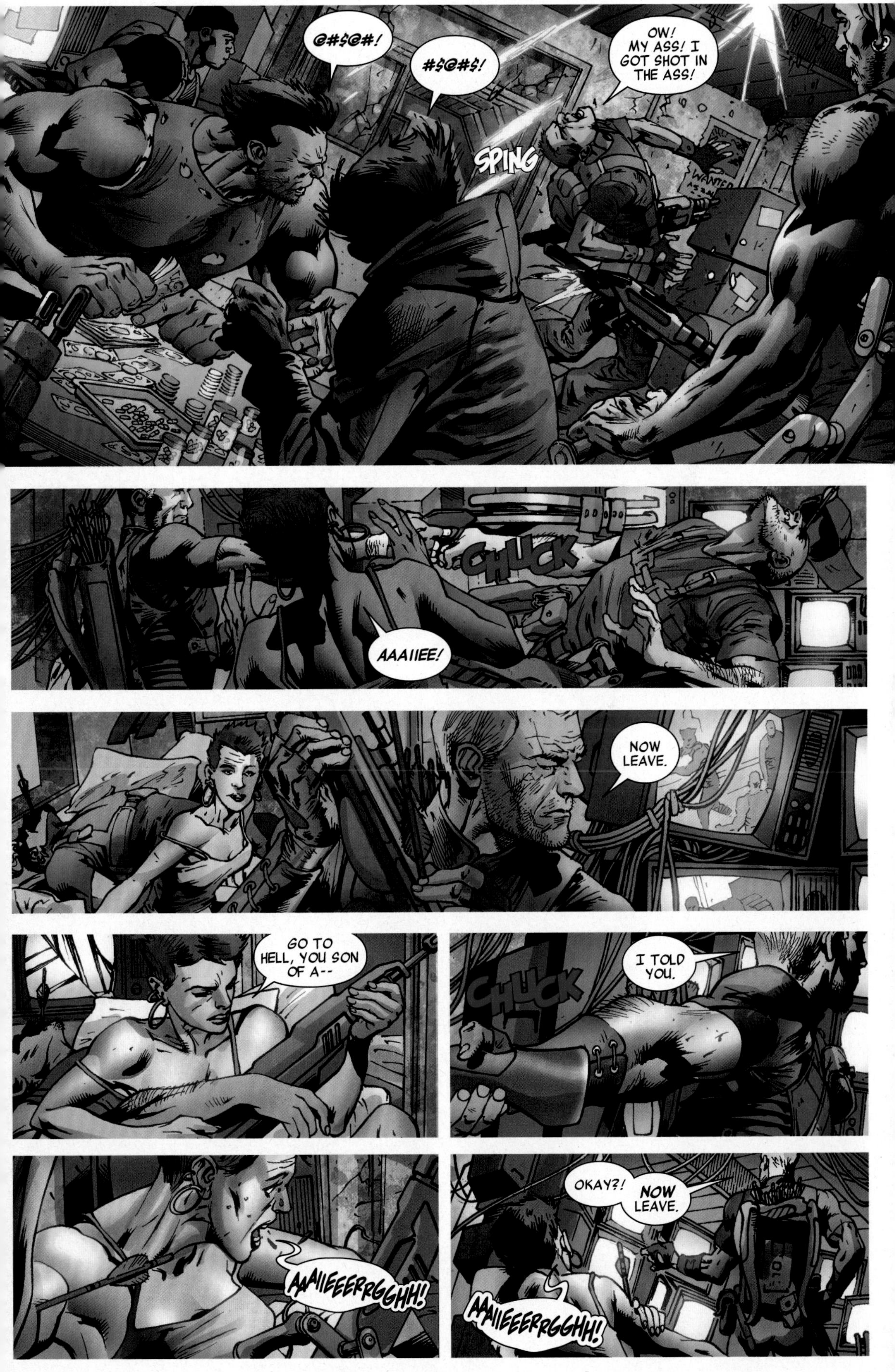
@#$@#!
#$@#$!
OW! MY ASS! I GOT SHOT IN THE ASS!
SPING
CHUCK
AAAIIEE!
NOW LEAVE.
GO TO HELL, YOU SON OF A--
CHUCK
I TOLD YOU.
AAAIIEEERRGGHH!
OKAY?!
NOW LEAVE.
AAAIIEEERRGGHH!

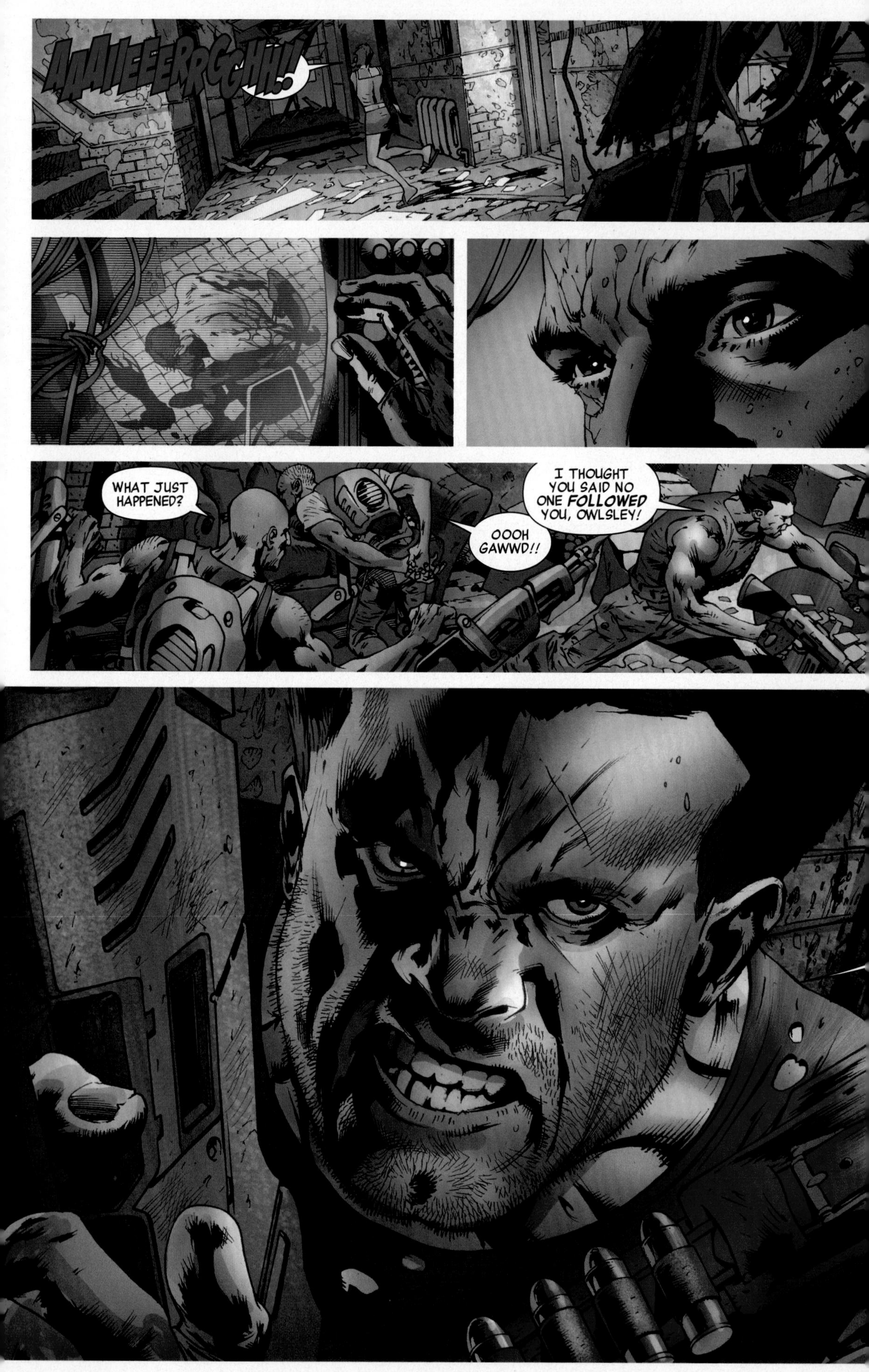
AAAIIEEEERRGGHH!!
WHAT JUST HAPPENED?
OOOH GAWWD!!
I THOUGHT YOU SAID NO ONE FOLLOWED YOU, OWLSLEY!

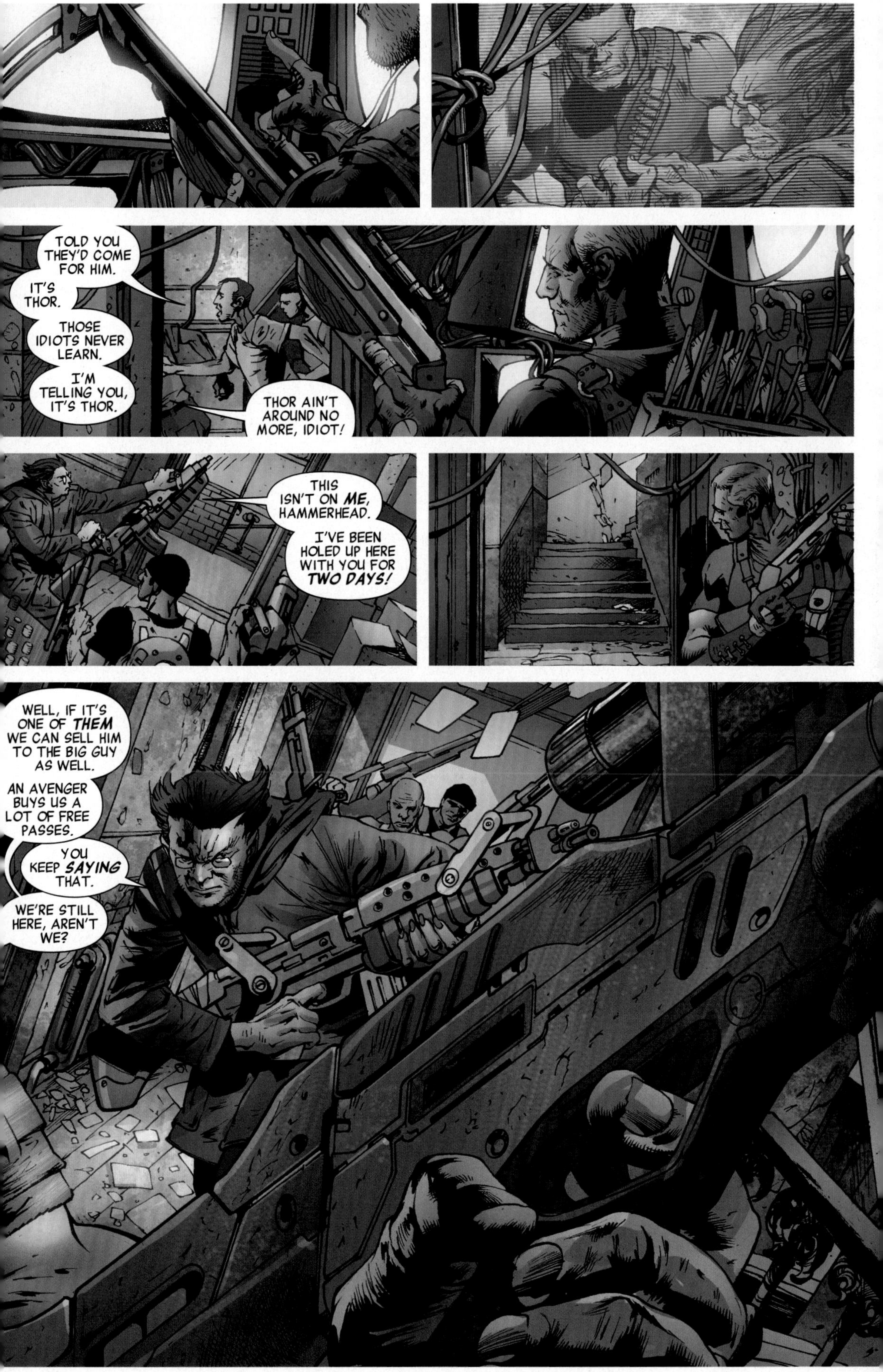

TOLD YOU THEY'D COME FOR HIM.
IT'S THOR.
THOSE IDIOTS NEVER LEARN.
I'M TELLING YOU, IT'S THOR.
THOR AIN'T AROUND NO MORE, IDIOT!
THIS ISN'T ON ME, HAMMERHEAD.
I'VE BEEN HOLED UP HERE WITH YOU FOR TWO DAYS!
WELL, IF IT'S ONE OF THEM WE CAN SELL HIM TO THE BIG GUY AS WELL.
AN AVENGER BUYS US A LOT OF FREE PASSES.
YOU KEEP SAYING THAT.
WE'RE STILL HERE, AREN'T WE?

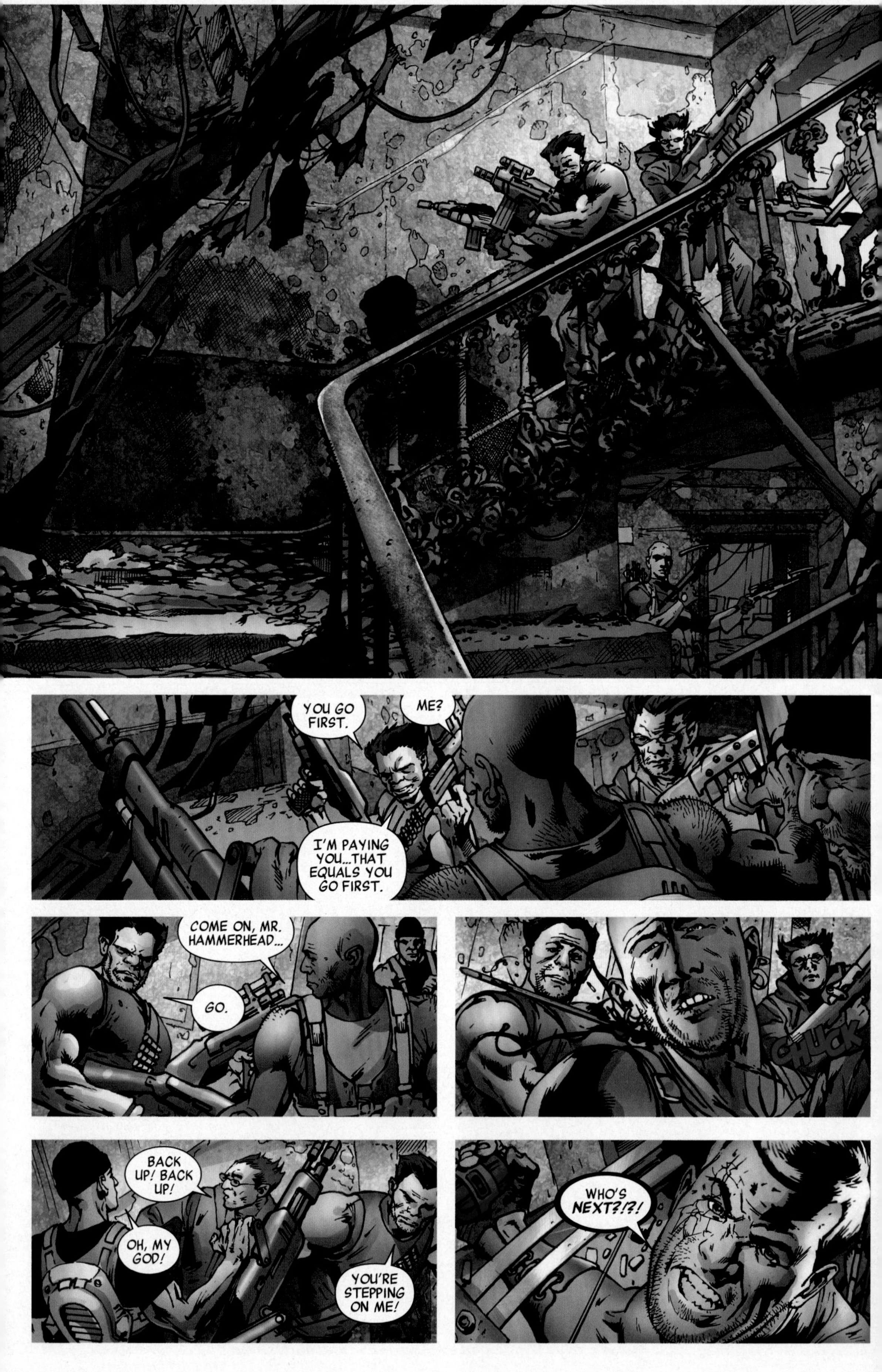
YOU GO FIRST.
ME?
I'M PAYING YOU...THAT EQUALS YOU GO FIRST.
COME ON, MR. HAMMERHEAD...
GO.
CHUCK
BACK UP! BACK UP!
OH, MY GOD!
YOU'RE STEPPING ON ME!
WHO'S NEXT?!?!

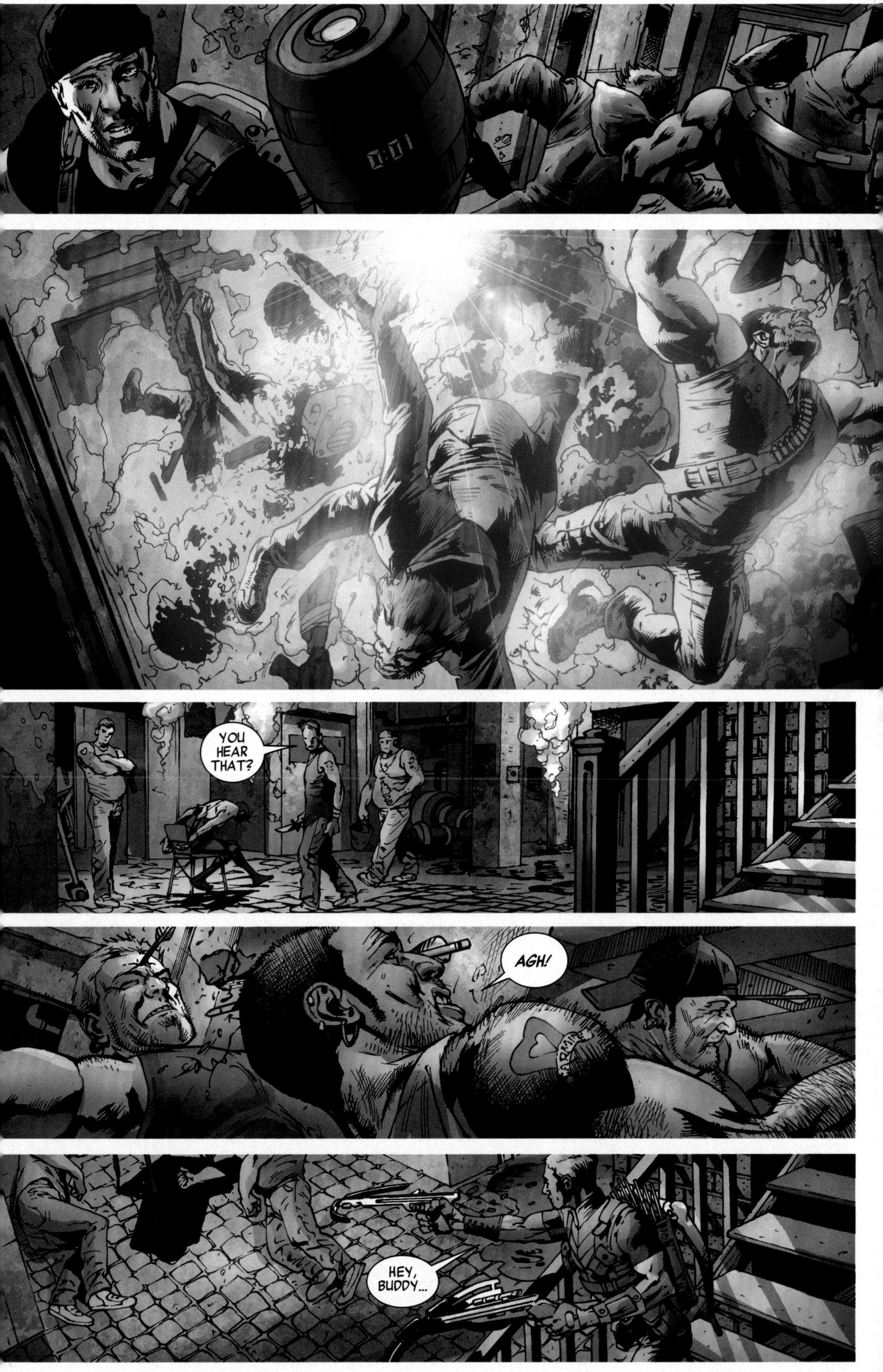
0:01
YOU HEAR THAT?
AGH!
HEY, BUDDY...

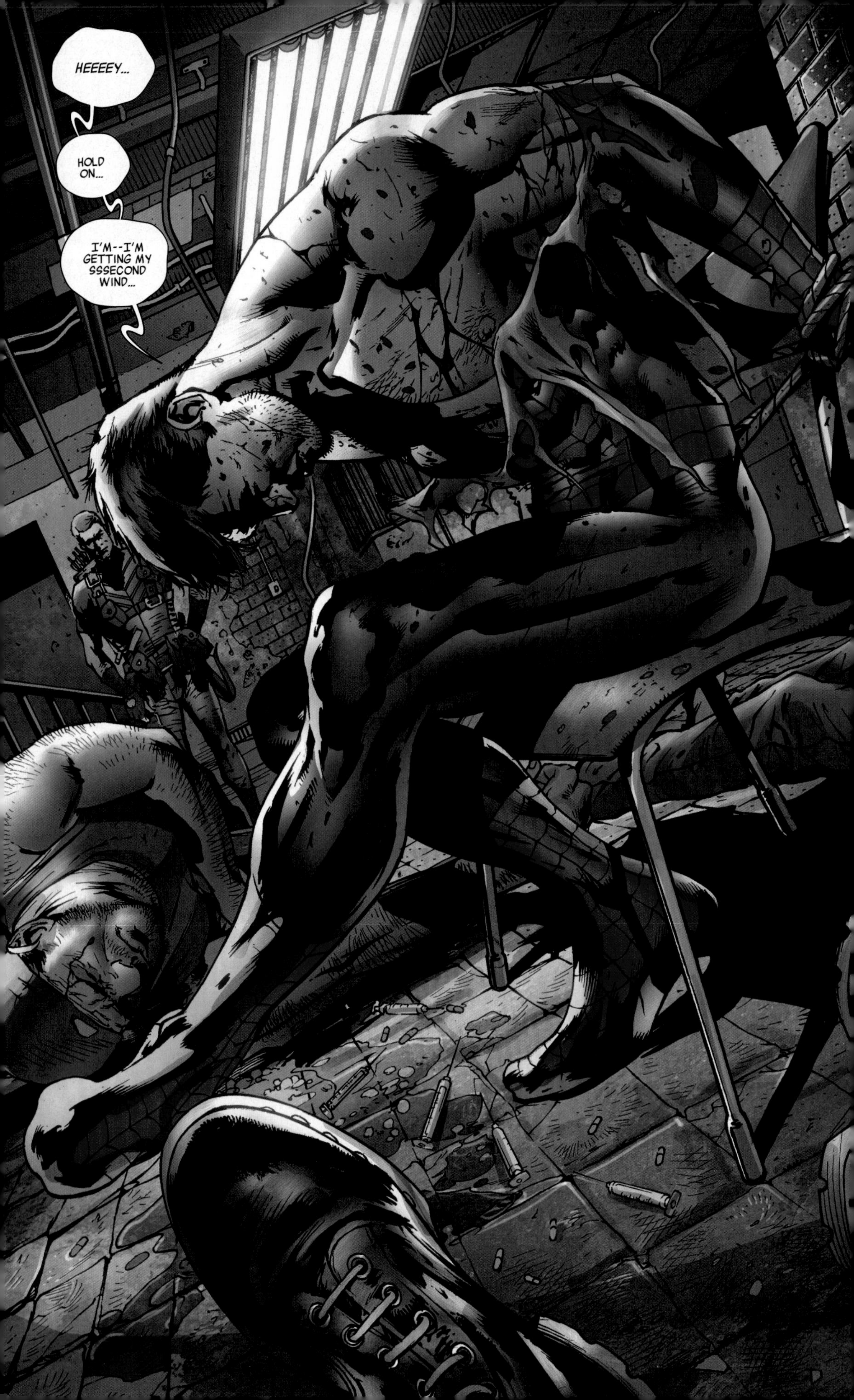
HEEEEY...
HOLD ON...
I'M--I'M GETTING MY SSSECOND WIND...

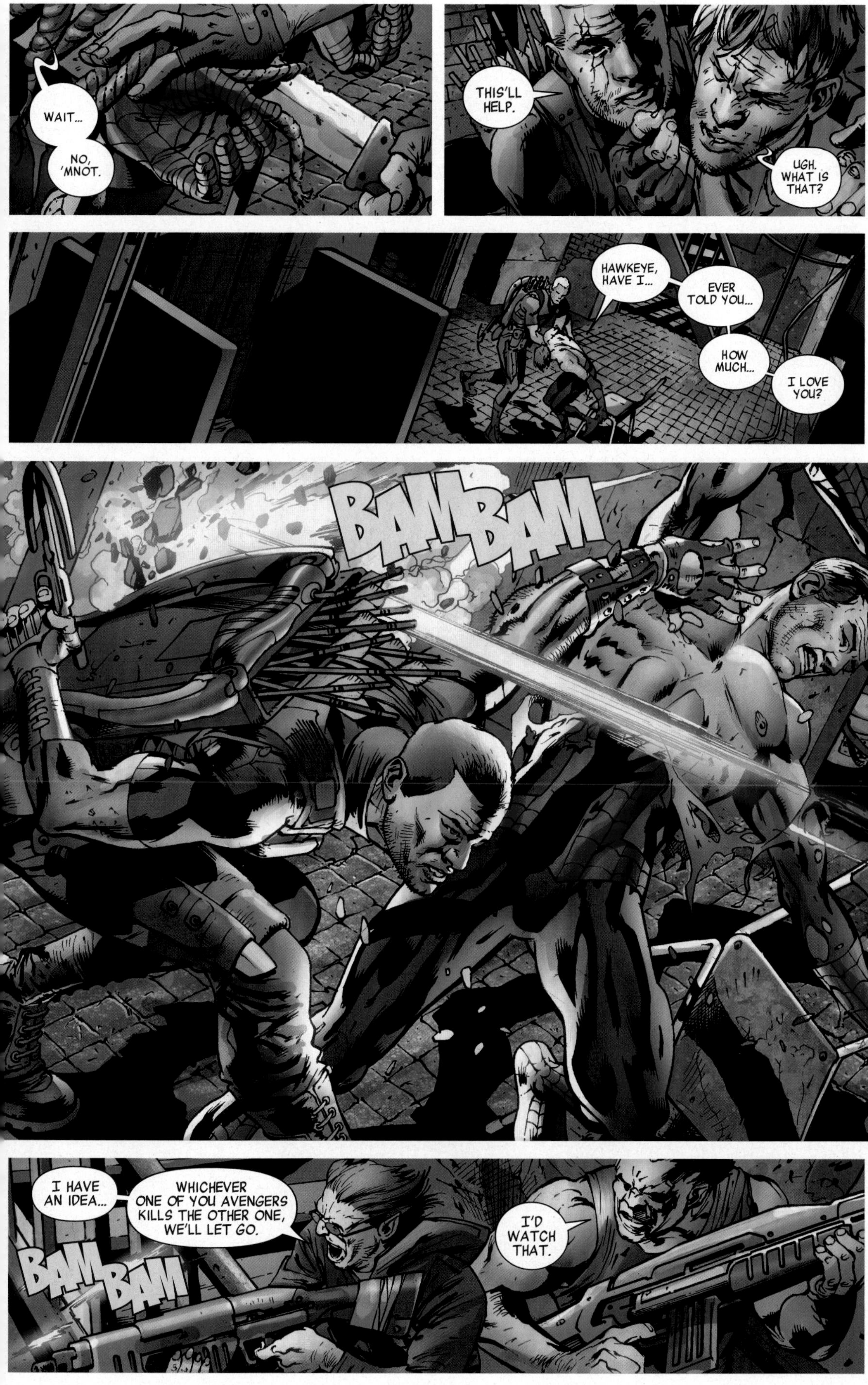
WAIT...
NO, 'MNOT.
THIS'LL HELP.
UGH. WHAT IS THAT?
HAWKEYE, HAVE I...
EVER TOLD YOU...
HOW MUCH...
I LOVE YOU?
BAM BAM
I HAVE AN IDEA...
WHICHEVER ONE OF YOU AVENGERS KILLS THE OTHER ONE, WE'LL LET GO.
I'D WATCH THAT.
BAM BAM

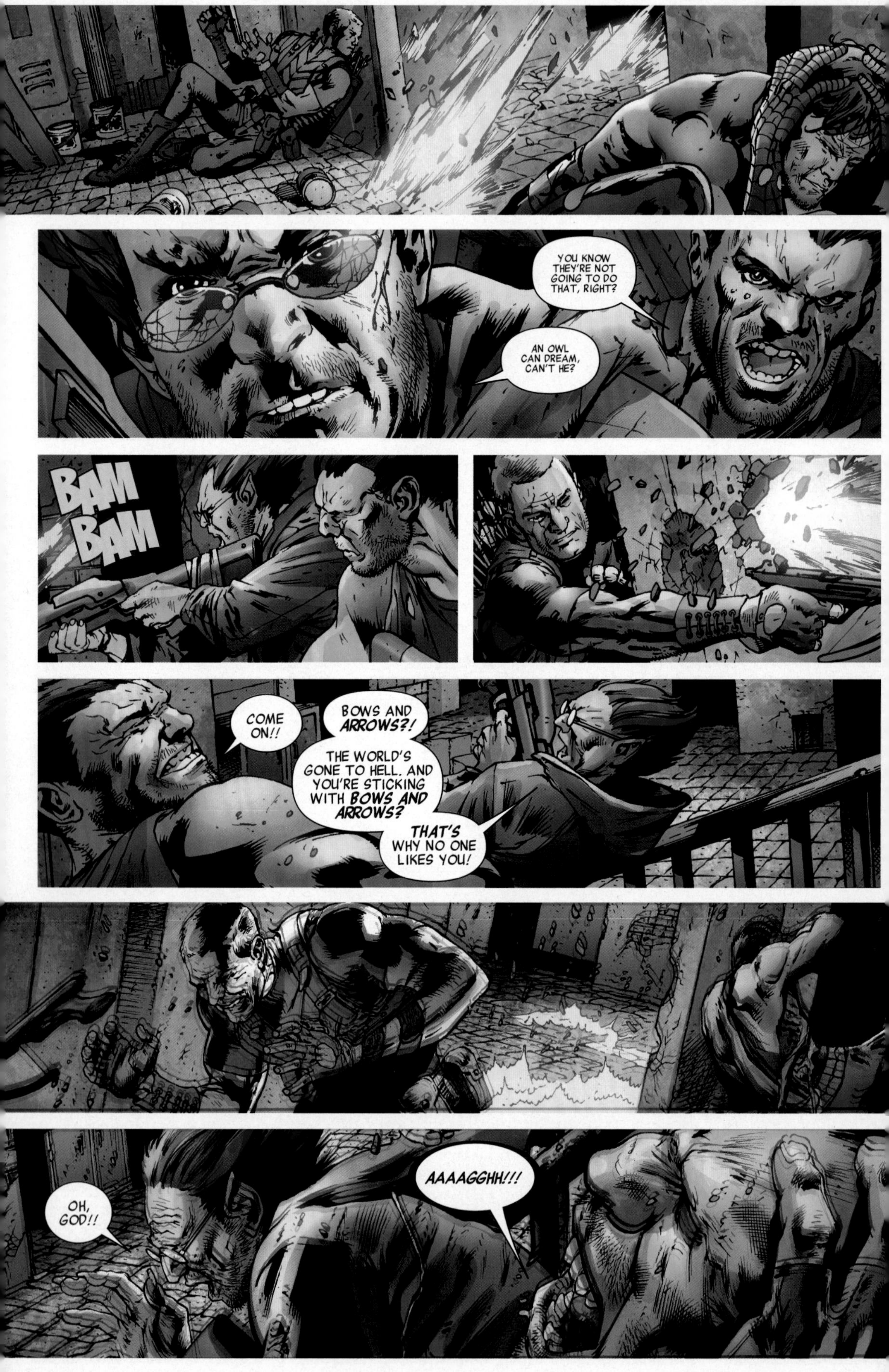
YOU KNOW THEY'RE NOT GOING TO DO THAT, RIGHT?
AN OWL CAN DREAM, CAN'T HE?
BAM BAM
COME ON!!
BOWS AND ARROWS?!
THE WORLD'S GONE TO HELL. AND YOU'RE STICKING WITH BOWS AND ARROWS?
THAT'S WHY NO ONE LIKES YOU!
OH, GOD!!
AAAAGGHH!!!

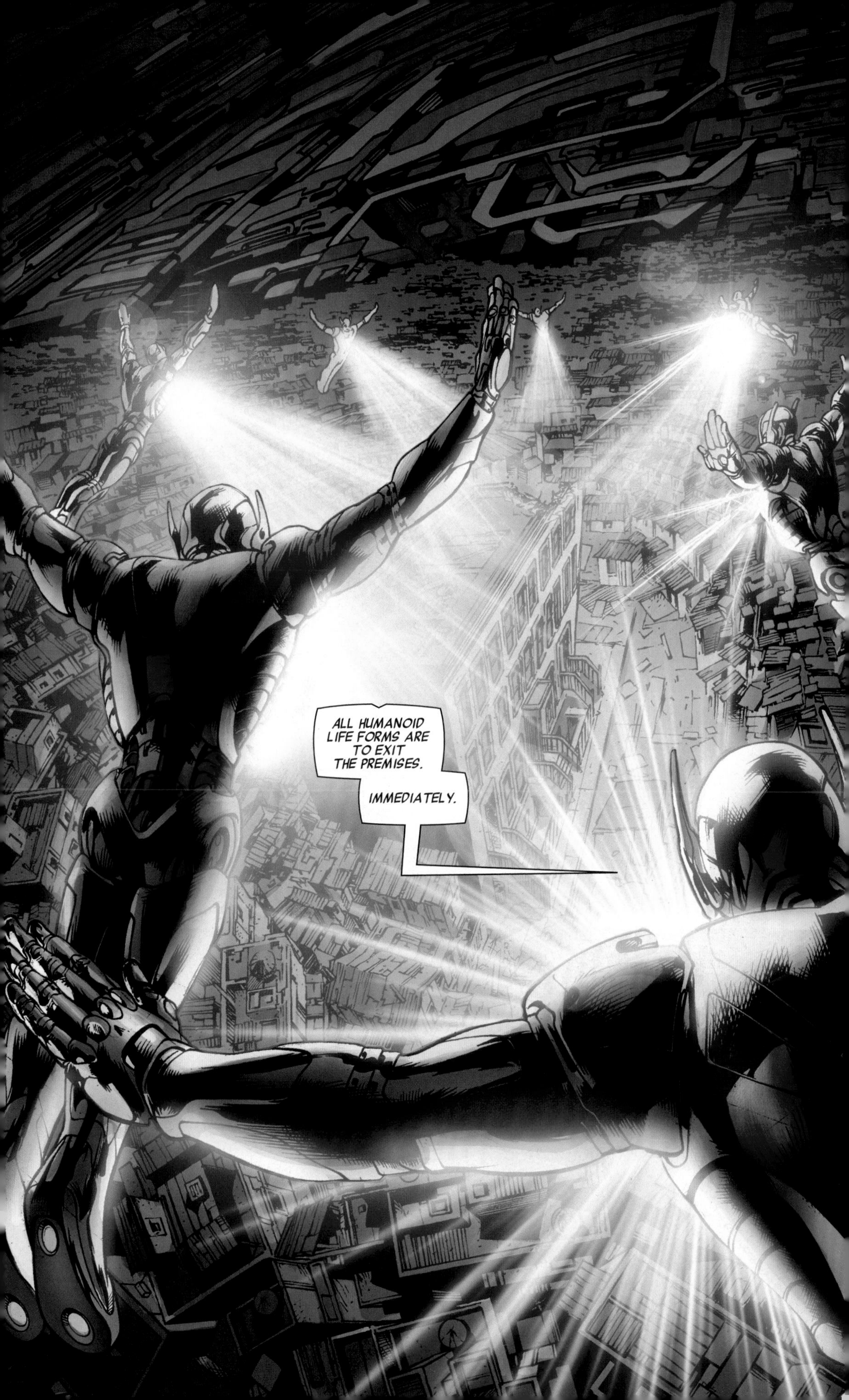
ALL HUMANOID LIFE FORMS ARE TO EXIT THE PREMISES.
IMMEDIATELY.

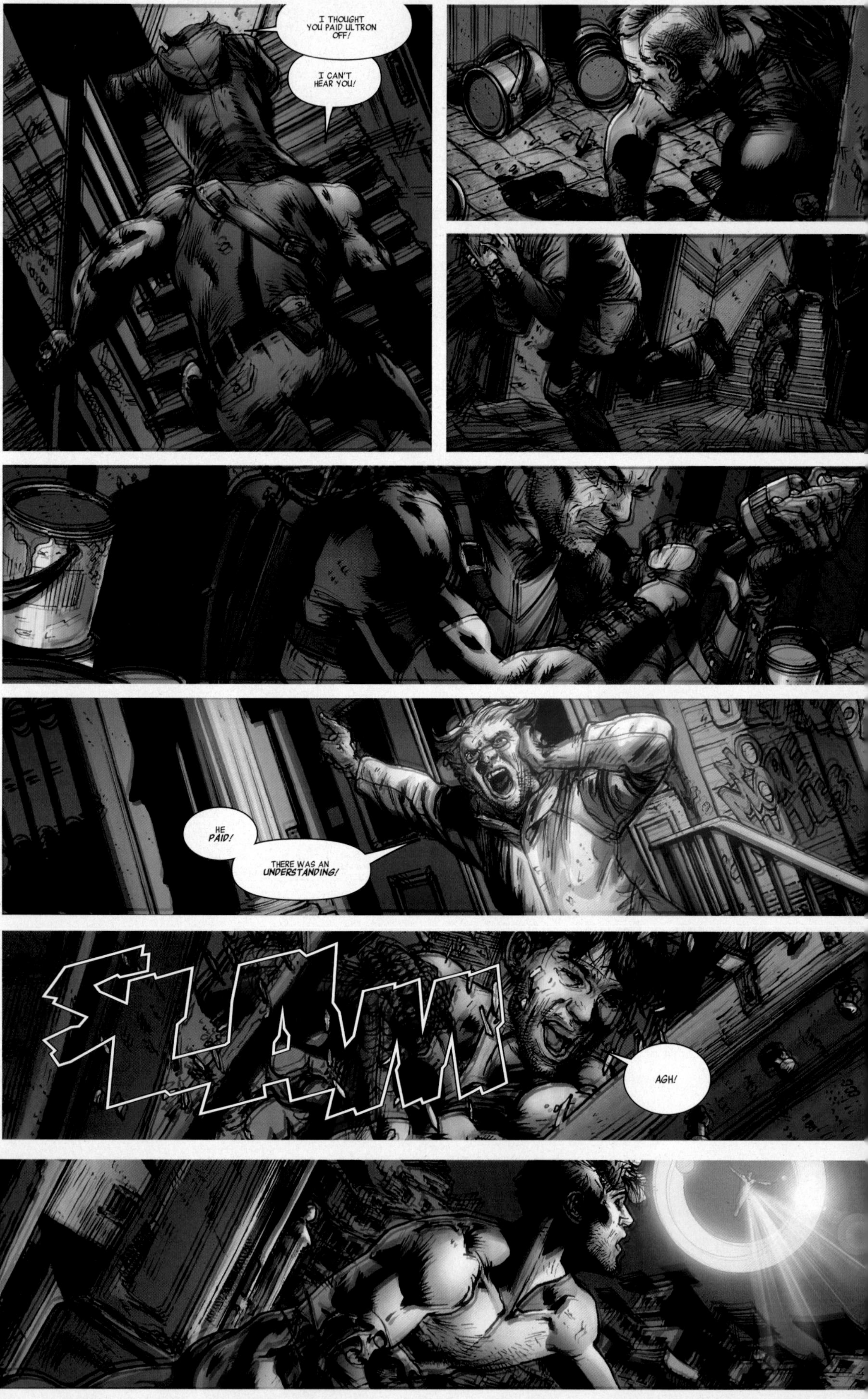
I THOUGHT YOU PAID ULTRON OFF!
I CAN'T HEAR YOU!
HE PAID!
THERE WAS AN UNDERSTANDING!
SLAM
AGH!

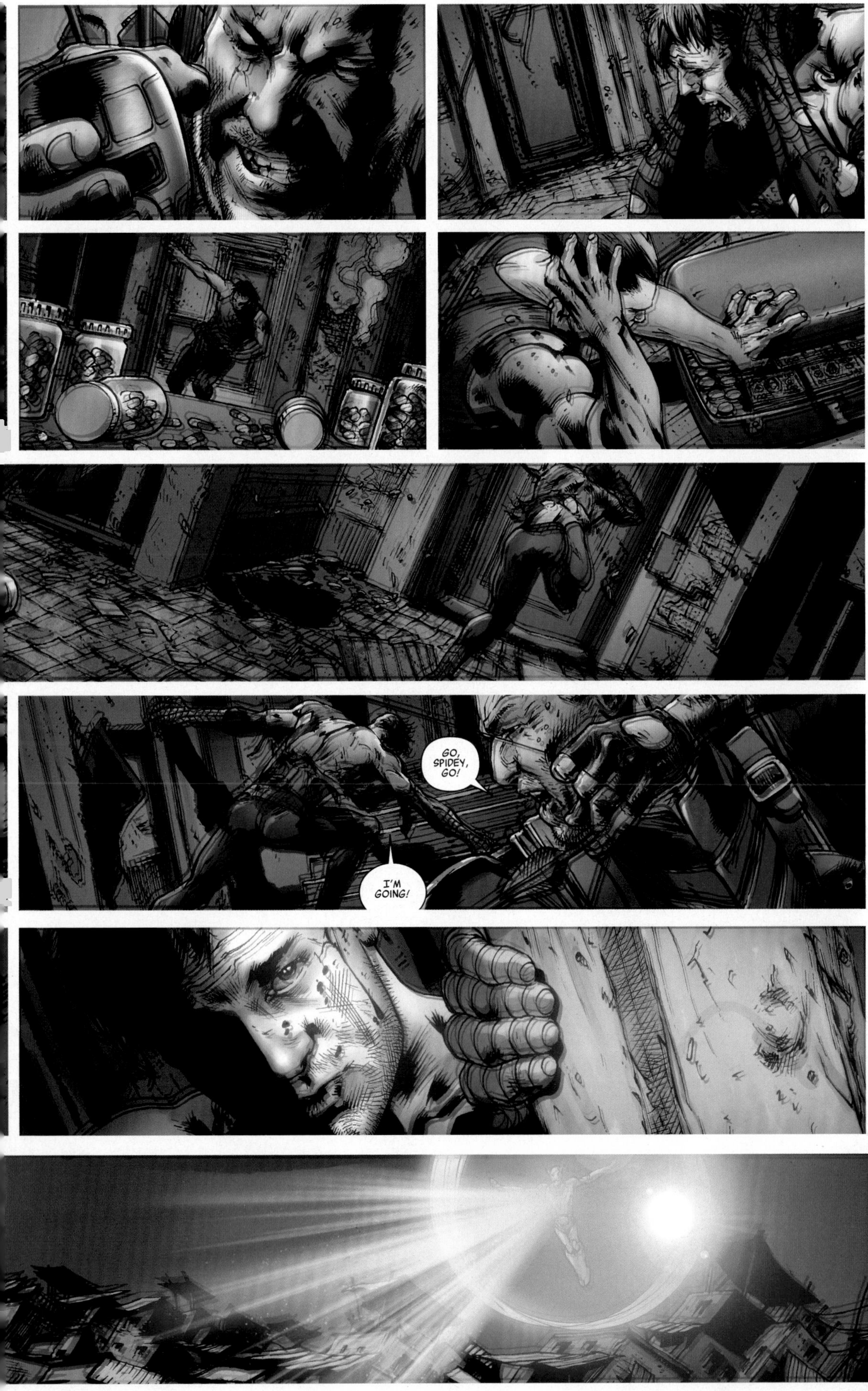
GO, SPIDEY, GO!
I'M GOING!

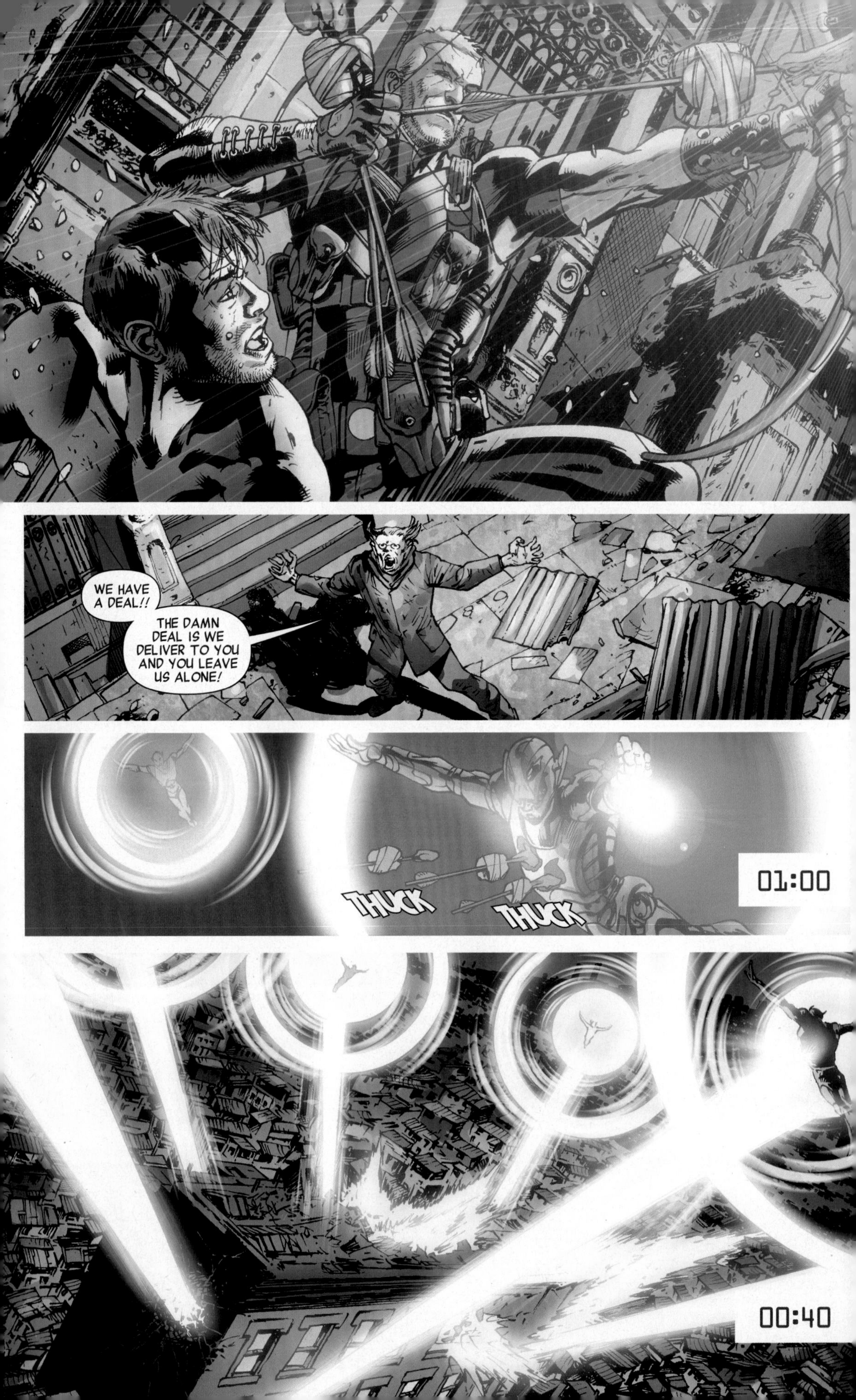
WE HAVE A DEAL!!
THE DAMN DEAL IS WE DELIVER TO YOU AND YOU LEAVE US ALONE!
01:00
THUCK
THUCK
00:40

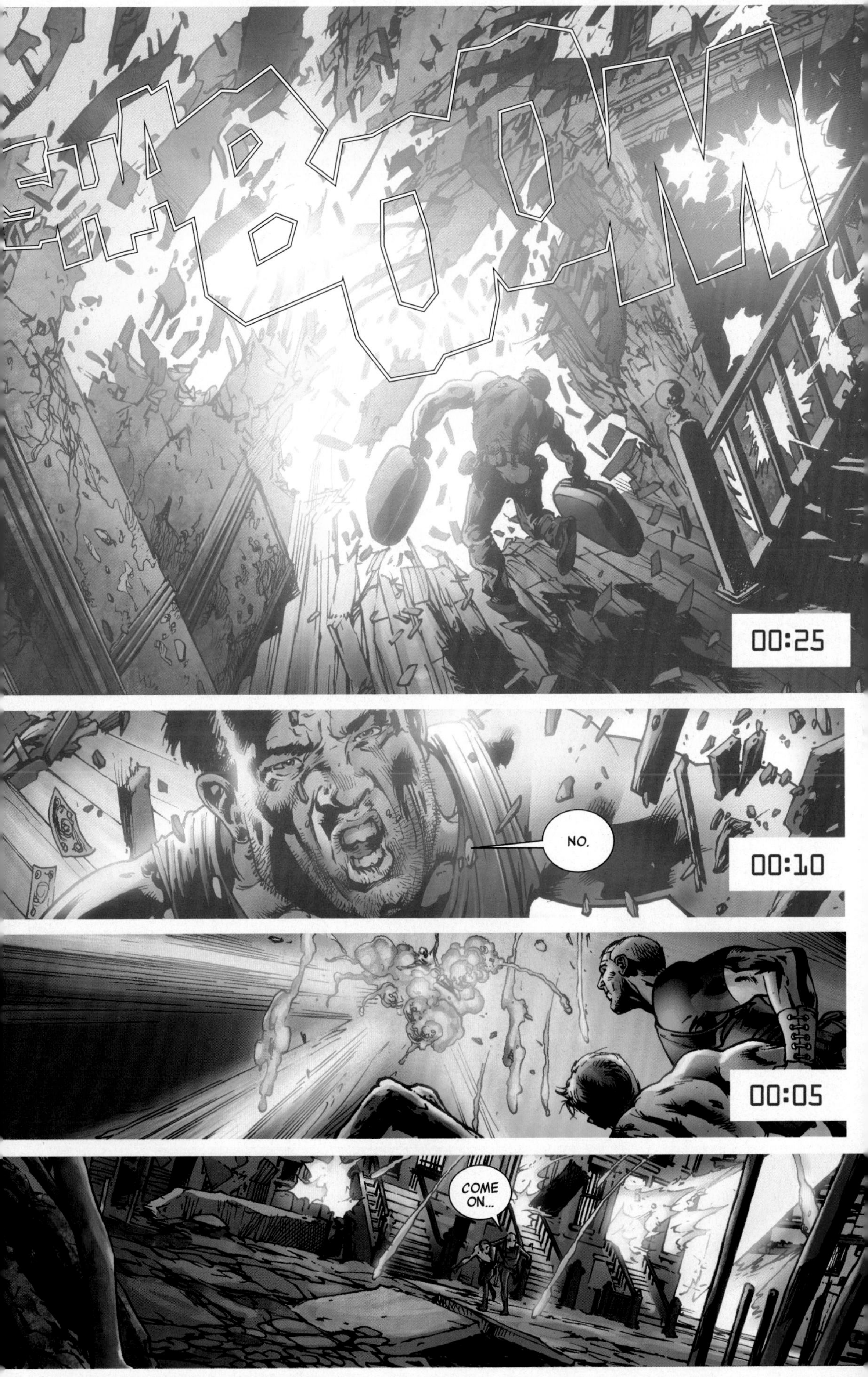
KA-BOOM
00:25
NO.
00:10
00:05
COME ON...

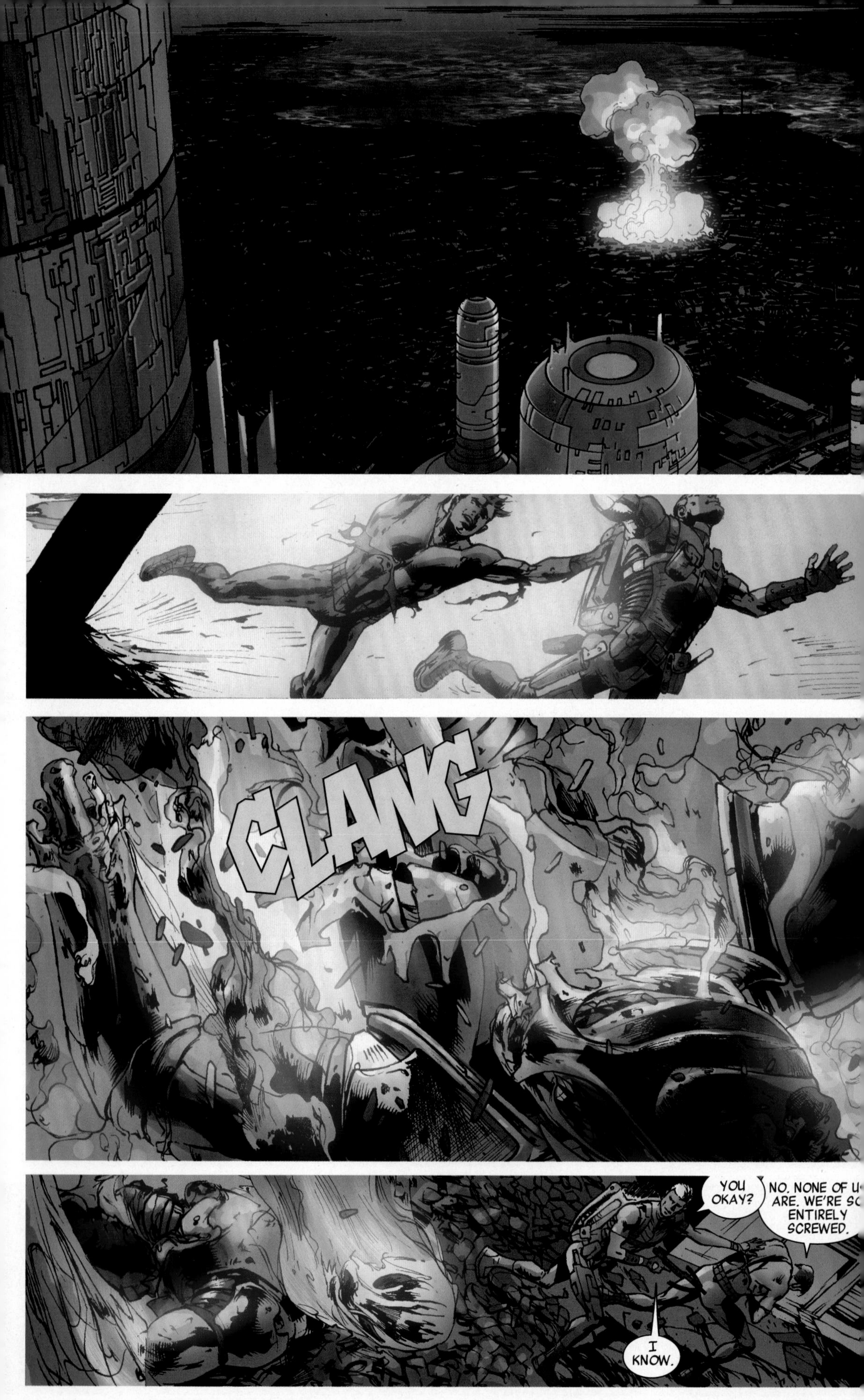
CLANG
YOU OKAY?
NO. NONE OF U
ARE. WE'RE S
ENTIRELY
SCREWED.
I KNOW.

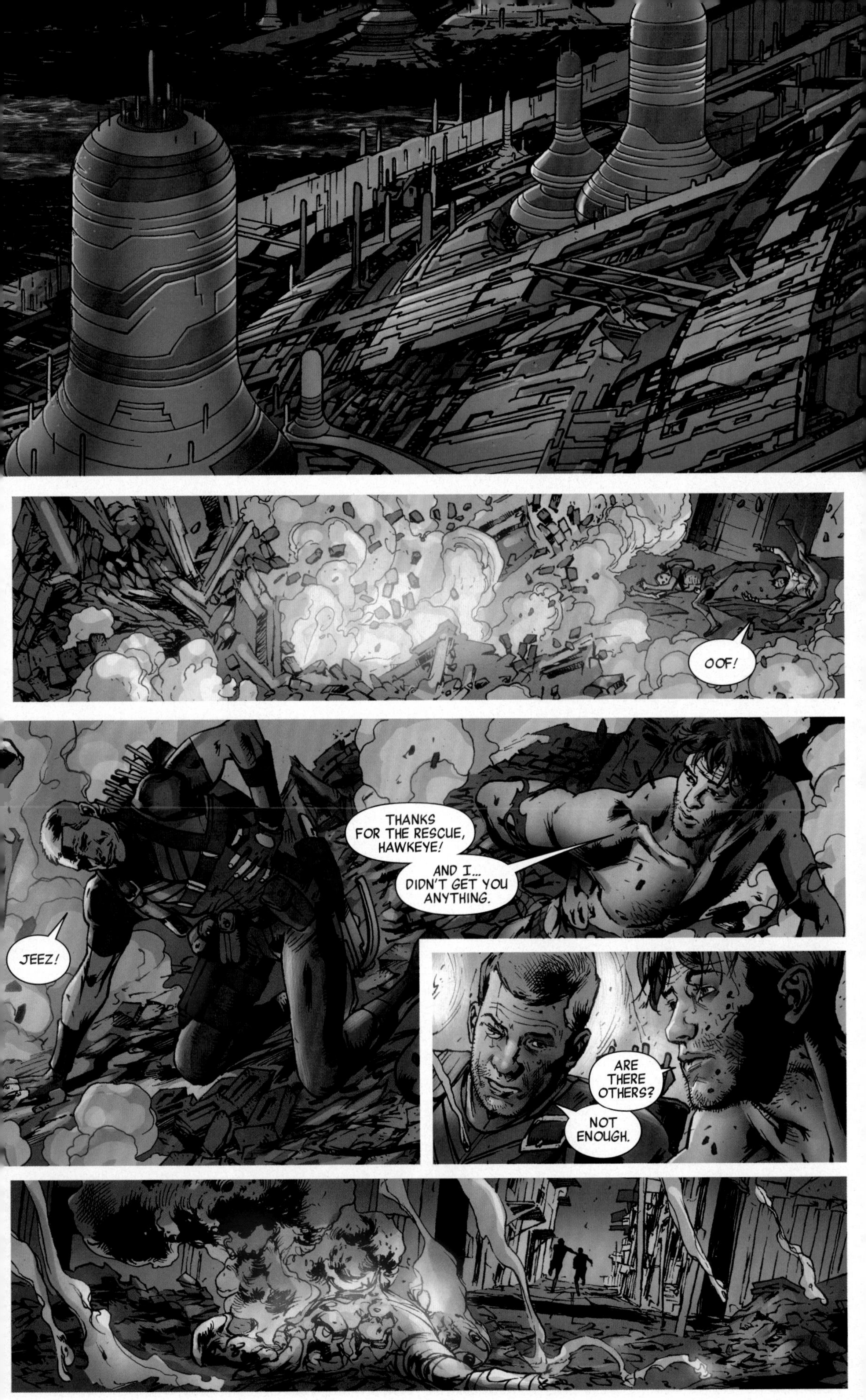
OOF!
THANKS FOR THE RESCUE, HAWKEYE!
AND I... DIDN'T GET YOU ANYTHING.
JEEZ!
ARE THERE OTHERS?
NOT ENOUGH.

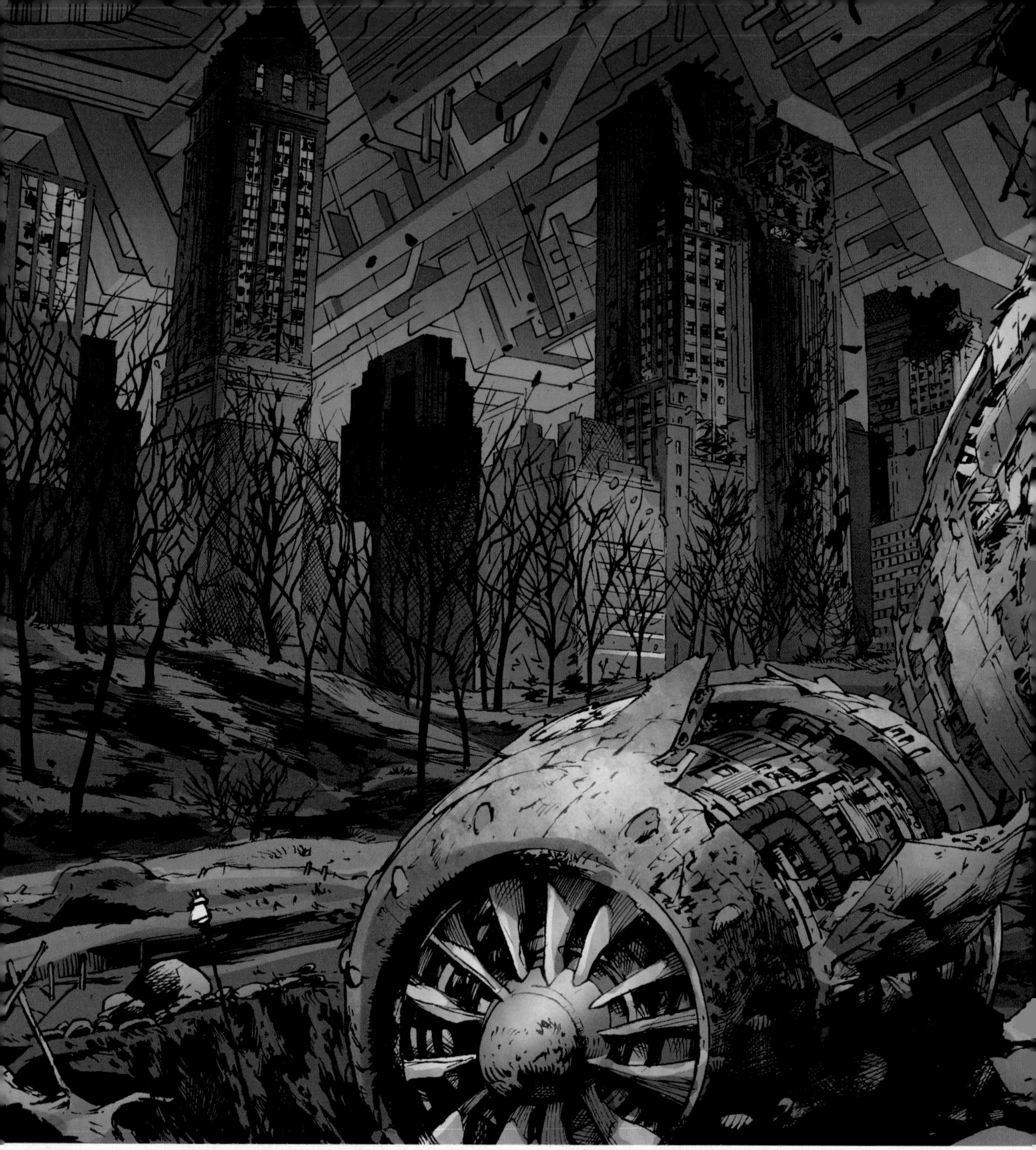

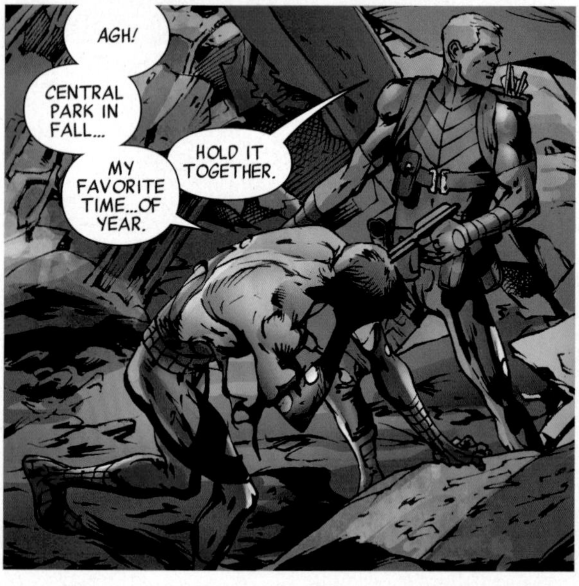
AGH!
CENTRAL PARK IN FALL...
MY FAVORITE TIME...OF YEAR.
HOLD IT TOGETHER.

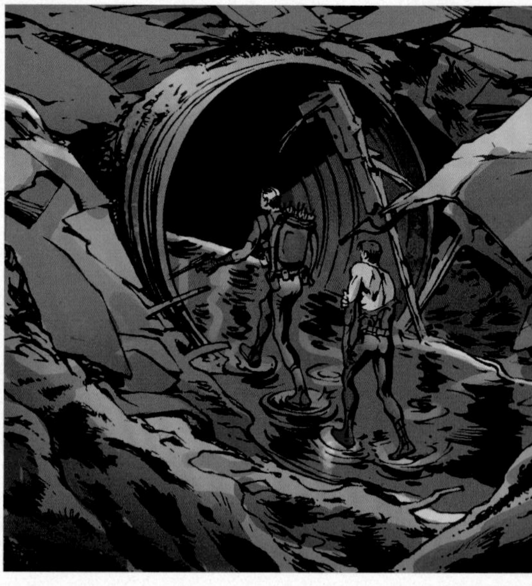

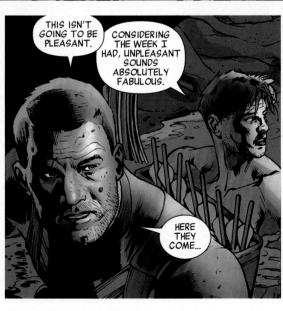

THIS ISN'T GOING TO BE PLEASANT.

CONSIDERING THE WEEK I HAD, UNPLEASANT SOUNDS ABSOLUTELY FABULOUS.

HERE THEY COME...

GUYS, HEY...

COME ON! COME ON!

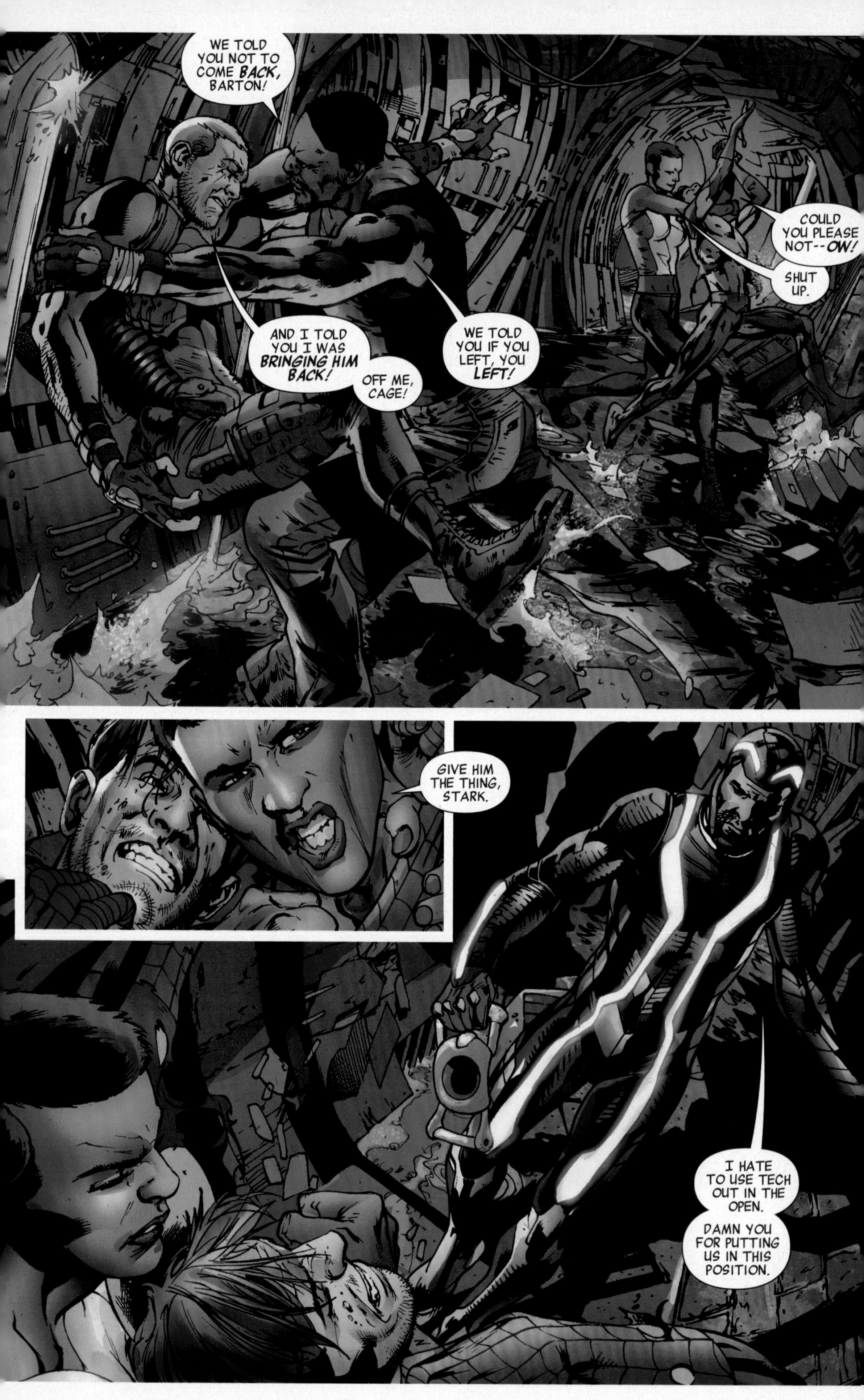
WE TOLD YOU NOT TO COME BACK, BARTON!
AND I TOLD YOU I WAS BRINGING HIM BACK!
OFF ME, CAGE!
WE TOLD YOU IF YOU LEFT, YOU LEFT!
COULD YOU PLEASE NOT--OW!
SHUT UP.
GIVE HIM THE THING, STARK.
I HATE TO USE TECH OUT IN THE OPEN.
DAMN YOU FOR PUTTING US IN THIS POSITION.

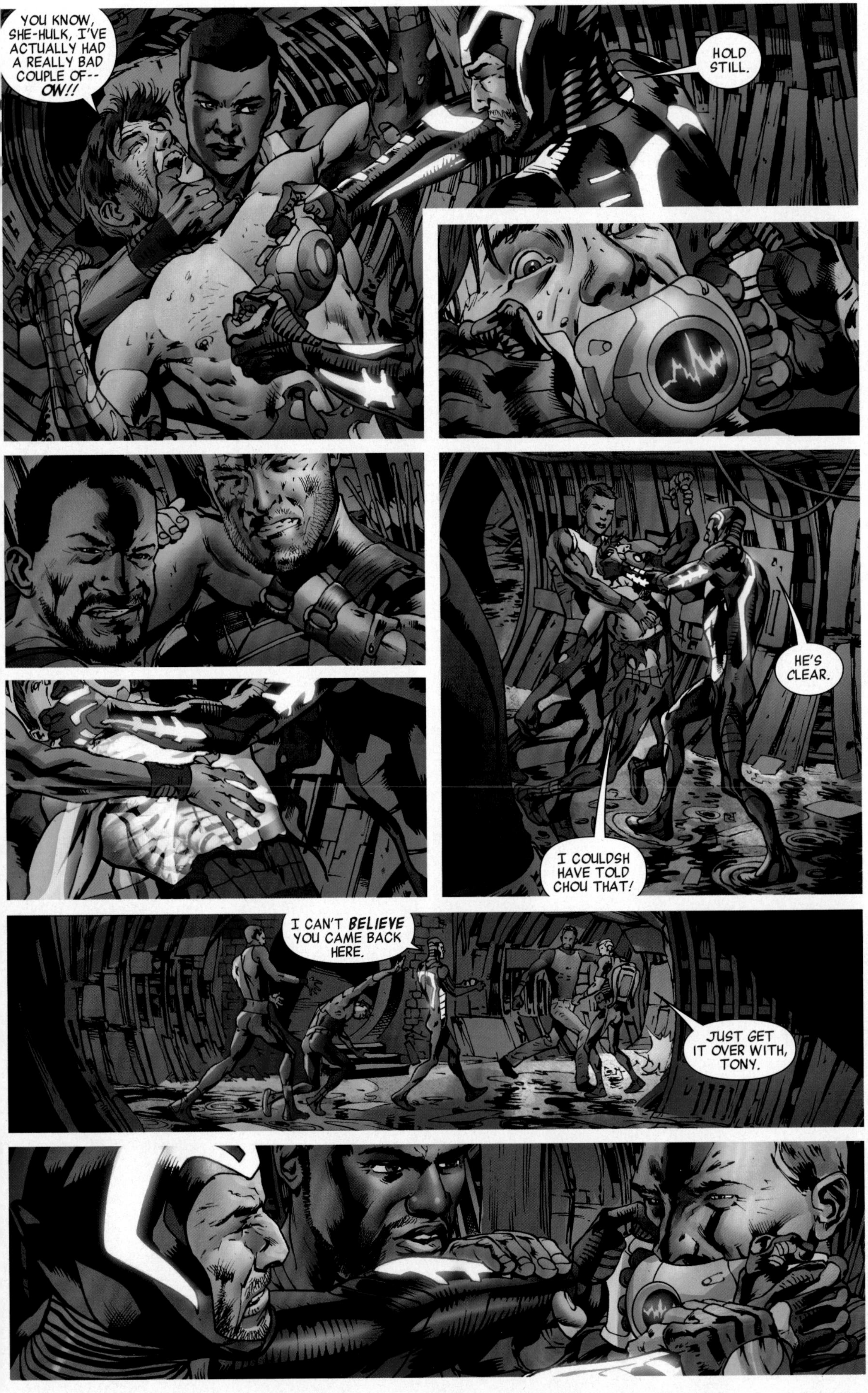
YOU KNOW, SHE-HULK, I'VE ACTUALLY HAD A REALLY BAD COUPLE OF-- OW!!
HOLD STILL.
HE'S CLEAR.
I COULDSH HAVE TOLD CHOU THAT!
I CAN'T BELIEVE YOU CAME BACK HERE.
JUST GET IT OVER WITH, TONY.

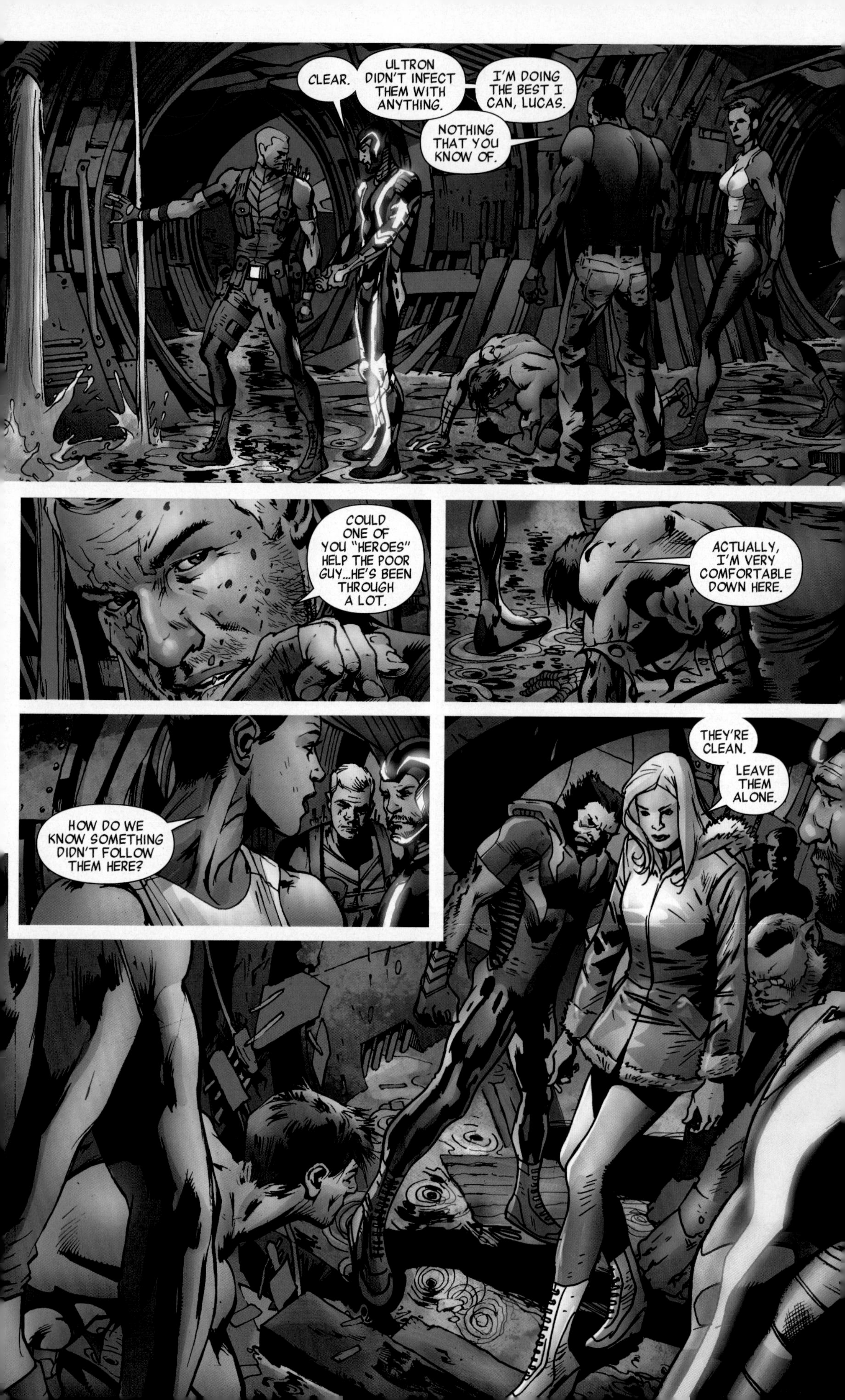
CLEAR.
ULTRON DIDN'T INFECT THEM WITH ANYTHING.
I'M DOING THE BEST I CAN, LUCAS.
NOTHING THAT YOU KNOW OF.
COULD ONE OF YOU "HEROES" HELP THE POOR GUY...HE'S BEEN THROUGH A LOT.
ACTUALLY, I'M VERY COMFORTABLE DOWN HERE.
HOW DO WE KNOW SOMETHING DIDN'T FOLLOW THEM HERE?
THEY'RE CLEAN.
LEAVE THEM ALONE.

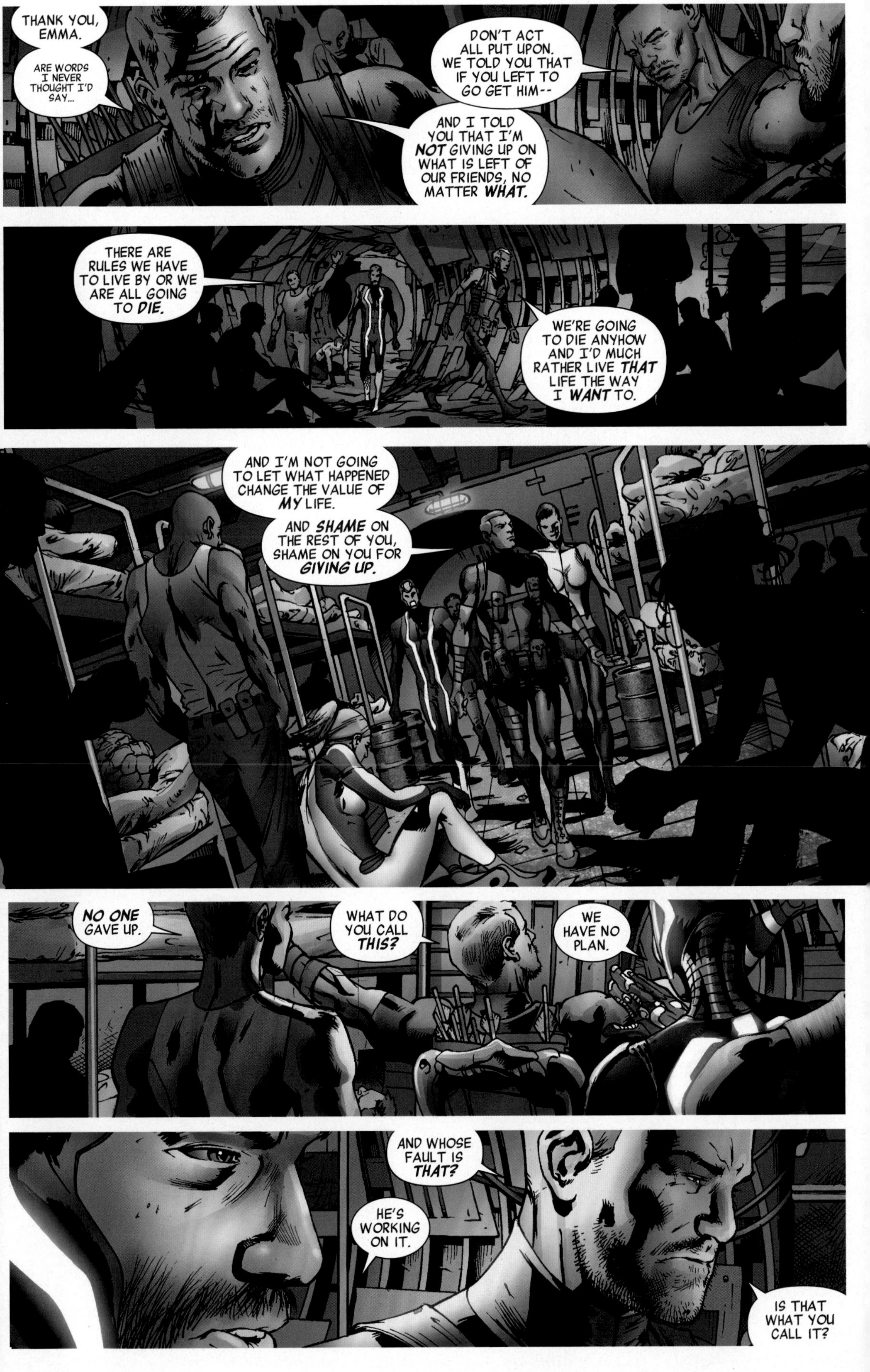
THANK YOU, EMMA.
ARE WORDS I NEVER THOUGHT I'D SAY...
DON'T ACT ALL PUT UPON. WE TOLD YOU THAT IF YOU LEFT TO GO GET HIM--
AND I TOLD YOU THAT I'M NOT GIVING UP ON WHAT IS LEFT OF OUR FRIENDS, NO MATTER WHAT.
THERE ARE RULES WE HAVE TO LIVE BY OR WE ARE ALL GOING TO DIE.
WE'RE GOING TO DIE ANYHOW AND I'D MUCH RATHER LIVE THAT LIFE THE WAY I WANT TO.
AND I'M NOT GOING TO LET WHAT HAPPENED CHANGE THE VALUE OF MY LIFE.
AND SHAME ON THE REST OF YOU, SHAME ON YOU FOR GIVING UP.
NO ONE GAVE UP.
WHAT DO YOU CALL THIS?
WE HAVE NO PLAN.
AND WHOSE FAULT IS THAT?
HE'S WORKING ON IT.
IS THAT WHAT YOU CALL IT?

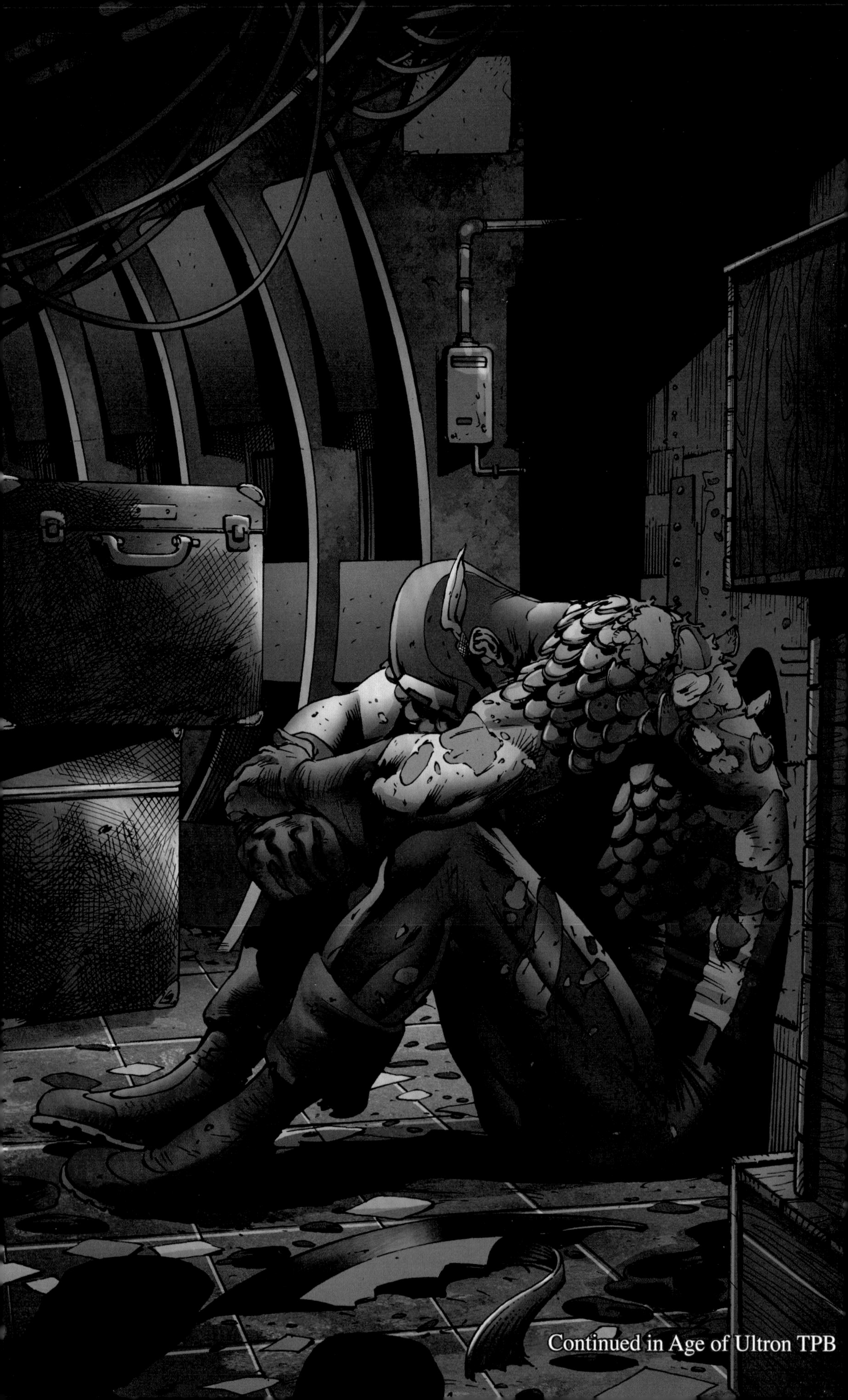

Continued in Age of Ultron TPB

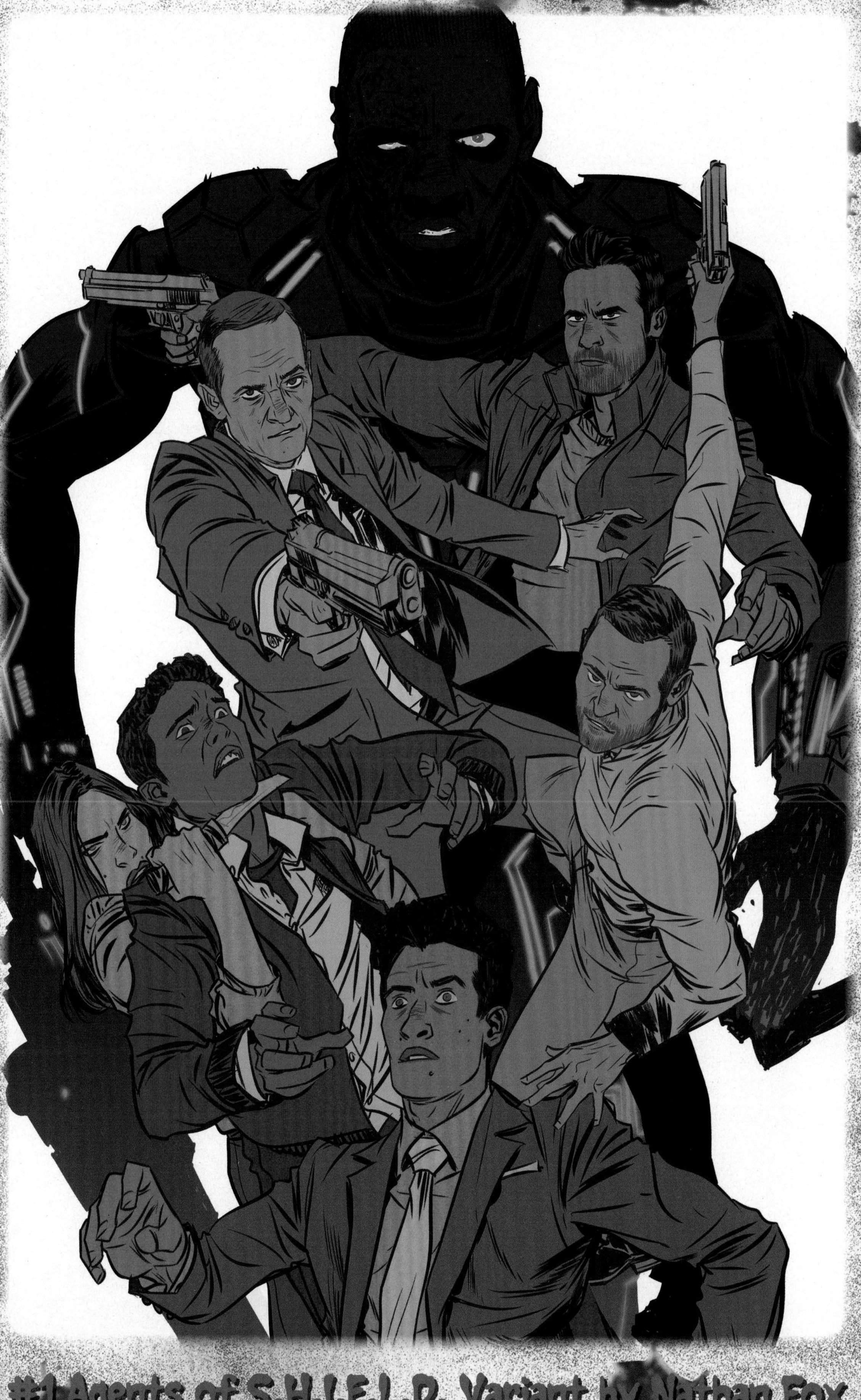

#1 Agents of S.H.I.E.L.D. Variant by Nathan Fox

#2 Variant by Alex Maleev

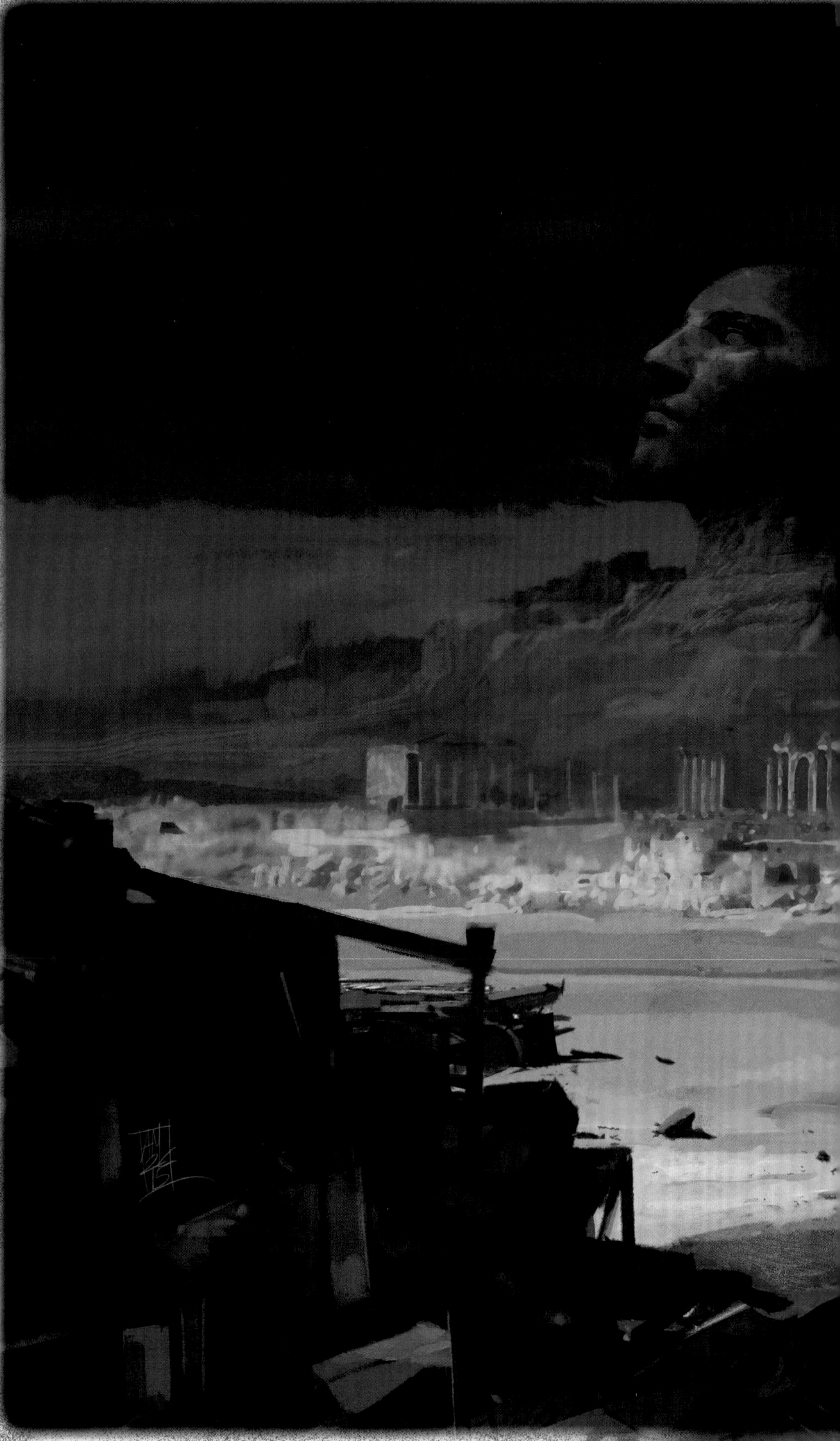

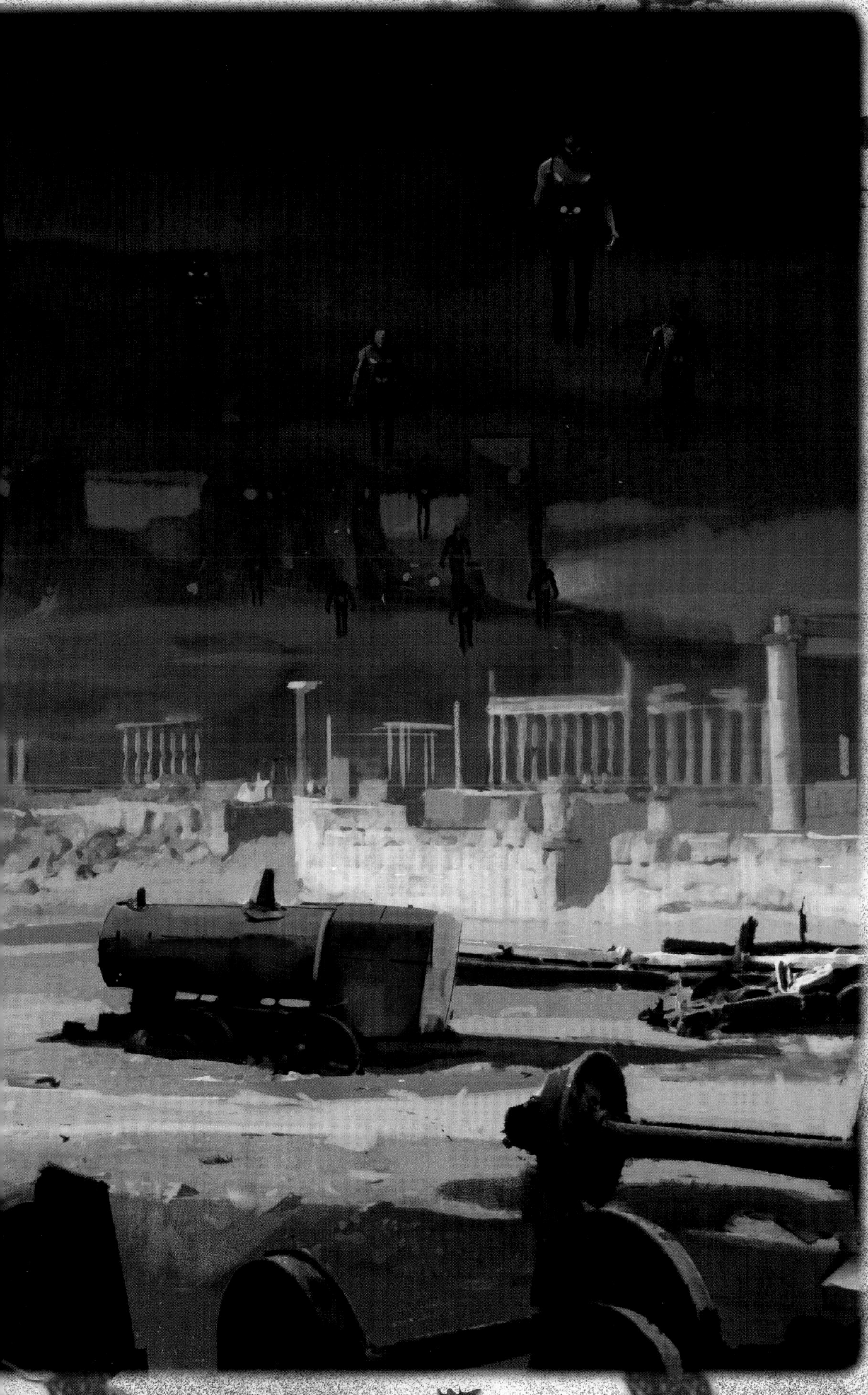

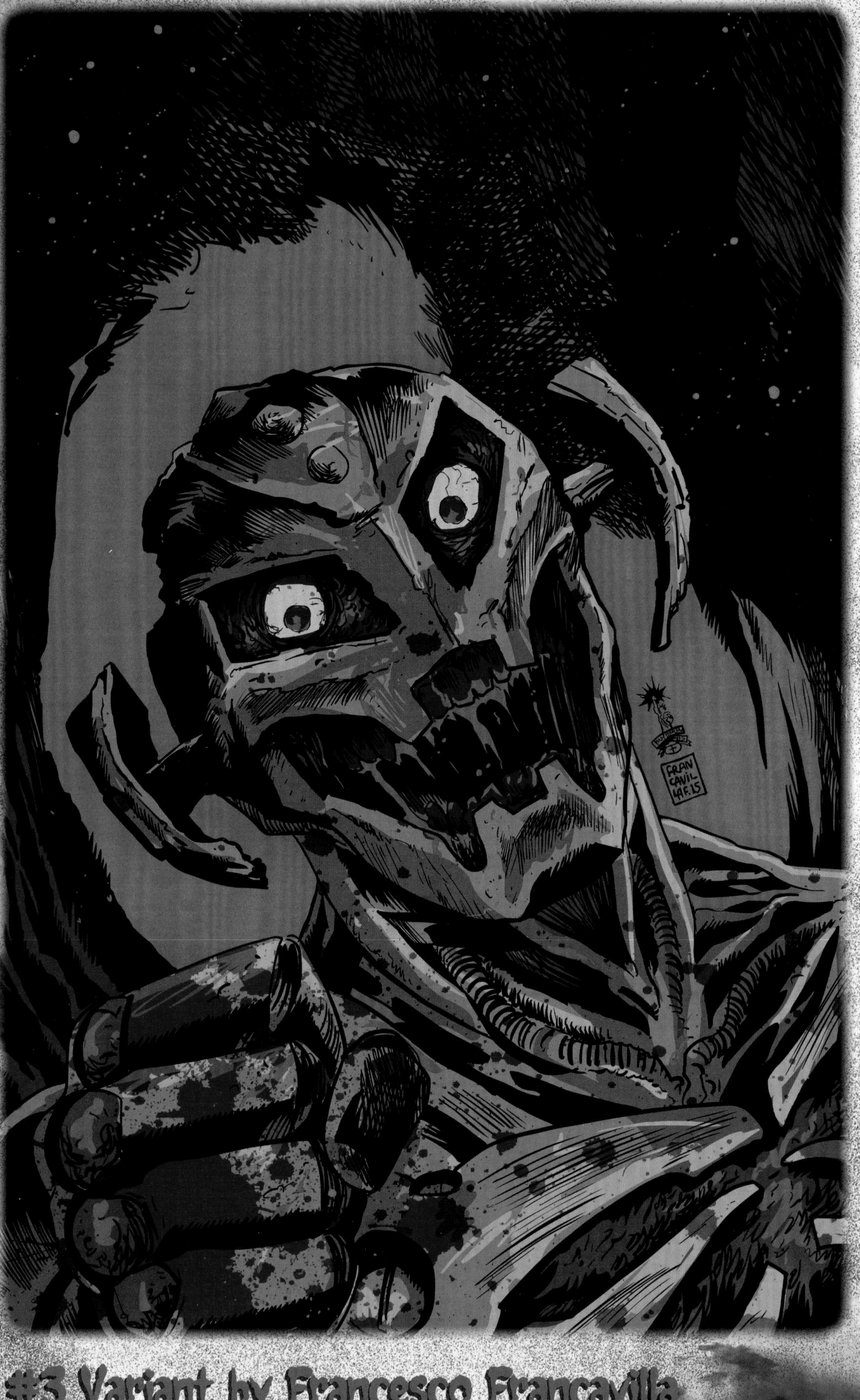

#3 Variant by Francesco Francavilla